FOSSIL COVE PRESS

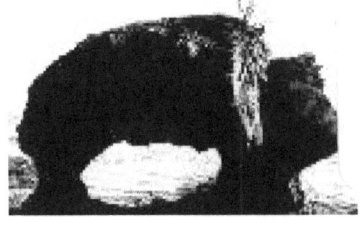

The Last PIRATE'S History of Doctor Who

The Final Journeys

by

D. G. Valdron

The Last Pirate's History of Doctor Who,

Fossil Cove Publishing. 90 Garry Street, Suite 1301,Winnipeg, Manitoba, Canada, R3C 4J4

Cover: A group of youths out to make their own version of Doctor Who, dressing up as Monsters and Aliens, and busily painting a traditional red British phone booth blue.

Art and Design by Roberto Gonzales Lara

http://www.robertogonzalezlara.com/

Issued in print and electronic formats ISBN: 978-1-990860-91-1 (ingramspark pbk); ISBN: 978-1-990860-31-7 (ebook); ISBN: 978-1-990860-30-0 (audio)

Visit our Website at:

http://www.denvaldron.com

Text set in Garamond

The Last *PIRATE'S* History of *Doctor Who*

TABLE OF CONTENTS

INTRODUCTION: THE FACES OF THE DOCTOR

Can you believe it? Here we are at the third and final volume. I never expected or intended to write so much. If you're starting here, welcome aboard. If you've stuck it out through the previous volumes, well, kudos and thanks.

I started this Odyssey because a long time ago, I met something that wasn't supposed to exist: Barbara Benedetti, a Woman Doctor who starred in real adventures, a series of them, all the way back in 1985. And I fell in love with the Benedetti Doctor, just the same way I'd fallen in love with the Tom Baker Doctor. She was the Doctor, no question. It didn't matter that she wasn't official, she was simply the Doctor.

And on this quest, I've found more women Doctors, Sharon Horton, Lily Daniels and Krystal Moore.

I found black doctors like Spencer Kennedy, Dominic G. Marten and Jevocas Green.

I found Romanian Doctors, Italian Doctors, New Zealand Doctors, Stage Doctors, Audio Doctors, Cartoon Doctors. So many variations on the Doctor, and all of them wonderful. So many stories.

I've ended up watching a vast number of Doctor Who films, many terrible, a surprising amount watchable, and a few that were genuinely brilliant. And I've ended up watching a lot of people play the Doctor, a great many failing, but in there, many successes, and a few that were extraordinary.

This is my discovery.

The Doctor can be anyone, white or black, Asian or Hispanic, man or woman, you or me.

What makes the Doctor has nothing to do with skin colour or gender. The surface doesn't count, what counts is the spirit, the style, the eccentricity.

There's an online meme attributed to Moffatt that I'll refer to. I'm probably getting it wrong: "When they made the Doctor, they didn't give him a weapon, they gave him a screwdriver to fix things; they didn't give him a vehicle, they gave him a call box because communicating is more important than fighting; they didn't give him a purpose, they gave him two hearts because that matters more." That's it in a nutshell.

The Doctor is about humanity, it's about always being kind and never cruel, it's about compassion and respecting everyone you meet. It's about being intelligent rather than brutal, being clever rather than violent. It's about trying to make things better, helping others even if they're strangers, and standing up against the bad things even when they're winning.

There's eccentricity and charm, there's passion and anger, curmudgeonly grumpiness, youthful exuberance. That's just framework. I've seen a hundred different versions that somehow were all the Doctor. It comes down to humanity.

You want my advice? Based on what I've learned from all these films. The Doctor can be anyone. The Doctor can be you.

Be the Doctor.

How's that.

CHAPTER 13: THE ANIMATED DOCTOR WHO

Lost and Found in the Second Dimension

"**Hawkspur** *(as he will be called), an alien menace in the far future manages to kill the McCoy Doctor, but is ultimately defeated.*

However, the creature travels backwards along the Doctor's timeline into the past. There, it interferes to prevent the fourth Doctor from regenerating. Instead, it saves him from death and packs him off to a mental institution to keep him out of the way.

With the fourth Doctor a drugged out has-been in a mental institution, Hawkspur then proceeds with its plan for the destruction of the human race.

In the future, the succeeding Doctors are in trouble as their timelines wink out. Sophie Aldred's character, identified as Dorothy but really an Ace who has never met her Doctor, has to figure out what's going on. The Brigadier gets involved, and the two of them try to help the Fourth Doctor find himself."

Welcome to *The Dark Dimension* aka, *Lost in the Dark Dimension*. The legendary lost and abandoned 1993 thirtieth anniversary special. Consigned to the abyss of the unwanted, unloved and unmade.

Reanimated twice. What the hell?

Yes, it seems that Ian Levine decided to re-create this one, and then in 2014, a handful of fans decided to re-create it again as an animated serial. On further reflection: What the hell?

Actually, it's not half bad.

Okay, pause for a second.

What the hell is the *Dark Dimension*? And why should we have any interest in watching an animated fan video of the *Dark Dimension*? For that, we need to look into the muddy waters of history.

Once again, we go back to 1989: Doctor Who is cancelled. It's officially on hiatus. But really, that's just to keep the fanboys quiet. It's cancelled, and cancelled with a stake through the heart, mouth stuffed with garlic, body dismembered, burned to ashes, buried at a crossroads and pissed on for good measure kind of cancelled. There are reasons for that. For those of you who skipped ahead to this chapter, let's just say that grudges were involved.

Anyway, the point is: Cancelled, not coming back, and the BBC is pretty happy about that. Not all of the BBC though.

The BBC has spun off a commercial arm for overseas sales, product licensing etc., which it has, in a burst of imagination called 'BBC Enterprises.' A few years later, they had another burst of imagination and renamed it 'BBC Worldwide.' I imagine it took months to come up with that.

BBC Enterprises has the thankless task of selling the BBC's productions worldwide, selling BBC videos and DVDs, licensing out tosh merchandise, whatever. Doctor Who is one of their cash cows. It sells terrific. But it's also cancelled. You can figure, that they're a bit concerned about that. For the time being, there's a huge catalogue, lots of product. Unfortunately, the world moves on, though, and sooner or later, without new product, that catalogue is going to start looking stale and old fashioned.

The clock winds on. 1989 turns to 1990, which turns into 1991. Still nothing on the Doctor Who front, that hiatus just keeps on going. 1992 comes along, and now we are coming up on the thirtieth anniversary. So if for no other reason, excitement starts to mount. There's a sense of anticipation.

BBC Enterprises saw an opportunity to make some real money. They're marketing people. Their job is to sell things. When you are selling things, you look for occasions, opportunities to cash in, and ways to move the product. Anniversaries are big time cash cows.

First up is John Nathan-Turner, who sends in a memo in July, 1992, suggesting a 30th Anniversary story. Nathan-Turner's career stalled out after the show was cancelled. In 1990, he'd quit the BBC and started his own production company, but it didn't really take off. The last few years of the show had left his reputation in tatters. He pitched a number of productions, but his name was mud at the BBC, and he didn't have much in the way of connections elsewhere. Nothing much seems to have taken off.

A lot of his subsequent work, tended to drift back to Doctor Who. He did conventions, he did documentaries, he provided commentary for DVD releases. Through the 90s he often seemed to be living on his connection to the show.

So suggesting a 30th Anniversary Story wasn't exactly rocket science on his part. But he's not well liked back at the BBC, so no one cared. His suggestion probably went in the circular file.

It's also around this time that Tom Baker starts to feel a little nostalgic. The thing was; he played the Doctor for seven years. But seven years playing a single character... that gets exhausting. There's a sense of boredom and frustration, there's a sense of life passing you by, opportunities coming and going untapped. He'd gotten pretty sick of it. So when he left, he basically wanted out. No coming back for the *Five Doctors*, no public appearances in the scarves. He wasn't going to be Adam West, patching up the seams in his old Bat-suit. No, Baker wanted a clean break from it. He wanted leave it behind.

But now?

Its twelve years later. He's kind of missing the old long scarf. He lets it be known to someone, perhaps several someones, that he wouldn't mind playing the Doctor one more time. That's what sets the ball rolling – particularly for BBC Enterprises, because if they get Tom Baker back... well, everything in his old catalogue is new again!

At this point, it's not exactly clear what happens next or how it comes about. However, the key character in this whole drama seems to be the improbably named Adrian Rigelsford, who is in various eyes, the hero, the villain, the fool or a minor supporting player in the piece. As to what his exact role was, opinions vary. But I think he was more central than the official histories, what there are of them, suggest.

Rigelsford's claim to fame is that he wrote the script for Dark Dimensions. He has a smattering of other writing credits on the internet movie database, nothing terribly memorable. Mostly, he seems to have been a media writer – he ghostwrote for Peter Sellers and Brian Blessed, published magazine articles, wrote specialty books on Doctor Who, Blake's 7, etc. This is a respectable career as a writer. It paid the bills and got his name out. But there are no script credits.

There was nothing to indicate that this was the guy to write the thirtieth anniversary story.

Did I say respectable career?

Maybe not so much.

There were little inconsistencies, unsourced and unverified and rather suspicious seeming quotes from William Hartnell or Roger Delgado. There was the wee boner of leaving the entirety of season 18, Tom Baker's final season, out of 'The Doctors: Thirty Years of Time Travel.' And how exactly does something like that happen?

In fact, it turns out that a certain amount of his media work appeared to be sloppy and unsourced, in terms of errors and quotes from dead people. Rigelsford's work was peppered with a lot of unverifiable quotes from 'final interviews' with persons since passed on. So he kind of garnered a poor reputation among the hard core fans.

Here's a typical gag floating around from the day: Some fan says he was at a séance. Another fan asks, *"Was Adrian Rigelsford there conducting interviews for his next book?"*

Apparently, he published the last interview with Stanley Kubrick before his death… Except that no record or recording of that interview was found to exist, and it's now considered to be fraudulent, particularly by Kubrick's close associates. There appears to have been a certain amount of this kind of thing with Rigelsford.

There was also the matter of theft – apparently, he stole a few photographs from the Daily Mail/Associated Newspapers Archive library and sold them. Fifty-six thousand pictures over eight years, to be exact, sold for seventy five thousand pounds in all. He spent eighteen months in jail over that in 2004. I'm astonished – 56,000 photographs? Even over eight years, how the hell does one manage that? That's 7000 photographs a year. 600 a month. Assuming the Archive

Library was closed on weekends and holidays, that amounts to stealing 40 pictures a day. How does that happen? Did he show up every day with a suitcase? Or did he just drive a forklift over once in a while? How was it that no one noticed?

Rigelsford, deservedly, earned the reputation as a fraud artist, a thief, a dubious person all the way around. Which is a shame because it seems so unnecessary.

Riglesford already had a career, he was a wunderkind. He was knocking out books in his early 20s. The Dark Dimensions saga takes place when he's about 23. He was getting professional magazine sales, which is impressive.

All of this suggests that there must have been some talent there, some hard work and genuine drive, underneath that youthful sloppiness and moral sketchiness.

Or maybe not?

Maybe sleazing and lying is how you get to be a Wunderkind. Or maybe he's just a young man that got the wrong kind of lucky breaks, came too far too fast, cut a few corners which worked out well enough to turn into long running bad habits which eventually caught up with him.

I think that in literary terms, Adrian would be what we call an unreliable narrator. But he also seems essential to the story. Anthony Frewin, an associate of Stanley Kubrick, the fellow who wrote the article about Rigelsford and blew the lid on his fabricated interview (and my source for the Séance joke), had this to say about him:

"Anyone who has worked in the film industry will instantly recognize the type. They hover around on the margins. The Sammy Glick figure forever on the verge of the Big Break, no more morality than is strictly necessary, constantly hustling, chasing chimeras, talking up deals that evaporate at the 11th hour through no fault of their own. So, in this respect, Rigelsford is part of a great tradition."

I think that's probably spot on. I've met a few of those myself. The truth is that at its most basic level, that describes a lot of the film and television industry. It's almost random. Just atoms in a box, ceaselessly bouncing off each other, ideas, personalities, proposals, notions, every now and then, by sheer fluke, things coalesce and a project gels. Usually it breaks apart or disintegrates back to its constituent atoms. But once in a while, when the moon is right, everything lines up all the way to the end and something gets done, and the participants have maybe a better shot at another project.

There's the factory level of course – the money, the television stations and movie companies, the BBC, the established power players… the ones who make productions happen on a regular basis. But the people in those factories all have to come from somewhere, and at the earliest points, they might not be that different from Rigelsford. Mostly, in the entertainment business, it's just atoms randomly colliding, searching for the right combinations to amount to something.

I read somewhere that at any given time, there are a million scripts bouncing around Hollywood. Can you believe that? The late Spalding Grey, best known for *Swimming to Cambodia* and *Monster in a Box* had a cable show where he'd go up to completely random people in L.A. and say 'Tell me about your script!'

And every time, they'd have one!

Jeff Hirschfield of LEXX and Zixx once told me *'this whole business is built on failure, every now and then, something happens and we're all astonished.'*

So Rigelsford is now branded as a fraud, a thief, and a sketchy, skeevy person. That's a hard reputation to overcome. He may well have been all of these things way back in 1992, but few people appreciated that back then. He was so new the taint of history had not yet begun to cling. What he really was, basically, was a hustler looking to make a connection, which in a sense, describes almost everyone in the entertainment business.

I have nothing against Rigelsford, from what I can tell, his sins are long in the past, and he seems to have paid for them. He's just a part of the story. Apparently, he wrote a novelization of the script, and a book about the almost-making of the *Dark Dimensions*, but neither was ever published. That's kind of a shame.

Anyway, back to the story. Tom Baker apparently says 'I'd like to be Doctor Who again' to someone, just in time for the 30th Anniversary. Somehow, this suggestion makes its way to BBC Enterprises where a couple of Senior Producers, Penny Mills and David Jackson take it up, and push it all the way to BBC Enterprises Senior Manager, Tony Greenwood, who says 'let's do it.'

All of this seems to bear the fingerprints of behind the scenes politicking. So if I had to take a completely unsupported guess, I think it was Rigelsford who seems to have been doing Doctor Who books and magazine articles at the time, who would have been talking to Baker, and then conveyed this sentiment to both the BBC and BBC Enterprises, until he found someone to pick up the torch. Rigelsford's best connections would probably have been at BBC Enterprises. They were in charge of licensing, they'd be who he dealt with on the books and they'd pretty much inherited the defunct show.

Why do I think this? No direct evidence. But Rigelsford, a fan and a media-book writer, gets tapped to write the script, with no film or television experience at all? That's a WTF moment. Even Andrew Cartmel had taken a few workshops. In industry terms, Rigelsford has no apparent qualifications – it's like giving the job to a chimpanzee. The only way that makes sense to me, if he's involved up to his elbows behind the scenes. To my thinking, he has to be a prime mover, or connected to a prime mover, to land the job, otherwise, they'd have gone with someone with actual television writing experience, Terrance Dicks, for instance.

At this point the project is a 'direct to video' release – not intended for broadcast. BBC after all does the broadcasting. BBC Enterprises does the video release. It's a peculiar thing that BBC Enterprises is actually getting into production. But maybe they've caught the Hollywood bug. Everyone wants to make their mark, find a place in the sun. The entertainment industry is funny that way, deep down no one goes to Hollywood to become an accountant.

According to the story, Rigelsford brings Graeme Harper on as Director. Harper had done *Caves of Androzani* and *Revelation of the Daleks*, so no complaints there. But again, this is something that makes me very suspicious that Rigelsford was more than just a hired hand scriptwriter, but was more along the lines of an uncredited producer. Script writers don't recruit directors.

By the way, in 1996, Harper and Rigelsford co-wrote a book together about the making of Harper's Doctor Who serials. At another point, they seem to have collaborated on a 'wilderness era' pitch to license the right to produce Doctor Who from the BBC. There's some history between the two.

Then the turf war starts up. November 1992, BBC Controller Jonathan Powell, no fan of the show, gets wind of the project and objects to it, since it's a production and that belongs to BBC proper. Powell, as we recall, despises Nathan-Turner, so he's well out of it. The high command of the BBC are still pretty vindictive about the whole Who thing. But since BBC proper has no intention of doing it, BBC Enterprises presses on.

Then the BBC decides it will sign on. This may have something to do with Allan Yentob replacing Jonathan Powell as BBC Controller.

So far as I can tell, Yentob didn't have the same messy history with the show that Grade and Powell had.

Or perhaps the BBC itself signing on is a decision that if they can't stop it, then they can at least protect their turf as the production arm and maybe grab some of the credit.

Dates come and go.

New dates are set.

They're talking a release for 1994.

Then suddenly it's advanced to 1993.

It's no longer direct to video, now its broadcast.

Except wait, the video edition will be a special edition with extra scenes and stuff!

Generally, when you see that level of confusion, you start to wonder if there's a train wreck in the offing. There's very much a sense of a game of hot potato going on, not a clear sense of the direction, not a lot of sense of organization or progress or the duckies lining up in sensible ways.

Five weeks into production, as artists and designers start doing their thing, it dies a sudden death. Kaput! Just like that.

Done.

There's some nifty production work done – a 'deaths head' Cyberman, a new sort of heavy weapons Dalek. But apart from some artwork, not much else was accomplished. It died on the operating table.

What killed it? There's a lot of talk and a lot of reasons, some of them good, some of them just wind.

There's certainly politics involved. The key meeting that killed the production takes place when all the proponents are out of town and unable to defend it.

But fundamentally, it all came down to this: Someone who actually knew how to read a budget got a look at the project. Game over.

The financial structure of the project made no sense at all. In particular, they were listing the same items in both the revenue and expense category. Film financing, and particularly film revenue generally involves some spectacularly creative accounting. But this was in a class by itself. This wasn't just fiddling with numbers; this was speaking French to wolverines.

There were a lot of other problems that showed up on the post-mortem. A big one was the fact that they hadn't gotten around to signing any of the other Doctors, and were likely to have trouble getting them to sign on – Tom Baker got half the script to himself. Pertwee, Davison, Baker and McCoy got about 12 minutes apiece and not a whole lot to do with the plot. Even Sophie Aldred and Nicholas Courtney had bigger and more integral parts than the other Doctors.

For the four other surviving Doctors, it was a slap in their collective faces, shitty parts delivered to them in demeaning ways – it would have taken some fancy footwork to get any of them to buy in. They weren't doing fancy footwork though; their approach seems ham handed and half assed. Added to that, it doesn't look to me like they'd secured the rights to the Daleks, Ice Warriors or the Cybermen. So that was going to be a problem. Terry Nation's agents, in particular, were known to be pretty hard to deal with.

Then there's the innumerable production issues – this script looked expensive to put on, you had time vortexes left and right which sounds like a costly kind of thing, all sorts of sets and locations, a big sprawling cast of supporting characters, post-apocalyptic landscapes, royal banquets, it was going to be a production managers budget busting nightmare. There's not a lot of evidence that BBC Enterprises had the resources or the talent on tap to make it happen.

There's also talk of the rival projects in the wind around this time, the Daltenreys Doctor Who movie project, and a proposed American series. So there were some other turf wars in the background. But I don't take that too seriously. It was there, in the back of people's minds. But I don't think it was make or break. Bottom line, it died.

John Nathan-Turner, who had been left shivering in the dark, alone and unwanted, came roaring back with Dimensions in Time. This handily crystallized everything that was wrong with his approach to Doctor Who in less than fifteen minutes. We will say no more about. Ever.

So what do we have here?

Well, this is the internet age, so if you want to read an actual rehearsal script, banged out on an actual typewriter (even in 1993 an anachronism) with authentic typos, you can do it. You just need to poke around a bit.

Before we get too deeply into the review, let me address a couple of points.

First, it was always going to be Tom Baker's show. Sorry, that's just how it is. Tom Baker had been the most successful and long running Doctor ever. He had the most stories. He was the most widely known internationally. On a good day, Tom Baker had pulled in 13 million viewers and better; he had 7 years, 41 stories, 172 episodes. On a bad day, McCoy struggled for 3 million viewers; he had three years, 12 stories, 42 episodes. If it came down to dollars and sense, Tom Baker's Doctor made sense.

Plus, it was going to have to explain why and how Tom looked fifteen years older, fatter and a lot rougher around the edges. So they took that issue, met it head on, and made it central to the plot and character. This is a good decision.

It's one of the reasons why Star Trek the Motion Picture, which tried to ignore the fact that its cast had gotten older, is disliked, and Wrath of Khan, which actually accepted that they were long in the tooth is considered a classic.

I suppose it's one of the reasons that the visible aging of Jon Pertwee and Patrick Troughton in the Five Doctors and Two Doctors encourages the Season 6B theory.

It's actually got real potential – Tom Baker playing a *'Lion in Winter'* version of his Doctor. Sort of the *'King Lear'* Doctor. It would be something very new to do with the character, quite possibly a man who liked going over the top, as Baker did, could really sink his teeth in and run with that. Equal chance he'd turn it into a spectacular, incandescent mess. But there's real potential for greatness here.

That decision, once it gets made, means that the status and existence of the subsequent Doctors is in trouble. That's a very logical follow through. Pretty reasonable decision there, although the specifics might be challenged.

The Third Doctor gets shoehorned in as a kind of Jiminy Cricket memory construct. Again, a pretty reasonable decision, creatively, though not actually necessary. These guys are all time travelers, so the Third Doctor could just as easily have popped out of his Police Box. But it at least allowed for scenes with Baker and Pertwee together.

But then, you kind of come up against a problem – Doctors 5, 6 and 7 are basically on ice in story terms, Doctor 3 is a memory, and Doctor 4 has been put in a trap – he's stuck being the passive victim. Which is always a risk: A protagonist who doesn't do much, isn't much of a protagonist, it undercuts your drama. So who is carrying the action?

This means you need other characters to bust things out – enter the Brigadier and Ace/Dorothy – and run around connecting things to other things. So really, the actual driving characters, the ones who are pushing the story, and holding the narrative together, are the two companions, with literally all the Doctors kind of boxed out. They don't really connect up with the narrative, but rather, are connected to the companions.

Well… the show is Doctor Who, not '*The Adventures of the Brig and Dorothy Bouncing Amongst Doctors.*' That's kind of a problem, narratively speaking.

The solution, such as it is, is to turn it into a bunch of chase sequences, as our supporting heroes are chased up and down halls and corridors all Scooby Doo style by Daleks, Cybermen and Ice Warriors.

Okay, well that amounts to some good decisions, some bad decisions, but overall, Rigelsford's story is workable and hangs together structurally. It gets really complicated, I don't know why some writers have to treat Time Travel like a Chinese puzzle box, sometimes it works, but mostly it just annoys. But we can live with this.

You're going to get continuity porn. Of course you are. This is a thirtieth anniversary special, driven by the sole objective of BBC Enterprises merchandising its ass off. You're not going to avoid that, and it's insulting to think you might. I'll leave it to the purists to complain. But you were always going to get some classic monsters.

As it turns out, the thirtieth anniversary came and went. *Dark Dimensions* was much talked about, but ultimately abandoned.....

Until much, much later, perhaps decades later, somewhere down the line, Ian Levine became involved in the *Mission to the Unknown* animation project, and got the bug to do his own Doctor Who. The results were twelve fan films, new editions of *Shada* and *Downtime*, lost episodes like *Mission to the*

Unknown recreated, productions of unmade serials like *Gallifrey* or *Yellow Fever* or the fabled *Dark Dimension*.

And what casts he recruited! Sylvester McCoy appeared a couple of times, Lalla Ward, Carole Ann Ford, Frazier Hines, William Russel have all shown up in person or on voice on his behalf.

It speaks, I think, to Levine's deep pockets and decades of contacts that he was able to do it, able to hire or recruit the cast members that he did, hire the animators, retain or engage in the production. Bits of it show up, for a while his version of Shada could be found online. Maybe it still can. There's a YouTube compilation of his trailers. His work is mostly hidden away, which may fit with Levine's personality. Maybe he gets a kick out of having this body of work to be talked about, but held just out of sight - contributes to the 'Legend of Levine.' Or maybe Levine did all this stuff for his own and perhaps for his friends enjoyment, and it's not more complicated than that. Perhaps he just did it for the fun of doing it.

There's talk that he's offered some of this to the BBC, I think that he would deeply love to be a creator of some officially recognized or acknowledged canon. That seems to be the recurring thing, particularly with his version of *Shada*. But if he has, that speaks to a profound and abyssal ignorance of how the video and television business works. The BBC doesn't accept unsolicited fan videos, particularly of products that it owns the copyrights to anyway.

Levine created his own version of the *Dark Dimension*, as a Reconstruction. Why do it this way? Simplicity and cost. As I've pointed out over and over, actually making a video is hideously difficult, even for a fan production, and one way or the other, it's an expensive proposition. Audio and still pictures are much more manageable.

Paul Jones, an impressionist, assays the voice role of Tom Baker as the Fourth Doctor. The big wrinkle is that Sylvester McCoy and Sophie Aldred actually voice/play their characters in the story.

McCoy has participated in some of Levine's other fan creations, which is fairly mysterious to me – either Levine is writing big cheques, McCoy is incredibly fond of the gentleman or there is the matter of a certain amount of blackmail.

Also notably, Peter Miles stars as Hawkspur. The role was originally written for cult comedian, Rick Mayall, who had unfortunately passed away. Peter Miles was originally to be cast as Mayall's assistant, so here he steps into the role. Miles had originally played Davros sidekick, Nyder, in Genesis of the Daleks.

Ian Levine's *Dark Dimension* was completed in 2012, premiered before a small group of friends, and has been largely unseen. There's a five minute clip available on YouTube, but it's possible that the entirety of the work will never be generally available. But then again, you never know. It's surprising what will show up online.

But there was an unforeseen consequence: Word of Ian Levine's *Dark Dimension* inspired James Walker to produce his own animated *Dark Dimension*...

Review: The Animated Dark Dimension

A Fan Animated Serial Epic

Okay, the animation is computer based flash. Flash animation is a peculiar thing.

I had a friend who was an animator, did short films, did bits for Sesame Street. Real animation, the pen and ink drawings on paper, that's incredibly time consuming. Basically, that's creating a film painstakingly one frame at a time. Thirty six frames a second, sixty seconds to a minute. Even a five minute short was thousands of drawings, first penciled, then inked, then painted, then sound tracked, rough cut, answer print, negative cut, etc. He spent years working on a single ten minute cartoon, months doing Sesame Street shorts.

For a major project, a full length movie or TV series, you need an animation studio. An animation studio, Disney or Nelvana or the Japanese or Korean places, is like an army battalion. There is just so much painstaking work, by so many people, acting in coordination.

It's changed a bit over time. Hanna-Barbera perfected the art of limited animation, still pictures and static backgrounds, with only limited motion cycles for body parts. Fred Flintstone could run a marathon, but the only thing that moved were his feet. It worked: a 24 minute Flintstone cartoon could take as little as 4000 drawings. But it was barely animation. Critics of the old Hanna-Barbera shows used to call them 'radio with pictures.' And a lot of their old projects have vanished away, the clunky, marginal animation no longer able to pass muster in the modern marketplace.

The Japanese developed the technique of stretching their animation with long artistic shots of motionless characters gazing at things. When you become aware of it, you really start to see the shortcuts taken in a lot of animation. But even the most limited conventional animation is still incredibly time consuming. In real life, for a dedicated fan, or even a group of dedicated fans to try and animate Dark Dimension in a conventional way, they'd need lifetimes, or an army of artists locked in some cavernous warehouse basement.

Which takes us to Flash animation. Among the many things that computers have done is given us an opportunity to create animation that simply wouldn't be within the human capacity. The trouble is that it's one of those satanic bargains. Yes, you can do animation, cheaply, efficiently and at home. But it's often going to look and feel pretty stilted and awful, particularly compared to what we are now used to from companies that actually do keep armies of Korean animators locked in a warehouse drawing away.

So, fair warning. Flash animation. If you know it, and you're okay with that style and format of animation, then good. If your only concept of animation is the Simpsons or Japanese Anime, then not so good. Sometimes it works very well, sometimes not so much. The handicaps or roughness or the 'crappyness', however, feels a lot like the limitation of the animation format though.

You're basically moving characters on a computer screen and doing some pretty limited motion cycles, there are some pans and scans, some zooms. It's crude, but at least it does the job. Animation is tough; it's a heartbreaking consumer of time and energy. So it's the sort of thing you have to lay in some forgiveness for.

The animation of the Dark Dimensions is, within that framework, not bad at all. It is more than adequate in depicting the actions and interactions of the characters. You can watch it and be able to tell what's going on. Even without dialogue, you could figure out who was who, who was up to what and who was doing what to whom by the animation, and that's actually pretty reasonable. I've seen professional live action films that had trouble accomplishing that.

As to the Dark Dimension's artwork? The foreground animation, the characters are all over the map. The fourth Doctor, an aged Tom Baker, is rendered lovingly and with strong detail, as we'd expect for a central character. There is a continuum that extends from Tom and the Daleks at one end, through the Doctors and principal cast, to quite crudely drawn supporting characters who are barely tolerable.

One nice touch is that all of the Doctors are rendered as they were in 1993. So Pertwee is definitely old and Colin has a much more butch haircut. The Doctors poorest rendition is Davison, but I could have predicted that. Peter Davison is blandly handsome, there's no distinctive feature to anchor a drawing on.

The Daleks are clean, detailed and animation friendly, the Ice Warriors almost so, the Cybermen, not quite. The Brigadier is well done, Dorothy/Ace not so much. Again, I think that Sophie Aldred's features just didn't provide a distinctive element to anchor the drawing. Tom Baker or Jon Pertwee? Well, you just start with those noses, or those bushy heads of hair. Davison or Aldred. What do you do?

The renditions of the supporting background character? Well, mostly that doesn't start off reaching very high, and it declines fast. There's a group of time soldiers jumping back from McCoy's time, and they're just painful to watch.

Consistently, the artwork for the characters is almost crude – while individuals vary, there tends to be a lack of perspective, a lack of dimensionality, a lot of the supporting characters come across as flatly drawn figures, which are then frustrated by the limited animation. It's a feature of this kind of animation, I suppose.

The backgrounds vary in detail. Some, the ones that need to be, are quite impressive. Many are pretty perfunctory, they're there, they depict what they're supposed to in terms of where things are taking place, but they're not especially detailed or impressive. They make up for that by simple strong colour schemes.

Nevertheless, you'll be surprised to hear me say this, but the artwork and animation are entirely serviceable. This isn't television quality or high end professional animation. This isn't Disney, or Fox or Warner brothers. There is no army of Koreans or Japanese.

According to producer James Walker, almost all of the animation is the single handed work of one man, Jay Hale. When you consider that I'm comparing Hale's work to the output of entire commercial animation teams, that's astonishing. It is literally amazing to see a single man accomplishing this much. I'd love to see what Hale could do with real resources and an animation team under him.

As I've said, you can watch it, and follow it. You know who is who, who is talking to who, who is doing what to whom. The flow of characters and consequence is clear and discernible. That's not an accomplishment without merit; I've seen professional animation that couldn't meet those standards.

If some of it is rough, I've seen much worse on some of Adult Swim's offerings. It's well within the boundaries of tolerance and some of it is quite good. That's an astonishing feat considering the very small production team.

Ultimately, the biggest challenge may be time. Computer animation technology keeps moving ahead. In a few years, or a decade, the animation software available to the consumer may simply outstrip these *Dark Dimensions*.

So be it. It's still worthwhile.

This production is a group of dedicated fans doing it for free, for the love of it, who are putting a lot of time and work in and maybe learning as they go, pushing the limits of their talent, because they feel it is important. You need to respect that, and make allowances.

Where the production stands out is in the voice acting and direction. We have Paul Jones playing the lead role of Tom Baker, playing the fourth Doctor. Nothing Meta there – we're not talking some esoteric layer on layer performance. He's doing a straight on Tom Baker imitation which is actually pretty good. Apparently, he's made a bit of a living off of it. I believe he did Baker's voice for Ian Levine's versions of *Shada* and *Dark Dimension* (might have been Jon Culshaw). He's also apparently done a fair amount of work for Big Finish. Anyway, he does the job – you hear that voice, and it's got that familiar timbre to it. Maybe he doesn't quite bring the nuance and personality of the actual Tom Baker. But it sells.

Playing a small role as the sixth Doctor is Steven Warren Hill, known from the Federation for his uncanny rendition of Colin Baker. The rest of the voice actors are mostly unknown to me. There is theatre performer Jennifer Knighton and video game actor Graydon Schlichter. James Walker singles out Tegan Harris (Ace) and Jonathon Carley (Third and Fifth Doctor). But there's a full cast of them – the internet movie database lists twenty-five voice actors in the animated *Dark Dimensions*.

The sheer variety of unique voices give the production a professional edge. We're so used to television animation making use of only a small voice cast, that a large voice cast actually gives the project an auditory cachet. It feels bigger, more real, more credible.

This is a crucial thing. Fundamentally, almost no animation, unless you're Disney, can produce the complexity and nuance, the richness of detail of real life. Quite often, it doesn't even try. It's made as cheaply as possible, and there are all sorts of tricks to try and stretch that product, to try and escape having to make a few drawings here and there.

What makes animation work is the voice work. The foley effects, but mainly the voices, the sounds, the sense of conversation. Voices move, they rise and fall, lilt and lumber. Voices convey anger and panic, amusement, satisfaction, a rich range of emotions. And if you're not watching for it, good voice work will carry you over bad animation. We'll watch a cartoon, and it comes alive for us, not because of the limited animation, but because of the terrific voices and sound mix.

Aidan Clark, the sound designer notes, *"Thankfully we're living in an era where cheap or even free software can let us do in an hour what would have taken days and thousands of pounds of equipment to achieve 10 or 20 years ago. We're also in the enviable position of having no real deadlines, which means that we can take as much time fine-tuning the sound as is necessary. We also have over 50 years of inspiration from the brilliant work of the BBC Radiophonic Workshop and their successors!"*

In fact, try this right now. Go back and watch one of your favourite cartoons as a child. Watch it with the voice off. Or watch it, but focus on the actual movement. You'll be shocked by how lively and dynamic it is in your memory, but how stilted and limited it is when you're actually watching it. The difference then, the difference now, is the voices that made it come alive, that made stilted and static sequences of images shimmer and dance.

We humans are visual creatures. I've read synopsis for the *Dark Dimension*. I've even read the script. But I didn't get much out of it. Seeing it played out visually just added dimensions to it, no pun intended. I could watch the animation, and I could see through it to Tom Baker and Sylvester McCoy, I could take that step to visualize the performances of Sophie Aldred and Nicholas Courtney. It wasn't perfect. But it took me close to the actual experience of what the *Dark Dimension* might have been, way back in 1993.

I found it easy to just stop being a critic and become engrossed in the story, which is a good sign. Which, I suppose, brings us back to the story itself, and the big question of whether the story is any good? Because, hey, not all stories are good.

I'm going to say yes. Credit to Rigelsford. This is an interesting story well told, both in terms of the script, and particularly in terms of the animation and voice action. This gives us a different and interesting take on the Fourth Doctor, it's a decent role for the supporting characters, the villain/monster is interesting and devious.

There's a nice moment with the villain Hawkspur, where he reflects that when he first started out, he had real doubts about the morality of genocide, but now that he's spent a few decades getting to know humanity, he can't wait to put us down.

I think that if I'd watched it without any background or historical context, I just watched this as the work of some fan pulling some random out of thin air and just deciding to animate hid own little Doctor Who epic, I'd be pretty impressed. I think that the work, on its own terms, is strong enough to hold up.

But then, we can't avoid that historical context, can we? What we are looking at is the expression of a strange chapter in

Doctor Who history, a wild roller coaster ride of ambition and nostalgia, hustling and infighting, the rise and fall of Adrian Riglesford, Tom Baker's last hurrah, Sylvester McCoy's slap in the face. Knowing all that, how could you not want to watch this? How could you not want to see this, and through it, glimpse a reflection of what might have been and never was? I couldn't.

So, go check it out.

CAST: Paul Jones - Fourth Doctor; Kurt Bergeron - Seventh Doctor; Jonathon Carley - Third Doctor; Sharon Holmes - Summerfield; Matt Dale - Hawkspur; Tegan Harris - Ace; Wink Taylor -Brigadier Lethbridge Stewart; Dan Armitage - Swift; Stony Hill - Snyder; Bob Brinkman - Mason; Catherine Curtis - Flemyng; Mike Bell - Sanders; Nick Hilton - Everitt; Jennifer Knighton - A J Manson; Philip Austin - Tony McCabe; Graydon Schlichter - Alex Stewart; Gary Davison - Deavish; Neil Ray - Hammond; Steve Pearson- Spaulding; Andrew Foster - Keller; Scott Burditt -Frelane; Danny Lavery - Sampson; Hazy Holden - Librarian; Louise Armitage - Secretary; Steven Warren Hill - Sixth Doctor; Trish Walker - Librarian

CREW: James Walker - Executive Producer, Director, Editor; Adrian Rigelsford - Writer; Jay Hale - Cinematography and Animation; Aidan Clark - Music.

Reviews – The Fan Animations

A Strange and Wonderful Assortment

It turns out, that Doctor Who has had a very long, lively and successful career in fan created cartoons. This is probably because animation, while time and labour intensive, may still be easier than actually getting an entire film production team together.

You can do more, your expectations are lower and you can get away with being very short.

One of the earliest Doctor Who fan films is actually a three minute Super 8 cartoon from 1977, called *Doctor Hoo*. It's the only widely accessible fan film from that era. Look it up, it's on YouTube.

A few year later, 1984 and 1985, we had a couple of other Super 8 animations *Dial D For Dalek* and the *Hues of Doom*. Also on YouTube.

After that, things seemed fairly quiet through the 1990s.

Things didn't really take off until the 2000s, and the advent of YouTube. Again, it's a case where technology and opportunity drives creativity. The earlier cartoons had been drawn and shot frame by frame on film, Super 8 film, but still film. By definition, it's time consuming to create your film one frame at a time. Super8 cartridges only ran for about two to three minutes. So you were pretty much stuck with short subjects. No one had the inclination to do a lengthy epic, and the technology didn't really support length. Three minute shorts were fine.

In the 1990s, the medium for fans was videotape, which wasn't really friendly to frame by frame animation. There was no such thing as frame by frame camcorders. On the other hand, you could shoot a lot of video. You could easily record an hour or two at a shot. It just became easier and more desirable to make a lengthy, twenty minutes or hour long, fan video, than to do a short animation.

Video was the medium that allowed fan films to be traded back and forth, from hand to hand. It tended to be a waste to only have a three or four minute film on an entire tape - people wanted more substantial stories. So the medium worked against animation and drove longer stories.

Suddenly, the medium of transmission changed again with YouTube in 2005. Anyone could put up a short five or ten minute video. Suddenly, the short subject was back on. Five or minutes was all you needed. In fact, YouTube preferred short subjects. Long features are a comparatively recent development on YouTube.

The YouTube era is also the time that people started finding they could do different kinds of animation on computer, from scanning in traditional line drawing, to flash animation, to different kinds of motion with puppets and dolls. There's so much out there, that cataloguing it all would be impossible, instead, we'll just highlight some of the more interesting works in no particular order.

The Puppet Doctor is a stop motion series created by Alisa Stern. The characters are silent, with music and occasional sound effects highlighting their actions. It is unspeakably sweet and engaging. Puppet renditions of real Doctors come to life.

Then there's the *Doctor Puppet*, from Jay Tyson, sometimes operating as *99 Acre Woods*, which makes use of muppets to tell clever little stories. Shorts include *Genesis of the Moleks*, with a David Tenant puppet, and *A Leak in Time* featuring a Tom Baker puppet. It's flat out brilliant.

Doctor Wow is a muppet series from Barry and Belinda Noble. This one in black and white and aimed at children. It's a loving tribute to the Hartnell era, and feels very much like the 1960s Doctor recast as a children's puppet adventure.

Speaking of muppets, there was a theatrical *Muppet show* in England, featuring the *Pigs in Space* sketch, on different nights, both David Tennant and Peter Davison appeared as their Doctors. It's not a fan film, but they're both entertaining, and it's nice to see each of them having fun with the role.

Anime Doctor Who is a thirteen minute short from Paul Johnson, aka 'Otaking.' It features the Pertwee Doctor in Tokyo, battling Cybermen, Daleks, and the Delgado and Ainsley version of the Masters, using dialogue sampled from the classic series, and drawn in a 1980s, anime/*Macrosse* style. Framed as a long trailer, with scenes and shots from a hypothetical full length work, it's gorgeous and insane. If I ever win the lottery, I'm going to find this guy and hire him to spend a couple of years doing the full length version. It's that good.

Slipback was a six episode, sixty minute, radio serial by Eric Saward, with the voices of Colin Baker and Nicola Bryant. This was from 1985, the year that Doctor Who was cancelled, so instead of the 23rd season planned, we got this as a consolation prize. It's not really well regarded. A fellow named Jon Scatman has taken it upon himself to use the radio serial as a platform for an animated version. Surprisingly, it works a lot better that way. The animation is fun, and you can finally see that Saward was trying to channel Douglas Adams and his comedy style. Sadly, the work is incomplete, with only the first two episodes animated. But it's well worth searching out.

The Pescatons, from 1976, written by Victor Pemberton, is a strange little mutant. Originally, it was, and I guess still is, a 46 minute, two part, audio adventure featuring the Fourth Doctor, Tom Baker, with Liz Sladen as Sarah Jane Smith. It was released on LP, and isn't really one of the better stories, despite the mellifluous tones of Baker. Matthew Woodhouse has used this as a platform for an animated version. As with Slipback, it's incomplete, with only ten of the forty-seven minutes complete, but as I've said, it's worth searching out.

Doctor Stew is a more conventional animated series. It's a sly hybrid of Doctor Who and the *Family Guy*, funny, sarcastic, and somehow managing to do justice to both of its inspirations. It's well worth seeking out. Watch for the guest appearances by *Inspector Spacetime*.

Although it doesn't quite fit here, I'll give a shout to *Inspector Spacetime*. It started off as a running gag, a fictionalized version of Doctor Who for the television series *Community*. The actor, Travis Richey, picked up that ball and ran with it, turning the Inspector into a running web series, which for legal reasons; he retitled Untitled Web Series About a *Space Traveler Who Can Also Travel Through Time*.

Anermay Film's Jon Gransden has produced a Claymation version of Doctor Who - *Lord of the Daleks*, where the 4th Doctor confronts Davros and his minions.

Jon Gransden also collaborated with Christopher Thomson and John Hutch for *Christmas With the Enemy*. Davros captures the Doctor and is about to do fiendish things, but somehow, the Doctor and a future incarnation, manage to teach Davros the true meaning of the holidays. It's polled as one of the ten best Doctor Who fan films of the noughties (2000 to 2010.

The Animated Doctor Who Series written, directed and created by Tom Cowell, with James O'Neill as the Doctor, Felicity Stonehill as Riley, and Anna Beaumont as Emma. Done back in 2008, this production ran seven episodes, running from 6 to 24 minutes, with aliens, demons, Yeti, the Great Intelligence, Daleks and Davros, and sundry.

There's a heroic little group called *Altered Vistas*, created by Stuart Palmer, which among other things produces 3D CGI movies, animating mostly stories from the comics. Their shtick was that you sent them a blank CD and they'll burn it and send it back to you. They produced a fan version of the *Curse of the Daleks* stage play, now withdrawn. But they've also done Doctor Who and the *Invasion From Space*, an animation of an original Doctor Who novella from 1966, featuring the Hartnell Doctor. Other productions include an adaptation of a Cyberman comic story called *Black Legacy*, the adventures of *Absalom Daak - Dalek Killer*, as well as a whole series of *Dalek Chronicles*. They've done a lot of animations of Doctor Who comic strip stories. No less than Alan Moore, comic book legend, is a fan of their work.

Of course, there's no avoiding *Lego Doctor Who* by various enthusiastic amateurs, ranging from simple figures and voices, up to increasingly sophisticated stop motion, and even to professional CGI Lego.

Since we're playing with toys, I'd also like to acknowledge Matthew Toffolo, aka Batman-march and his *Action Figure Adventures*. It's basically exactly what it says - a staggering number of small adventures, using posed action figures, homemade miniature sets and occasional limited animation. The sheer volume of it is worth respecting.

Another prolific action figure series is Doctor Who *Online Adventures*, by Brendan Shepherd. The series ran an astonishing seven seasons, roughly 140 (short, eleven minutes or so) episodes, compiling into 52 stories. Visually, the direction is fresh and interesting, there are a lot of cool miniature props and sets and the series is aided by some remarkably sophisticated effects and camerawork.

The Dalek that Time Forgot, written and animated by Lee Adams. This is an entirely CGI production chronicling the journey of Dalek Caan in his fall through the timestream between *Evolution of the Daleks* and the *Stolen Earth*. There's a lot of impressive Dalek 3D CGI. I think they're easy to animate - they're essentially just cones or tubes that glide around, not a lot of erratic moving limbs and joints. *Flight of the Daleks* and *Tyranny of the Daleks* are live action fan films that make impressive use of Dalek CGI.

Another notable Dalek CGI video is Dalek Seth's *Emperor of the* Daleks, the Trial of Davros, which we've already covered.

An extremely ambitious piece of work, is *DALEKS!* A five episode CGI serial, hosted on the Doctor Who YouTube site and made with BBC support. It features the Emperor and Strategist Dalek confronting an enemy force from another universe and forced to ally with their old rivals, the Mechanoids. It consists of five episodes averaging thirteen to fourteen minutes.

There are a lot of fan made CGI Dalek videos, far too many for me to list here. As I've said, they seem to be easy to animate, and there seems to be something compelling about the psychotic pepperpots that draws people.

Real Daleks, in the form of full sized props or small models are also used in comedy shorts.

Derek the Dalek is a series of comedy shorts from Matt, at Mattaf Productions. The premise is that Daleks have invaded earth, but due to a transmission glitch, they got the dimensions wrong, and have materialized as toy sized. This is the tale of one toy sized Dalek, Derek, and his much put upon room-mate, Matt.

Dalek Gary is a series about a full sized Dalek, Gary, who ends up on Earth and tries to fit in. He's also the subject of a documentary by a British crew, who want to follow the lives of immigrant workers in the United States. Daleks, meet the The Office. According to the YouTube listing, it's from Michelle Ossorio.

This is just the tip of the iceberg. Doctor Who animation takes many forms, from different sorts of stop motion, hand puppets, muppets and marionettes, regular animation, CGI, flash, Lego and action figures.

Typically, it's short. *The Dark Dimension* is the lone epic. Some of the more ambitious ones are incomplete. Ultimately, it's mostly pitched towards skits and short jokes with punchlines and payoffs. It's like popcorn Doctor Who. It's just fun.

Let me leave you with an anecdote. Before I did these books, I would do online reviews and discussions. Just trying to promote films and shorts, getting my writing and my ideas out there.

One day, this woman wrote back to me out of the blue. She was a single mom, raising her twelve year old son, who was a Doctor Who fanatic in the way that only twelve years could be. She'd loved my articles and posts about the animations and short pieces, the cartoon doctors, the puppet doctors, even the action figure adventures. She was able to share them with her son, who was wild for them. She was writing to thank me. I felt like I'd done something good, that I'd actually helped make someone's life a little happier in some small way. That I'd done something worthwhile. It was a nice feeling, and I think, as much as anything, it decided me on writing these books.

Review – Out of Time

The Fourth and Tenth Doctor Meet

"The David Tennant and Tom Baker Doctors accidentally meet up at a Cathedral outside of time and space. Before you know it, the Daleks are invading. Will the greatest Doctors of the classic and new eras be able to save the Universe? Of course they will. The fun is seeing them do it."

The world of Doctor Who, and the world of Fan creativity is rapidly moving.

When I first started writing these books, we were coming off the high of Matt Smith's international success, Peter Capaldi was still finding his feet and no one had ever heard of Jody Whittaker. The animated recreation of old serials was barely getting off the ground.

In fandom, the final episodes of the Dark Dimensions animated serial had yet to air. The first episodes of Devious hadn't been released. Bedlam had yet to unleash I See You. DW2012 was barely starting its third series.

I remember talking about how profoundly new technologies were changing fan films, and even how these technologies were affecting animation, allowing single fans to do what took armies of animators in the past. Some of it was rough, but the technology was evolving constantly.

Which brings us to Josh Snares extra-ordinary, hour long, animated story, Out of Time, featuring the 4th Doctor, voiced by Tom Baker, and the 10th Doctor, voiced by David Tennant. I am utterly astonished that this even exists, and more so by the fact that on the whole, it's quite well done.

Wait! What? Where the hell did Josh Snares get Tom Baker and David Tennant from? Well, actually, he didn't. Out of Time is actually a Big Finish Audio Adventure, you can buy it as a CD or download, and I certainly recommend you do so. What Snares has done is used that audio track as a framework to hang his animation.

We've seen earlier fan animators try the same thing with Slipback and Colin Baker, and the Pescatons with Tom Baker, although in those cases, less advanced technology and sheer amount of work meant that the projects seem to have been abandoned halfway through. And to be blunt, using an audio track (and Tele-Snaps for reference and storyboard) is exactly what the BBC did when it animated the old serials. So Snares is simply following a well-established tradition.

Out of Time is part of a Big Finish line that pairs up Tennant's 10th Doctor with several of the classic Doctors. Others in the series have Tennant's Doctor meeting up with the Davison and Colin Baker Doctor. Overall, it's not a bad story. The 4th and 10th, each travelling alone at low point in their lives and hoping to get away from it all, have gone visiting a Cathedral located outside time and space. The Universe, or perhaps the Cathedral being what it is, of course they accidentally run into each other.

Tennant's Doctor knows exactly who Tom is, while Tom eventually figures it out. The Daleks show up to provide complications. It feels like a bit of a standard runaround, I miss the old serials with all their nested plots and subplots. This is a more linear story, more in line with the feel of an extra-length episode of the new series. But what really elevates it are the voice works of Tennant and Baker, and the clear fun they're having with each other. It's simply terrific to have the two of them back slipping into their old characters, and to have them together is sublime. There's a little bickering – multiple Doctors? There has to be. But bickering isn't the point, there's clearly a lot of mutual affection between the Doctors and the actors, and the cat and mouse fencing is entirely engaging and not even a little mean spirited.

As to the animated version, Snares has been quite brilliant. He's stuck it up on Youtube without a sound track. Instead, he provides instructions on how and where to buy the Audio Adventure from Big Finish, and synch it up. Fair warning though, you have to do quite a bit of jigging to get the audio and animation to synch up properly and this can get frustrating. But it's a small irritation compared to the reward. The audio and animation complement each other beautifully, each elevating the other, and creating a whole experience greater than the sum of the parts.

Perhaps for this reason, Big Finish hasn't objected to a rather obvious and massive infringement on their copyright. But then again, why should they. The animation is basically a 59 minute billboard for their product, they'll lose absolutely nothing because of it, and may well rack up additional sales. It certainly started me buying online from big finish.

Besides, Big Finish are basically ascended fans, so they may be more tolerant. I suspect that they're flattered, and perhaps a little astonished.

The animation was a two year labour of love for Snares. Out of Time was released as an Audio in 2020. The animated version was released April, 2022.

And frankly, Snares had been building up to something like this for a long time before that. Years ago, Snares started out making fan films playing the Doctor, quite a lot of them. Almost from the start, he was a heavy user of greenscreen and CGI effects, and rapidly began to get interested in attempting to animate missing episodes using Tele-Snaps as a base. You can still see a lot of Snares earlier experiments and efforts on his YouTube channel.

The point is that he'd kind of been working towards this sort of thing for years, before he took the plunge. It's not like he was some random guy who woke up one morning and casually said"I think I'll commit two years of my life to making an animated episode." By the time he started on this project, he'd made something like a hundred or so YouTube videos, knew what to do with a camera, understood the show, and had been tinkering with animation and effects.

Ironically, Snares couldn't draw, rather, he commissioned an artist, Lucy Crewe, to do a set of basic drawings, and then fed that into 3D modelling and line animation software. This makes it sound altogether casual, and it's actually extraordinary that software packages have evolved to the point this could be done at all. But I'll again remind you: Two years of hard work. The software made it feasible and even easy, but not that easy. As with many modern fan film makers, the project is curated, with Snares also putting up a fascinating "How I did it" video, well worth watching on its own.

With all that said, how does the whole thing hold up? I watched it, first silent with subtitles, and then with the Big Finish Audio synched up. It really is quite remarkable.

It's not perfect. The basic artwork is quite good, though all the characters basically feel like variations on each other – a basic template just dressed up differently each time. Mostly this is fine and not noticeable. Tennant and his Doctor are captured quite well. The Tom Baker Doctor, not quite so much, it's hard to really capture Tom's looming larger than life quality and expressiveness. But if that's a quibble, it's easily overlooked – the drawings and characters are distinctive and fine.

As to the animation, the most irritating thing is that all the characters, even background characters, tend to slowly wave back and forth like they were seaweed in a current. That's slightly off putting – traditional animation involved a lot of arduous line drawing, so unless you were Disney, almost no one was putting unnecessary motion in. The constant waviness draws attention to itself, as does blinking and funny walking. The Abess' crucifix and the 4th Doctor's scarf seem to be made of rubber, as they bounce when the characters walk .

Beyond that, there are some shots, great vistas and perspectives that you don't normally see in normal animation. It feels more overtly cinematic as opposed to animated, if that makes sense. . But these are pretty forgivable distractions. And frankly, the backgrounds and 3D modelling give the production a real sense of scope and an epic quality.

It also comes across as overtly talky. Which makes sense, since it's originally an audio story, and designed for audio storytelling.. There are some scenes or conversations which translate only awkwardly in visual medial. But it's not awkward enough to ruin the enjoyment, it's just a reminder that telling audio stories is itself a distinctive art form from telling visual stories, just as that's distinct from prose.

None of these criticism should get in the way of the fact that I love this to pieces. Without an actual time machine we will never see Tom Baker and David Tennant together in their primes for a television episode, this is as close as we can come.

While an Audio adventure is a treat, the fact that this exists as an animation is delightful.

And, as I've said, it's well done. The lip synching of the animated characters is effective, apart from the walking and seaweed waving effects, the animation is quite well done. You always have a solid sense of location, with visually striking backgrounds, and the motion and character interractions are good.

Compared to the professional animations over the years, this easily beats Richard E. Grant's *Scream of the Shalka* from twenty years ago, and it's definitely better than *Dreamland* or *Infinite Voyage*, Tennant's two animated specials from a decade earlier. That's not to disparage this prior work, but to acknowledge the many factors, including technology, that come into play.

It's easily comparable to the modern BBC recreations, and perhaps better, the recreated serials are flowed in their own way with perhaps too much fidelity to the Tele-Snaps. In contrast, Snare's animation is looser, easier on the eyes, moves more freely and feels like it's rooted in the animation medium, rather than trying to be an animated version of live action.

So yes, it's that good – easily on par with, or exceeding the BBC's various official animation efforts. Perhaps that's faint praise if you're not enamoured with the BBC's efforts.

But the BBC has budgets, and staff and contractors, armies of them on the one side. And on the other side, there's just Josh Snares, spending two years on a dream. So it's not faint praise at all, it's straight up praise.

So look, just buy the Audio Adventure, go look up the Animated adventure, and just watch them together. That's all I have to say.

One of the interesting things about this is the future potential. The fact that one talented, dedicated young man can do something so remarkable, something that would have been flat out impossible not so long ago, suggests that we may see more of this in the future. Certainly the basic raw material is out there – Pertwee's two radio plays from 1993, Tom Baker's *Pescatons*, Colin Baker's *Slipback*, all those lost serials, not even mentioning the massive audio libraries of the BBV and Big Finish.

Even that's just the tip of the possible iceberg. There's nothing to stop fans from writing their own scripts, doing their own voice tracks. Indeed, writing directly for animation, rather than adapting an audio script might work better.

Indeed, the evolving technology may actually drive things towards animation. Traditionally film making, including fan films, has been a collective effort. It took a lot of people to get things done, and the fewer the people, the less you could do, so 80's and 90's fan films were often the product of fan clubs or de facto film clubs. Nowadays, the changing technology, nowadays, allows for more individual effort… which has downsides. But animation actually works better for solo effort than live action.

It is stull, an intimidating amount of work. There aren't that many Josh Snares out there, with that unique combination of extensive prior experience, relentless dedication, and the willingness to put two years into a project, or months into some shorter projcct.

But here's the thing – the *Altered Vistas* crew, the *Dark Dimensions* crew, and now Josh Snares, shows us what is increasingly possible and the changing frontier of what is doable, there's simply a mountain of stuff out there, calling for attention, and every day, the software and the artware becomes more sophisticated, more user friendly, more accessible.

So odds are that in the near future, maybe ten years, maybe five or less, we're going to see more and more and better and better fan animations, steadily approaching or sometimes matching professional quality. I think that's something to look forward to.

CAST: *Tom Baker – The Classic Doctor; David Tennant – The New Doctor; Kathryn Drysdale – Jora; Nicholas Ashbury – Zenna & Kivali; Claire Rushbrook – Abbess & Marna; Nicholas Briggs – Daleks*

AUDIO CREW: *Big Finish Productions; Producer – David Richardson; Director – Nicholas Briggs; Writer – Matt Fitton; Music/Sound – Howard Carter;*

ANIMATION CREW: *Producer, Creator, Animator, Intro-Narration – Josh Snares; Character Art – Lucy Crewe.*

Reviews – The Official Animations

If At First You Don't Succeed

Doctor Who's history with animation, like so much of its history, is full of left turns and strange detours, both in terms of the official production and in fan work.

There's a recurring rumour that the first commercial Doctor Who cartoon, may not have been a Doctor Who cartoon at all. The story goes that back in 1979/1980, the BBC almost made a deal with Hanna-Barbera to license a Doctor Who cartoon.

In itself, that's not a crazy idea. Hanna-Barbera and other animation companies were chugging out all kinds of lunatic stuff for Saturday mornings, Doctor Who was still at the heights of its popularity, Tom Baker was still the Doctor and the show was starting to break through on PBS stations in America.

The story goes that the deal eventually fell through, but Hanna-Barbera took the idea, sketches and development work anyway, pasted Ron Howard and Henry Winkler, and turned it into *Fonzie and the Happy Days Gang*. It seems that Fonzie, Richie Cunningham, and Ralph Malph are having milk shakes at Arnold's, and a time machine materializes in the parking lot, piloted by a teenage girl, with an unbearable

Bronx accent, named Cupcake. Fonzie helps to fix the time machine, and the next thing you know, the gang is bounding across history as the defective machine takes them through time and space.

It's actually pretty dire stuff.

The central characters, Fonzie, Richie and Malph are voiced by the actual actors, but are rendered as hideously ugly caricatures. The animation is minimal. The stories are shallow. It's a testament to misconceived ideas executed badly.

There are a few things that make you think this might be Doctor Who with the serial numbers filed off. The teenage pilot, despite her Bronx accent, might well have been intended to be Susan, or any of the Doctor's young female companions.

The idea of a time machine that lands unpredictably in time and space is classic Doctor Who. The first time trip is to the age of cavemen - shades of *Unearthly Child*, the next is to a race of Robots about to attack humanity - shades of the *Dalek Invasion*. The most persuasive bit of evidence is the Time Ship's console. The time ship itself looks like a chubby flying saucer, though it's arguably bigger on the inside. But the console bears a real resemblance to the Tardis console. So you can see how the rumour got started.

On the other hand, it's a pretty sketchy case. There's no particular resemblance to Susan or anyone else, the stories are pretty generic, time machines never ever land where they're supposed to, that's a staple of fiction. Cavemen and Robots- cliché. As to the console, that's mounted at the center of a round ship? Could be a coincidence.

Happy Days was a retro series from the 70s and early 80s, set in the 1950s, so really the notion of taking that dissonance and extending it to time travel hijinks isn't that out there. Hell, the animated Laverne and Shirley had them joining the army. Hannah-Barbera was just doing weird things. Ultimately there's nothing beyond rumour that makes this a distaff Who clone.

Colour me skeptical.

There was a genuine attempt to produce a Doctor Who cartoon in 1990. After the cancellation of the live series in 1989, *Nelvana Animation* in Canada began development on a Who cartoon. Unlike Hanna-Barbera which had specialized in very stiff, limited animation, Nelvana, was next generation, using new technology and Asian drawing houses, and was a part of a renaissance of action cartoons that dominated Saturday mornings in the 1990s. Their big claim to fame, apart from *Rock and Rule*, and the *Care Bears* movies, was that they had created Boba Fett for George Lucas. That's right; Fett's first appearance was in a cartoon they did for the *Star Wars Holiday Special*. They'd also done *Star Wars* spin off cartoons - *Droids* and *Ewoks,* in the early 1980s.

Nelvana's Doctor Who seemed to be a pretty serious effort - there were a lot of production drawings, at least four scripts were actually written, then suddenly after all the development, the plug was pulled. A number of pieces of the Nelvana artwork by Ted Bastien are on line and are quite interesting.

Their Doctor was still in flux, not based on any existing Doctor. Some versions in the artwork depict the Doctor as a funny old man; other versions go for a more heroic Jeff Goldblum/Harold Ramis/Peter O'Toole look. There's a teenage girl companion, K9, a cyborg Master that is half-robot and half Sean Connery, and new visions of Daleks and Cybermen.

Some might be put off by the fact that this was going to be Who adapted for Saturday morning animation, and geared towards a younger audience. I'm actually quite intrigued as to how it might have turned out; there was some quite impressive stuff back then.

I'm not sure what the story is behind Nelvana's effort. It takes place during the post-cancellation era when all sorts of private groups were trying to obtain the license to produce a movie or a new television series.

Maybe Nelvana approached the BBC. Perhaps the BBC approached them. It may have started off as a tie-in to another Who related project. Given the poor odor of the show with the BBC in 1990, it seems surprising that they'd have considered commissioning an animation company. Take that with a grain of salt.

The word from Nelvana is that the BBC approached them to do it as a sort of continuation of the live action series, and was intended to be their biggest show to date.

The story is that the project ended when a British animation company, possibly Cosgrove Hall, intervened, claiming that they could do it cheaper. If so, that other project never materialized. There's not even a rumour.

After that, if you were jonesing for cartoon Doctors, your best bets were the occasional Tom Baker Doctor cameos that would sneak up on the *Simpson*s from time to time.

Then beginning in 2001-2002, BBCi started to webcast its own Doctor Who animation, starting with *Death Comes to Time,* starring Sylvester McCoy and Sophie Aldred, with Nicholas Courtney showing up as the Brigadier. Among the cast is Stephen Fry, playing another renegade Time Lord called the Minister of Chance.

Calling it animation might be a stretch. What they did was commission a lot of drawings, and then put them up and used zooms, pans and cuts to give a sense of motion to the static images. It may have resembled Reconstructions with drawings instead of photographs more than anything else. It was early in the internet and there wasn't a lot of bandwidth, for genuine animation, so it was what it was.

Death Comes to Time is generally considered non-canonical, given that the McCoy Doctor shows a lot of previously unknown superpowers and eventually dies in it. I think that the idea was to spin off the Minister of Chance into his own web series, as a sort of successor to the Doctor.

Anyway, this was succeeded by *Realtime*, starring Colin Baker in 2002, and then by yet another version of *Shada* with Paul McGann and Lalla Ward in 2003, all of them done in cooperation with Big Finish Audio productions.

BBCi did well enough with this, that they were inspired to launch Doctor Who as a fully animated web series.

They created a new ninth Doctor, played by Richard E. Grant, who starred in an ambitious, flash animated, six-part, ninety minute serial called *Scream of the Shalka*, written by Paul Cornell.

For a time, Richard E. Grant was the BBC's official ninth Doctor, and a second serial, *Blood of the Robots*, was in development.

Then Russell T. Davies brought in the new series with Christopher Ecclestone, and the *Shalka* Doctor was de-canonized. It's still an interesting project.

You can still find *Scream of the Shalka* out there on DVD, and probably online.

After that, during the David Tenant era, there were two animated specials – the cartoon *Infinite Voyage* and the CGI animated *Dreamlands*.

Each was originally broadcast in three minute segments, but have since been compiled together onto DVD releases. Each of them, in their own way, captures the feel of the Tenant series, while doing things that couldn't be done in a live action series. They're a bit scattered, these are essentially compilations of three minute segments and that format will do terrible things to narrative coherence, but worth tracking down.

Finally, somewhere along the line, in the David Tenant or Matt Smith eras, there was apparently talk of doing an animated series which would feature the classic Doctors. I'm not sure what the story behind that is, or how far it got.

Reviews: Reanimating the Classic Adventures

Old Adventures, New Life

Ultimately, the proposed cartoon series failed to launch. Nelvana died stillborn, the *Shalka* Doctor was strangled in the cradle, neither *Dreamland* nor *Infinite Voyage* spun off into anything, and the proposed retro-series never materialized.

Instead, the BBC ended up looking backwards, not forwards for animation. It had a huge back catalogue of *Classic Doctor Who*. But there were gaps – partial stories that were only missing an episode or two! If only there was some way to fill those gaps – then you could market the whole thing.

Initially, one approach was to fill in a missing episodes with a Reconstruction. We've discussed those in *Marco Polo*. Fan Artists like Derek Handley, Ralph Montagu fond their work being taken up by the BBC.

Then, eventually, as sales of these re-released classic serials, supported by Reconstruction episodes, proved out, the BBC experimented with contracting out the missing episode to an animation company.

After all, they had the audio track, courtesy of fans for literally every serial.

There were also Tele-Snaps for visual reference for many serials, which, particularly with the aid of the Reconstructions, served as ready-made animation storyboards.

On top of those were scripts, director's notes, shot lists, even continuity photographs. And if you were doing one episode in a serial, you had the rest of the serial to get the idea and style. Even if you only had one live episode of a serial, it still provided a visual guide.

The earliest attempts were two episodes to fill out the Troughton serial, the *Invasion*, by Cosgrove Hall in 2006. Apparently it didn't turn out so well, or it was too expensive, since there was no follow up. A bit of both, I think. It would be seven years before the BBC tried again.

What happened? Well, in 2008, an American fan and animator, named David Busch pitched animating episodes to the BBC. He figured that the exchange rate between the US and UK made it viable. The BBC said no.

But Ian Levine, who appears often in our tales, said yes. He and Busch got together to create an animated version of *Mission to the Unknown*, which turned out very well. It was basically an audition pitch for the BBC, proof of concept.

Levine and Busch's animated *Mission to the Unknown* can still be found online, by the way. However, in 2019, a group of students from the University of Lancashire, with BBC approval, created a live action version of the episode, taking advantage of the fact that none of the main cast were involved originally. This rather unique experiment is also available online.

Levine had caught the bug. The next project was animating the missing episodes of *Shada,* in 2011, which reunited almost all the surviving actors except Tom Baker, and which Levine offered to the BBC. They didn't buy; eventually they did their own version of *Shada,* with all the actors plus Tom Baker.

But in a sense, it worked. Levine and Busch had provided the BBC with proof of concept, demonstrating that the old serials could be recreated with animation, that it could be done well, and that it could be done economically.

It's true that Cosgrove Hall had taken shot years before, and the BBC had decided not to pursue. They'd kept saying no.

But I think, genuinely, it was the work of Levine and Busch which persuaded them to go for it, leaving Levine and Busch behind, and out of the official history.

Levine, of course would just keep on going, getting weirder with his animated recreations through *Evil of the Daleks*, *Yellow Fever* and *Dark Dimensions*, and taking strange excursions into *Downtime* and *Destiny of the Doctors*, which …maybe he shouldn't have. But hey, it's his life.

In January of 2013, two missing episodes of Hartnell serial, *Reign of Terror* are animated. This is followed in November, 2013, by animating a missing episode of another Hartnell serial, *The Tenth Planet* (the first appearance of the Cybermen). All three episodes were created by an outfit called Planet 55.

That same year, 2013, a company called Qurios Entertainment does the animation work for two more episodes, fir the Troughton serial, the *Ice Warriors*.

In 2014, Planet 55 did two more episodes for the *Moonbase*, a Troughton/Cyberman caper.

This worked well enough that the BBC eventually decided to take the big leap and commission a fully animated *Power of the Daleks*, the classic lost Troughton serial, released in November and December, 2016.

Power of the Daleks was a major step up. This wasn't just one or two episodes to fill in the gaps. *Power* was completely lost, this was a story told completely through animation, with only the audio and the Tele-Snaps as a guide.

They followed it up with The *Macra Terror* in 2019, a Troughton serial.

Then two more serials, both with the Troughton Doctor, *The Faceless Ones* and *Fury From the Deep*, in 2020.

In 2021, Troughton's Evil of the Daleks, and Hartnell's Galaxy Four, in their entirety, plus the missing episode from Web of Fear.

2022 is the *Abominable Snowmen*. And that seems to be the end of the line for now.

The Wheel in Space feels like a good candidate for animation, relatively small cast, visually limited sets, available Tele-Snaps and fairly good quality audio. But that doesn't seem to be in the cards, currently.

All told, so far 49 of the 97 missing episodes, and seven of the eighteen completely or mostly lost serials, have been recreated through animation.

And it's honest animation – those are the real voices of the real actors in their real performances come down to us from the original sixties era broadcasts. The visual references, the Tele-Snaps, set photos and extensive fan and professional research means that this is a close to recreating the original episodes with maximum fidelity as you can get with current technology.

The only way to do better would be to use a time machine. Or hire live actors as lookalikes, train them to move with the same body language, rebuild the sets and film it all over again. No one is going to pay for that.

Actually, they did this for the *Mission to the Unknown* episode, but that was a single, unique stand-alone episode without any of the main cast. It's probably not viable for the rest of the lost episodes.

As to the animated episodes and serials themselves- your mileage varies. I found the earliest animated episodes to be pretty tough sledding. The figures are stiff, their motions and actions unnatural, there's very little of the flow you get with purposeful animation drawn for that purpose. There's a variation of quality.

They're trying to re-create a live television episode with line drawings or computer drawings, and often it's pretty tough going. A fan animation like *Dark Dimensions*, has its own drawbacks, but it also has strengths compared to the *Power of the Daleks* animation, which comes across quite wooden in comparison.

I don't know that the BBC recreation animations will wholly escape this woodenness. It may be baked into the very nature of what they're trying to do – recreating an old television episode from audio recordings and photographic references, and including limitations on the budgets.

But I do have the impression that they're getting steadily better at it, and more recent efforts like *Fury From the Deep* or *Evil of the Daleks* have been quite lively and even somewhat fluid.

Still, despite their drawbacks, an animated *Power of the Daleks* or *Fury from the Deep* is better than no *Power of the Daleks* or *Fury from the Deep*.

It's not clear where things are going to go from here. It may be that the Abominable Snowmen, or possibly the Wheel in Space, may be the last efforts.

The problem, you see is that the Tele-Snaps are running out. John Cura only started doing his Tele-Snaps of Doctor Who partway through the third series. There aren't really any Tele-Snap references for most of Hartnell's lost serials. As I've said, these have been essential visual references, practically the animation storyboards, and the work of fan reconstruction artists has been essential. Literally, a huge amount of key work in the animation process was done.

Without the Tele-Snaps and Reconstructions... well, it's a lot harder to maintain any kind of visual fidelity. And there just aren't that many left. From here on in, eventually they would have to start from the beginning and fly blind. That makes it a lot more expensive.

On the audio side, remember that the audio tracks or voice or sound tracks were all from fan recordings, taken off the television. The quality of these recordings varies, and some of it is pretty tough going. Restoring it to proper levels may be expensive even with today's technology. Some of it may be beyond today's sound technology.

The bottom line is that from the *Abominable Snowman*, creating these animations will be more and more difficult and expensive for the budget conscious BBC. Maybe they will, maybe they won't.

Of coure, the real deciding issues are economic, and particularly, it breaks down two ways.

First – how to pay for this? The current round of animations were jointly funded by the BBC and BBC America which is a separate enterprise. BBC America has ended its participation. Without its contribution of money, the BBC doesn't have the budget for further animations.

Well, technically, the BBC has a lot of money, but it also has a lot of demands, a lot of projects. It's unwilling to put aside sufficient funds to do this on its own, and requires a partner to share the costs.

The ultimate issue, however is simply an equation: How much money does it take to make these, and what revenue will they produce. If the animations lose money, they won't make them. Simple as that

But that kind of business decision is a moving target. Right now, Doctor Who is in a bit of a slump, the Whittaker era has not been well received by fans or the public. That probably affects the marketplace for Doctor Who spin offs like the animated recreations. But there's a new Doctor, and a beloved showrunner returning, so that may change.

The other variable is cost. And those costs are coming down, simply as a result of technology. Those same advances in technology that have made it possible for fans to create their own Dark Dimensions and Out of Time has also been making commercial animated productions faster, easier and especially cheaper. That's likely to continue.

So more popularity, more sales, cheaper production? I think eventually, we'll see all the lost episodes restored in animated re-creations.

Even if the BBC does re-create all the lost episodes, I suppose that raises the question:

What will they do when all of those lost episodes and serials are re-animated?

Where to from there? Doctor Who has proved itself out in animated form several times now, but never actually in mainstream animated venues.

So who knows?

Let me leave you with a final observation. The animated serials are terrific, I'm happy to have them, and I'm grateful to the BBC. I take nothing away from them

But these animated serials only exist because Doctor Who's fans built the foundations for them.

It was the fans that recorded the audio.

It was fans that dug out John Cura's forgotten Tele-Snaps and literally created an art form in Reconstructions that the BBC adopted and legitimized in its own releases.

Those Reconstructions paved the way and eventually became the blueprint for the animations. Something that fans were already searching for ways to do and attempting, well before the BBC came on board.

And in the end, it was the fans like Ian Levine and David Busch that created the proof of concept and persuaded the BBC that this was something they could and should do.

The BBC tried animation at various points along the way, and even tried animating missing episodes in serials. But in the end, they decided it wasn't cost effective and wasn't worth worth doing.

But with these efforts at *Mission of Doom* and *Shada*, they showed it could be done effectively.

I take nothing away from the BBC, but the often overlooked part of the story, is that animating the lost episodes is built upon the work, the inspiration, the impulses and ideas, the preserved records, research and proof of concept of fans.

And I think that is something admirable that we should remember and be inspired by.

CHAPTER 14 - THE AUDIO WHO

The Doctor That Became A Dalek

Let me introduce you to Doctor Who's Howard Stern, Nicholas Briggs. Okay, he doesn't have Howard Stern's hair, or Stern's raucous manner. But in the world of Doctor Who, Nicholas Briggs is the original Audio Doctor, and King of Doctor Who media.

Audio-Visuals, Reeltime, BBV, Big Finish, Stage Plays, documentaries, books, Daleks, Cybermen, Ice Warriors, Autons, writer, producer, Director, the BBC Doctor Who, *Sarah Jane Adventures*, no matter where you're looking, somewhere along the way, you'll find Nicholas Brigg, he's been everywhere, he's done everything, he's the voice of monsters, an ever present background presence.

Like the Mark Sinclair, Kevin Davies and Mark Ayres of the late 1970s, Briggs came to the world of Doctor Who through the official fan club, the Doctor Who Appreciation Society

(DWAS), which emerged as a sort of combined recruiting base, resource center and appreciative audience for fan activities.

Briggs started off in the early 80s, with Keith Barnfather, as an interviewer for Reeltime's *'Myth Makers'* series. Basically, these were a series of semi-professional video interviews with Doctor Who stars and actors, the video tapes sold in specialty comic and gaming shops.

During this period, Briggs worked on a spoof – *Myth Runner*. Briggs also appeared and acted in *Wartime,* starring John Levene, as UNIT's Sargent Benton, a character from the Pertwee era. This was first legal spin off featuring a Doctor Who character, forerunner of *Downtime, Shakedown*, the *Stranger* series, and all the rest. That was kind of a warm up act.

The real breakthrough was in 1985. Following season 22, at the end of 1984, Colin Baker's Doctor Who was cancelled, uncancelled, and then put on an 18 month holiday to return with reduced episodes and the *Trial of a Time Lord* in 1986.

During the hiatus, Eric Saward wrote a Doctor Who audio story for BBC Radio. *Slipback*. This was a wake-up call for two young men, Gary Russell and Bill Baggs. Basically, it showed them that Doctor Who could be done as an audio, it showed them how it was done badly, and it convinced them they could do better. The Audio Visuals were born.

Nick Briggs wasn't the original Doctor. That was Stephen Payne. But after the first Audio Visuals release, Briggs took the role and remained the Doctor through the rest of the four seasons of the Audio Visuals run. Twenty-seven audio stories, recorded on cassette tapes, from 1985 to 1991, passed from hand to hand, copied, traded and circulated among British fandom. Like Barbara Benedetti, Nick became the Doctor of the Gap. A fan himself, Nicholas was a regular at conventions, developing his Doctor's visual persona and style.

Briggs by this time had become so well known as an alternative Doctor, that his likeness and persona was used in the Doctor Who monthly comic strip in 1991.

In 1991, Bill Baggs, one of the original producers of the Audio Visuals decided to go pro, or semi-pro, creating the BBV to make videos and audios inspired by the Doctor Who universe. Briggs was involved in different ways in several productions.

In the late 1990s, Briggs came to work on a couple of significant projects with Baggs. The first was the *Auton* video trilogy. Briggs wrote and directed the first two, but the relationship between the two men was contentious. Eventually, there was a falling out with Baggs and took Briggs name off the third.

Meanwhile, Baggs and the BBV had decided to go back to its roots with a series of audio stories using thinly veiled versions of the Doctor. Sylvester McCoy and Sophie Aldred had several adventures as the Professor and Alice.

Briggs Doctor came back in a pair of audio adventures, *Cyber Hunt*, in 1998, and *Vital Signs* in 1999. He couldn't be called the Doctor, obviously. Instead, the character was a time traveller with amnesia who eventually calls himself Fred. I have the impression Briggs wasn't entirely comfortable. The cover art or photos, as well as Briggs voice and character, linked back to his Audio Visuals Doctor. His character, and these stories, would eventually appear as BBV novelizations.

Around this time, 1999, Briggs Doctor made another appearance in the comic strip in *Doctor Who monthly*, portraying a man who thinks he's the Doctor, but it turns out to be a hoax. Again, a means of finessing legal and canonical issues.

Briggs moved on from the Audio Visuals and BBV to join Garry Russell in helping found Big Finish Productions, around 1998. There he did a number of voice roles in Audio Adventures, including playing the Doctor in certain 'unbounded' stories – ones where the official actors weren't in the role. Mostly, I don't think, his portraits of the Doctor in these audios weren't related to his Audio Visuals Doctor, albeit the man and the voice is the same. Still the shadow lingers.

It's a weird sideways bit of fame, the man who was sort of the Doctor, for certain purposes, in a certain time and place and venue.

Briggs audio work, particularly doing voices for the Daleks, attracted the attention of Russell T- Davies, back when he was rebooting Doctor Who in 2005. Briggs got to be the voice of the Nestene Consciousness in the first episode, *Rose*. Since then, he's been on the show doing voices for Daleks, Cybermen, Judoon, Ice Warriors, you name it. The internet movie database lists 47 appearances as a voice actor on Doctor Who between 2005 and 2022, which may be some kind of record. If you've listened to a Dalek or Cyberman on television, it was probably Briggs.

He did Judoon voices for *Sarah Jane Adventures*, he actually appeared face and body in *Torchwood*. He was in the *Five-ish Doctors*, as a Dalek voice operator. He's done voice work for Doctor Who games, specials, documentaries, spin offs of every sort, animations, you name it. He's even appeared in *Lego Dimensions* and the *Lego Batman* movie as 'British Robots' (Daleks) voices.

And he appeared as the regeneration from the Scovell Doctor in Bedlam's production of *The Dalek Masterplan* stage play.

Along the way, he's written, directed, produced and done pretty much everything else. None of it is actually terribly huge, it's almost all small stuff, along the margins, and a great deal of it connects directly or indirectly to Doctor Who. But it's an impressive, even astonishing track record that just sprawls across every sort of media or expression.

I think the term for Nicholas Briggs is "Ascended Fan." He loved the show, and it seems that the show and the world of Doctor Who loves him right back, he's found a place in the official professional series, he's a big wheel in the parallel audio universe of Big Finish, and he's been everywhere, done everything. He's still at it, so I assume he's happy where he is. It's kind of nice.

It would be tragic if he got sick of it.

So, maybe the next time you're wandering through the Doctor Who universe, keep an eye out for Nicholas Briggs name. Just, for god's sake, don't make it a drinking game.

The Official Audio Productions

A Brief History, Cushing to Baker to Pertwee

This is a book about fan films mostly. I'm visual, I'm drawn to the visual component. Doctor Who is a television series after all. It shows up in a lot of different media, but first and last, it's a television series.

That said, there's also an audio only component to Doctor Who, one that overlaps strongly with the fan world and fan productions, so it's hard not to at least touch on the subject.

On the professional side, it amounted to Doctor Who dipping a toe in the audio medium, in a brief flurry of efforts, once a decade, in 1966, 1976, 1985, 1993.

For instance, 1965 and 1966 was a banner year for Doctor Who. The series was amazingly successful on television. We've talked about Dalekmania, the back to back Doctor Who movies starring Peter Cushing, Doctor Who comics, songs, even an original book, Doctor Who and the Invasion From Space. It makes sense that with a franchise that popular, there'd be some exploration of audio media in radio and records.

The first audio version of Doctor Who was actually based on the movies. Back in 1966, there was a BBC Radio program that specialized in presenting stripped down, half hour versions of movies. They'd fill in a lot of narration to explain what's going on; edit things down to key dialogue and plot points. It was like going to the movies, without the bother of actually having to waste time watching them. That doesn't make a lot of sense to me. It's a British thing, I suppose. One of their features was *Daleks Invasion Earth 2150 AD*, starring Peter Cushing, an adaptation of the televised Hartnell story, *Dalek Invasion Earth*. It's a testament to how popular the Daleks were at the time that they didn't even bother to mention Doctor Who in the title. Sadly, this program is now probably lost to us.

The second audio, also from 1966, was a pilot for a *Doctor Who Radio Series*, also starring Peter Cushing. This was produced by Bruce Stanley, a former radio pirate (there was indeed such a thing). The pilot was a half hour production called '*Journey into Time*' written by Malcolm Hulke, which saw the Doctor and his companions, Susan and Mike, get involved in the American Revolution. Mostly, the pilot episode wastes its time on set up.

Radio drama had actually been a lively thing back in the day – *Superman, the Shadow*, the *Lone Ranger*, the original soap operas, were all radio stalwarts in the 1930s and 40s. Radio drama was dead cheap to produce, easy on the actors who simply sat or stood at microphones, and special effects amounted to a Foley guy with a variety of noise makers. It was common and popular, and for a while it held its own against movie theatres. After all, you could enjoy radio drama, or radio comedy at home, but for a movie you actually had to go out to a theatre. At least until television came along.

Sadly, radio drama was a dying or dead form by the 1960s, so the Doctor Who radio series never took off. Bruce Stanley eventually moved to Australia where he became involved in film and television production. The audiotape for the radio pilot became the first 'lost Who.' And is still lost to this day.

The script for that pilot, though, has been rediscovered and fans have made their own audio version. So if you're curious, hunt it down.

Finally, Century 21 Records got into the act, releasing a seven inch record containing a very abridged episode of the Hartnell Dalek serial *The Chase*, based on the episode *Planet of Decision*.

After that, things went quiet. During the dying days of the Pertwee Era, in 1974, there was apparently an unaired ten minute radio sketch called *Glorious Goodwood*, which would be a terrific porn title. In it Sarah Jane Smith wandered around the Goodwood racing downs in the Whomobile, spoke to Jon Pertwee on the phone, and was menaced by Daleks. That was more a hiccup than anything else.

The next flurry of efforts was a couple of years later, around 1976, during the height Tom Baker era. Baker was an incredibly popular Doctor; so once again, there was that interest in exploring Doctor Who in new media. The most famous project during this time was Doctor Who versus the Scratchman, a feature film written by Ian Marter and Tom Baker himself, it was psychedelic and surreal, and it died in the planning stage. Which might be for the best, all around. Strange things were being done in movie theatres during this era.

Baker's first foray into the audio world was an appearance on a BBC Radio called *Exploration Earth*, a science series aimed at children. Tom Baker and Liz Sladen voiced their characters, the Doctor and Sarah Jane in an episode called *The Time Machine*. It is what it is, a children's educational radio play.

Baker and Sladen then followed up with a 46 minute audio play, released on vinyl, long play, in two episodes, called *The*

Pescatons. The story, by Victor Pemberton, who had written the Troughton serial *Fury From the Deep*, was about a race of humanoid sharks invading Earth because their planet is about to be destroyed. It's pretty terrible and that Pemberton writes as if Troughton is still the Doctor.

Radio drama had pretty much died off. But the vinyl record industry was huge, and the sheer volume and diversity of music recorded and sold on vinyl meant that there was an entire infrastructure – everything from recording studios to record stores. This infrastructure meant that artists were able to experiment and niche productions could find a market, even if that was just a box in the corner of the record store. Comedy records were pretty big in the seventies and eighties, with everyone from Rudy Ray Moore, to Bill Cosby, George Carlin to Monty Python releasing comedy records. There was a market for children's records, not just music, but children's fairy tales.

I have no idea if there was a market for audio drama on vinyl, I suspect not much of one. But record stores were always ready to take a chance on a novelty, and sometimes novelties took off, or even founded a genre. For a product as popular as Doctor Who, I can see the experiment being made. Remember that VCR's or DVD players didn't exist in the 1970s, the serials weren't being rerun, and the only way for fans to record them was by audio. So, at the peak of Tom Baker's popularity, branching out into vinyl audio adventures didn't seem unreasonable.

It didn't really work. Part of it was simply a weak story and a rather slapdash effort at production. But there was something more critical: Every medium, every art form has its own demands, its own requirements and logic. Radio or audio drama is the same, you can do things that television can't, but at the same time, there are things you can't do that television can, and there are things that just have to be done differently. The range of opportunities and obstacles is different. There had been a very successful history of radio drama. But that was decades in the past, and I suspect that many of those techniques and skills had atrophied, and the people behind them either weren't around or weren't recruited for the project. Tom Baker has a brilliant voice, but he's also a physically expressive actor. And I don't think that the form was really all that respected by that time. With all of that in mind, I suspect that Pemberton didn't really have any mastery of what was probably a pretty difficult form. Bottom line is that the Pescatons failed to go anywhere.

If Radio drama had been dead or dying in the 1960s, then by the 70s, it was long past resuscitation. The idea went nowhere. Things went quiet again.

Or maybe I speak to soon. BBC Radio wasn't a commercial enterprise; it had no special need for ratings and revenue. It just needed to fill air space. So there was remaining, a tradition of BBC radio comedy and drama. Douglas Adams, former script editor on Doctor Who, went on to fame and success with his *"Hitchhikers Guide to the Galaxy"* which started as a radio comedy in 1978. Eric Saward, who would become script editor for Who in the Davison and Colin Baker eras apparently started with radio dramas, featuring an Elizabethan swashbuckler named Richard Mace. Saward would even recruit a radio drama writer, Wally Daley to write for the show.

So perhaps the skills were still out there, and they just weren't applied to *The Pescatons*, which seems to have been a license venture rather than a BBC production. Perhaps the radio people who could have done it effectively were never invited.

Meanwhile, Terrance Dicks, who had been heavily involved with the franchise since 1968, acting as story editor, writing serials, stage plays and novels, pitched a Doctor Who radio series in the 1970s - presumably starring Tom Baker. Again, it's not clear why this never happened; perhaps it was simply a matter of 'turf' with the television side protecting its own, or radio not wanting to be involved.

The next big development in the world of Audio who was 1985. Doctor Who was off the air on hiatus as the show was cancelled and then uncancelled. With the show off the air, a BBC children's show called *Pirate Radio Four*, decided to run its own radio serial. The result, by series story editor Eric Saward, attempting to channel the spirit of Douglas Adams, was called *Slipback* and ran in six ten minute episodes. It was generally seen as a fill in for the missing series on television.

Slipback is an insubstantial piece of work – it's only an hour, and the requirement to break it into ten minute segments probably undermines it. It's available out there, if you want to find it, and it may be worthwhile to do so.

Slipback's biggest impact was entirely unnoticed. A pair of fans, Bill Baggs and Garry Russell decided that they could do the same, and do it better, and went on to found the Audio Visuals. More on them later.

That was it for a while.

Then thirtieth anniversary was coming up in 1993. The trouble was that the show had been dead since 1989. There was a sentiment among fans that this was it, the show was to come back in some form. *The Dark Dimensions* project got underway, collapsed and in its place was mounted the completely unrelated *Dimensions in Time*. There was a documentary. But by and large, television production was too expensive and ambitious and the BBC wasn't interested.

During this time, BBC Radio stepped in with a couple of radio plays - *The Ghosts of N-Space* and *Paradise of Death*, written by Terrance Dicks, and featuring Jon Pertwee and Liz Sladen. Jon Pertwee, by this time, had gotten pretty old, he was 74 years old, and you could hear it in his voice. He would pass away in 1996. The Terrance Dicks scripts were far from

Terrance Dicks' best work. But if you're a fan of the Pertwee Doctor and his era, these two stories represent both a call back and an addition, and are well worth searching out.

With the exception of some of the 1966 stuff, pretty much all the rest of this is available to be tracked down by dedicated fans, and for those who are dedicated to the classic era, that's a worthy undertaking. The consensus is that almost all of the official Audio releases were inferior to the actual television show at the time, but they're still worthy footnotes.

The Rise of Fan Audio Adventures

In the 1960s and 1970s, the only way that fans could record the show was on audio tape, with bulky reel to reel tape recorders.

Fans embraced them with open arms. These recordings formed a basis for early fandom. Back then, there was no such thing as reruns, no VHS or DVD releases. Legally, an episode could only be aired twice, so if you missed it, you were out of luck. Unless you or someone you knew had hooked up the bulky reel to reel and made an audio recording you could listen to.

But reel to reel tapes allowed fans to listen to audio recordings of serials gone from television. Reel to Reel was an old audio format, basically, these were big clunky box-like machines, the size of a suitcase, which played audio tapes almost the size of dinner plates. You would stick a reel on one axis; thread the tape through a reader, and onto a receiving reel. It was cumbersome as hell and inferior to vinyl, although still easier to manage than a super8 or other film projector.

But you could play music with it and have quality sound. With a microphone attachment, you could record with a high degree of fidelity. You could even hook up your reel to reel to your television and create an audio record of the program.

The Reel to Reel system hung around for a good long time, until the early 80s. I'm dating myself, but I remember being in University in the early 80s, singing along to 'American Pie' as a group of us listened to it on an old reel to reel. Technology often lingers, even after it becomes obsolete.

Here in the modern era, where we turn up our noses at DVD for Blu-ray and insist on 4 k, this seems… bizarre. Recording the audio of television? That seems so… incomplete, so inadequate, so empty. But there were a couple of reasons why this was so vital.

First, immediately prior to the age of television, there had been a lively era of radio drama. *Superman, The Shadow, The Lone Ranger* and many others had made it big as radio serials. So it wasn't as if audio dramas were completely alien to the culture. People, or at least their parents, were familiar with the format.

Another factor was simply that television was a bit different back then. In the 1950s well into the 70s, most television was black and white, usually on pretty small screens between 12 and 16 inches, the images were broadcast, subject to fading in and out and even at best, the cathode ray tubes of the time poor resolution… sometimes you weren't missing much. The writers often had a background in radio drama, or stage, so their stories were often dialogue heavy and character driven, rather than action oriented. So an audio recording of Star Trek or Doctor Who was innately more accessible then.

And finally, you couldn't record a television image – no VCR, no DVD, no downloads. So you took what you could get.

The culture of making and sharing audio recordings was a vital part of fandom. People came together to listen to these recordings, they copied and traded them. This wasn't just Doctor Who; people recorded the *Avengers, Star Trek, Gunsmoke,* all their favourites. The practices that would mature into the VHS trading networks and culture of the 80s and 90s began here.

Some fans were extremely thorough in making an audio recording of every episode. Six fans in particular, from those days are notable – from them, we have audio records of every single lost episode: Graham Strong, David Holman, Richard Landen, David Butler, James Russell and Allen Wilson.

In the long run, when the BBC began junking the actual episodes, these recordings would, in many cases, be all that was left, and would form the basis for reconstructions and animations. Literally all the lost Doctor Who episodes survive only through fan audio recordings and everything built on those audio records, is built on the dedication and efforts of fans. It's a remarkable thing to contemplate.

It's likely that fans began making their own versions of Doctor Who adventures on audiotape early on. One of the impulses that separate fans from the general audience is their impulse to create based on their inspiration - fans create, they do crafts and doilies, sew costumes, build props, publish fanzines, write fanfiction, do drawings, there's a whole body of naive and untutored art that comes out of the community of fans.

Fan created audio adventures were almost certainly a part of that. If so, most of these are probably lost to us, abandoned, discarded, sitting in trunks and drawers, obscure and undiscovered. There probably weren't much of them initially. You could record on Reel to Reel, and you could even get creative, but it was still a cumbersome format.

Then along comes the Cassette Tape. An audio tape on a small, self-contained cassette. Like Super8 film, these were designed to be really user friendly. Small, portable, hand held, no clunky reels to thread. You had a cassette, you popped it in, played it, popped it out.

The audio cassette format was released in 1963, and the first recorder was 1964, and so these likely were coming into use. But with any new technology, there's a lag where it takes time to spread, and another lag where it takes time for the quality to refine.

The audio cassettes remained a dominant format, into the early 21st century, even in the face of CD's in the 1990s. One of the reasons that the audio cassette hung on was the ease with which you could record and copy onto it.

By the 70s the quality of cassette sound was reaching the point where it could start to compete with vinyl records. Suddenly, you started to see things like ghetto blasters, walkmans, double track players, cassette players installed in cars, recording functions to record directly off of radio, or vinyl, or another cassette. You also started to see handheld tape recorders.

This was the era of the 'mix tape' when people started recording their own music, building their own music cassettes, mixing and matching music that they liked, rather than being stuck with the arrangements or songs of a particular album. The mix tape became an art form in and of itself. The cassette tape had come into its own, and it offered this wonderful bounty of possibilities. You could do things with it. You could create.

You could, with a couple of tape recorders, or a double cassette ghetto blaster, and some friends, write and produce your own audio Doctor Who adventure. The technology had made things so much easier. I've talked about this before, with Super 8, and with VCR's and Camcorders, these ongoing intersections of culture and technology, each of them changing, and with these changes, opening up new avenues for creativity.

And of course, Doctor Who was hard to find. Videocassette recorders were coming in and would quickly replace audio recording of episodes for fans. But the show was still on only for half the year or less, and while there was a huge backlog of serials, it would take time for those to begin circulating on videotape, either as commercial releases from the BBC, or as fan recorded tapes copied and circulated.

So if you wanted more Doctor who… well, tough luck. Unless you decided to make your own, then audiocassettes were an inviting friendly technology full of promise and possibility.

Fan Audios are simply easier to produce than Fan Films. The vast technical challenges of producing even an amateur film are immensely simplified. Forget about costumes, locations, forget about sets, forget about props, forget about schlepping giant piles of expensive and cumbersome equipment all over the place, forget about wrangling crews of actors, camera people, sound people, costumers, make-up artists. All you need is a few friends with voices, a microphone and a tape recorder. These days, it's more sophisticated audio equipment and software. Nowadays, your voice actors don't even have to be in the same room, or together on the same day. But even back in the early days, it was easy.

This made it easier and more tempting for fans to get their feet wet, to build capacity and ability to work up to a film production. Or, exhausted by an attempted film production, to try and do something in an easier format.

Another factor was that it was also easy to distribute. Making a copy was as simple as loading two cassettes into a ghetto blaster and pressing a button. The cassettes were small, portable and cheap, easy to pass hand to hand, or through the mail. They began to circulate through fan clubs always eager for new material to showcase at club meetings. The advent of the internet made things exponentially easier with uploading.

The earliest fan audio group that we have a record of was called 'Doctor Who Audio Dramas' (DWAD) dating back to

1982, right around the time that audio cassettes hit their stride. The *Doctor Who Audio Dramas* have active been for over thirty years and still going strong. You can find them online today, where they've claimed up to 70,000 downloads a month. Their website even has a writers guide. *DWAD* has actually had a longer continuous run than either the classic or the new series, and very nearly matches the combined seasons. They feature over 190 episodes or stories. The *DWAD* stories have featured six successive Doctor, some based on or influenced by existing classic Doctors, and some of them independent evolutions of their own. This body of work is so immense that I can't really do much more than acknowledge that it's out there. Essentially, they've created their own long running, self-contained, Doctor Who universe, for the unwary or enthusiastic fan to step in.

Since that time, there have been a lot of audio production groups. Far too many to list now, and probably more showing up from time to time. We'll just mention a few of them: *Best Fishes* was an audio group active around 2000 to 2003, which featured the first known woman audio Doctor. *BTR Productions* is an Australian audio series, not restricted to Doctor Who, which has been intermittently active since 1998. Another long running Australian group was *Crossover Adventures*, where the Doctor might meet anyone from Buffy the Vampire Slayer to the Muppets. Yet another crossover series is *Doctor Who: The Star Wars Chronicles* featuring Jaspreet Singh as the Doctor.

Between the success of *Big Finish* in almost single handedly establishing a vast commercial audio universe and the revival of the show, fan made audio productions have exploded in the last fifteen years.

Fan-made audio dramas remain a thing. Several of the production groups making fan films have also made audio dramas: Scovell and Thrush's *Bedlam Productions*, *Plymouth Productions*, *Teens Inc.* Even *Timebase* flirted with the idea of doing an audio drama for its anniversary. There are a number of groups which strictly, for artistic choice, or for resources, make audio adventures exclusively. As with all amateur productions, quality will vary. But there's likely brilliance among the dross.

The challenge of so many of these audio adventures is often in finding them. In the 80s and 90s, audio tapes were passed (and lost) hand to hand, ending up as forgotten relics in drawers and boxes. The internet offered new opportunities for access. But there was so much of everything on the internet, that even where you made an audio drama, finding an audience was like finding a needle in a haystack. The cozy old networks of fans and fan clubs gave way to a wilder and more anonymous world. People like David Nagel and Matthew Chambers, or forums like Gallifrey Base have become almost essential as central reference points. Even so, a lot of these audio productions vanish away, when hosting web sites come down.

The most famous and influential fan based audio adventures came in 1985, the year of the hiatus, from a group called the *Audio Visuals*. Founded by Bill Baggs and Garry Russell, their membership included Nicholas Briggs, Nigel Fairs, Chris Corney, Stephen Payne, Christian Darkin. From 1985 through 1991, the Audio Visuals group produced twenty-six audio adventures, most of them starring Nicholas Briggs as the Doctor.

The *Audio Visuals* were clearly born of the frustration from the cancellation crisis of 1985. There was an 18 month period where there was an active fandom, but no show to be a fan of.

Like Barbara Benedetti, Nicholas Briggs was a '*Doctor of the Gap*', called into existence by the extended period when the show was in limbo.

Without the hiatus, it's possible that they would not have bothered. Certainly, their continuing to go through the work of writing, producing and voicing their own audio stories reflected continuing disenchantment with the series after its return.

Gary Russell, one of the key *Audio Visuals* once told a fanzine, the Sonic Screwdriver, in Australia that Eric Saward *"...wouldn't know drama if it bit him."* I suspect that the BBC radio series *Slipback* probably helped to inspire the *Audio Visuals*. Fan produced audio adventures were already a thing, but *Slipback* was an official endorsement of the concept, and apparently, such an unsatisfactory one that it inspired the notion that they could do it better.

Basically, there was no Doctor Who in 1985, so they made their own. And more than that, there was a demand for it. The tapes circulated through fan clubs across England. Then when the show came back, they didn't like it all that much, so they kept on making their own. At their height, I'm told they were distributing up to 600 tapes for an adventure. That's an insane volume considering that these were all unpaid people literally doing this as a collective hobby.

The members of the *Audio Visuals*, particularly Briggs, Baggs and Russell, went on to bigger and better things.

Last Stand of the BBV

Bill Baggs moved on from the Audio Visuals to actual visuals, beginning with Colin Baker and Nicola Bryant as a very thinly disguised version of the Doctor and Companions in *The Stranger* series, between 1991 and 1995. In the wilderness years following the show's cancellation, that went over very well, and Baggs stuck with it.

The first three episodes of the *Stranger* were straight up Doctor Who. After that, there was some nervousness about the BBC, and the Stranger's background and history were revised, with Colin remaining and Nicola Bryant departing.

The Stranger was accompanied in 1993 by a one-off video called *The Airzone Solution*, which had nothing to do with Doctor Who, but managed to unite most of the living actors who had played the Doctor.

Following on both the Stranger and the Airzone, in 1995-1996, was *PROBE*, written by Mark Gatiss. This featured a former Doctor Who actress, Carolyn Jones, nominally playing Doctor Liz Shaw, former scientific advisor to UNIT and Pertwee companion in his first series. It was 25 years later, the connection was thin at best, but the *X-Files* was big and that was the vibe they were going for. The first of *PROBE*'s four episodes reunited four actors who had played the Doctor, much like the *Airzone Solution*. 1997 saw Auton and the beginning of the *Auton trilogy* on video.

But then in 1997-1998 Baggs and the BBV went back to doing Audios.

They didn't exactly give up on Video. *Auton 2* was released in 1998. *Auton 3* in 1999. *Do You Have a License to Save this Planet*, 2000, *Cyberon* in 2001. *Zygon* was shot and abandoned in 2003, before being revived in 2008. They kept chugging them out.

The thing with video though, is that it is immensely difficult. You need sets and locations, scouts to find locations, carpenters to build the sets, you need props and prop-makers, you need make up and wardrobe, a bevy of camera people to shoot, lighting technicians to make sure that the shots come out, and another sound crew to record, continuity people to make sure that everything matches from shot to shot, and once it's all done, there's a whole set of processes involved to make sure everything fits together.

It is, as Baggs found, and as the makers of *Downtime* and *Shakedown* found, an incredibly difficult, expensive, and protracted process, extremely hard to do well, very easy to do badly, and time consuming any way you looked at it.

In comparison, an audio adventure was much easier. Get the actors into a room with some microphones, a script, a technician to make sure your sound levels were right, maybe a Foley guy to add some effects, and boom! You have a product. In fact, you could create a dozen products, or adventures, on audio, for the time, the money and resources; it took to do a single one on video.

But there was another aspect to it. Back in the late 80s, the Audio-Visuals had distributed their adventures on Audio Cassettes, as many as 600 at a time. What this meant was that you literally had to physically record onto each Audio Cassette, one at a time, six hundred times. That was a giant pain in the ass. The cassettes could be copied from one to another, but each generation of copying lost sound quality, and eventually, the tapes would wear out.

But in the 1990s, audio Compact Disks started taking over the market, and that was much easier. All you had to do was feed the digital information, and you could stamp out an infinite number of Compact Disks, of pristine quality. With no moving parts, simply an emulsified plastic disk, the CD was immensely cheaper. The manufacturing and printing technology had become accessible to small producers. All you really paid for was the cost of packaging. The economics were changing overnight.

In contrast, video was still struggling with VHS tapes. DVD wouldn't appear until the end of the 1990s.

What this all meant there was a lot of incentive at both the back and the front end to go back to Audio, and by this time, the BBV had established itself in the marketplace – they were at Conventions, in specialty stores, available through mail order, everyone knew who they were and what they did. So the marketing work was done.

In fact, the BBV had already experimented with audio, in 1995, releasing a couple of audio stories as part of the Stranger series. These '*Stranger Chronicles*" audios filled in backstory for the Stranger's new history and teased the upcoming adventure.

Baggs enlisted Sylvester McCoy and Sophie Aldred to play a pair of travelers through time and space called the "Professor" and "Ace." Basically, the Doctor and Ace. Through 1998, they released a series of adventures – *Republica, Island of Lost Souls, Prosperity Island, Left Hand of Darkness, the Otherside* and *Guest for the Night*.

At some point, the BBC got a little peeved, Ace was after all Ace, played by Sophie Aldred, and on television, her character habitually referred to the Doctor as 'Professor.' Baggs had made a practice of tap dancing on the BBC's patience, but this was the second time he was literally flat out ripping them off.

This didn't even sport fig leaf that Colin Baker's Stranger had. Literally, Ace was Ace, and the Professor was the Doctor. So in 1999, they became the "Dominie" (Scottish for schoolmaster, or something like that) and "Alice," and they went on to appear *in Ghosts, Only Human, Guests for the Night, The Choice, Blood Sports*, with the "Dominie" on a solo outing in 2000 called *Punchline*.

That wasn't the only 'Doctor' Baggs had going. The former Audio-Visuals fan Doctor, Nicholas Briggs, came back twice, to play an amnesiac version of his Doctor, in *Cyber Hunt* in 1998 and *Vital Signs* in 1999.

In 1999, Baggs started to branch out, bringing out K9 and Mistress, in *Adventures in a Pocket Universe*, featuring the Tom Baker robot dog, K9, whose rights were owned by Bob Baker and Philip Martin. He also recruited Lalla Ward, who had played the second Romana in the Tom Baker era. Her character had been left behind in E-Space, which had been a, you guessed it, pocket universe. Romana and K9 had had a relationship, and K9 had habitually called her 'Mistress.' The apple is not falling far from the tree. This resulted in two audio adventures, *'The Choice'* and *'The Search.'*

At this point, in 1999, perhaps because of K9, Baggs and the BBV went a little wild obtaining rights for subordinate Doctor Who characters not directly owned by the BBC. Suddenly they were releasing audio adventures for Sontarans, Zygons, and even obscure critters like the Krynoids and the Wirn. There were adaptations or inspirations from a Who book spin off called *Faction Paradox*.

There were three exceptions to the BBV's audio circus of monsters. The Autons and the Cybermen. No idea about the Autons, except perhaps they didn't want to dilute the brand, as they were doing them on video. The others were the Cybermen and the Daleks, they couldn't get rights to either.

Terry Nation and his estate being notoriously litigious, they didn't dare come close to those.

But instead of Cybermen, they created Cyberons – basically Cybermen with their handlebars filed off, literally – take a look at the pictures. Cyberons bedeviled Nicholas Briggs amnesiac time traveler in *Cyber-Hunt*, in 1998. The came back on their own in the 1999 audio drama *Cybergeddon*. Then they ascended to video in a *Cocoon* rip off called *Cyberon* in 2001, and were brought back one more time to tweak the nose of the BBC in *Do You Have a License to Save This Planet*.

Of all of these, the most interesting was *The Rani Reaps the Whirlwind* from 2000. The Rani was a renegade female Time Lord, played by Kate O'Mara, and created by Pip and Jane Baker who had tussled with Colin Baker's Doctor in *Mark of the Rani,* and Sylvester McCoy's Doctor in *Time and the Rani*. She's also appeared as the villain in a *'Choose Your Own Adventure'* book called *Strange Matter*, again by Pip and Jane Baker, which had been the basis for the McCoy adventure. And she'd appeared, again played by Kate O'Mara (but not written by Pip and Jane) in the non-canonical *Dimensions in Time*. O'Mara was, at the time, quite a big deal, because she was starring in a hit American night-time soap called Dynasty.

The Rani Reaps the Whirlwind takes up pretty much where *Time and the Rani* leaves off, with our villain in the clutches of the bat-like Tetraps. Kate O'Mara returns to the role. Pip and Jane Baker wrote the thing. If you're a fan of classic villains, this is basically the fourth appearance of the Rani.

So what this amounts to is a surprisingly large body of 'Doctor Who with the serial numbers filed off. Sylvester McCoy played the Professor/Dominie on audio almost as many times as he played the Doctor on television.'

I can't imagine the BBC were amused by all this. Bill Baggs was tap dancing all over their properties, either side-licensing everything from K9, to Zygons and Sontarans, to the Rani herself; or blatantly thieving with only the thinnest pretenses – the Stranger might be overlooked, but then the Professor and Ace? Alice and the Dominie? Mistress? Cyberons?

Talk about burning bridges. He might as well have taken to leaving flaming bags of dog poop in front of the Comptroller's office.

The BBC would eventually license out Doctor Who for audio adventures, but to Big Finish instead. And there would be a condition – Bill Baggs was forbidden to ever be involved.

The BBV disappeared from sight sometime after that. *Zygon* got released in 2008, but very little was heard from them Baggs seems to be leading a revival post 2015, mostly around *PROBE* and *Faction Paradox*. Most recently, he's been doing these lo-fi six minute video diaries, PROBE case files, where he plays an operative named Giles.

There's something almost tragic there. In the 90s, particularly the early 90s, Bill Baggs was almost heroic. From 1989 on, Doctor Who was dead. And if you look at this body of work that he created or helped to create, if you look at what he inspired, at the people that he enlisted and recruited, and the pathways that arguably he paved or helped pave for others, it's awesome.

He had Colin Baker, Nicola Bryant, Sophie Aldred, Sylvester McCoy, Lalla Ward, Carolyn Johns, Nicholas Briggs, Mark Gatiss involved, John Pertwee, Peter Davison and Kate O'Mara, an open list of remarkable names representing past and future.

And at the same time, he burned bridges, with unkept promises, unpaid bills, selfishness and self-absorption, meddling and micromanagement, bad decisions, just plain rudeness and, I can't minimize this one, really pissing off the BBC.

He's like that Arthurian knight on the quest for the Holy Grail, who is good enough to be permitted to see it, but his flaws are such that he will never be admitted through the gates of the castle, to finally find the thing he's built his life around.

Big Finish and the New Who Universe

In 1996, former members of the Audio Visuals group, including Gary Russell, Nicholas Briggs and Gary Kurz, assisted and backed by Jason Haigh-Ellery, *Big Finish* productions.

By this time, *Reeltime* had done *Downtime*, the BBV had chugged out several videos, and *Dreamwatch* had come very close to financial disaster trying to do *Shakedown*. It had only been the financial intervention of Jason Haigh-Ellery that had salvaged the production.

I think that the consensus was probably that while doing Doctor Who spin offs was great, doing video was something of a nightmare. The object was to scale things back, and work on audio adventures.

The Big Finish crew weren't the only ones going in this direction of course. We've examined the BBV, and around this broad time frame there was an outfit called *Magic Bullet*, which was doing a thinly veiled Blake's 7 spin off called Kaldor City. Reeltime and the BBV were still messing about with videos, and Reeltime had released *Mindgame, Mindgame Trilogy* and *Daemos Rising*, and of course there were fan groups and fan productions like Timebase, Bedlam, etc. I don't think that anyone really had a clear or consistent notion of where the future lay. People were just trying stuff.

Now, let me digress. Back in the day, Doctor Who novelizations were being done by a company called Target Books. They did these slim, young adult novelizations of the serials that were shown on television, often by the writers of the serials themselves, or by the script editors for the shows. For the writers, it was an easy way to sell your work twice. And since re-runs and video-recording weren't things, it was one of the few ways you could experience the show after it played on air.

Target was eventually purchased by Virgin Books. In 1989, Doctor Who was cancelled, and Virgin had a problem – no new material for its Target line. So, Virgin asked for the rights to publish its own Doctor Who adventures, and eventually the BBC said yes. In 1991, Virgin started up the New Adventures book series, and started chugging them out.

The Virgin New Adventure series, perhaps more than any other factor, developed the style and the ideas and tone that would find its way into the rebooted Doctor Who series, and would develop and showcase a number of Doctor Who writers that would go on to working on the television show.

The New Adventures went very well, until about 1996. That was the year that Philip Segal and Universal produced the Doctor Who movie, and the BBC was all a twitter about the prospect of an American Doctor Who series and raking in scads of cash. So one of the things the BBC did, in anticipation of big money rolling in, was to cancel every contract it could.

Too bad for Virgin, whose contract terminated in 1997.

Virgin wasn't terribly happy about the whole thing. Their Doctor Who book line had been very lucrative.

But they had an 'ace' in the hole.

Along the way, a writer named Paul Cornell had created a companion for the Doctor named Bernice (Benny)

Summerfield. She was a kick ass space archeologist from the 26th century, and she became an extremely popular companion, appearing in forty-four books with the Doctor, before eventually being phased out.

The BBC didn't own Bernice Summerfield. That property belonged to Paul Cornell and Virgin Books.

So they just moved Bernice Summerfield front and center, and carried on with her rousing and remarkable adventures in the Doctor Who-ish universe, without the Doctor. It worked out fine, and everyone lived happily ever after, for an additional twenty-three novels, at least until 1999, when Virgin cancelled its entire fiction department.

But before they did that, in 1998, Virgin and Cornell licensed Big Finish Productions to do audio adventures with the character of Bernice Summerfield.

And once again, we see how profoundly half assed and lackadaisical the subject of copyright is in the Doctor Who universe. I'm betting nothing like this ever happens with *Star Wars* or Disney.

But this turned out to be critical.

The BBV's approach was to do grab bag of random monsters, the Rani once, a couple of K9's, a couple of Zygon stories, a Krynoid story, and gray-market tap dancing with things like the Stranger and the Professor. Not only did it annoy the BBC like crazy, it didn't really build or advance any kind of brand. The closest the BBV ever got to that was developing *PROBE* and messing with *Faction Paradox*, and they were pretty erratic about both.

Bernice Summerfield, on the other hand was an extremely well established character who had appeared in several dozen books and had her own following, and had built up a clear brand of her own beyond the Doctor. It was almost certainly a better, more coherent marketing strategy. And it didn't piss off the BBC.

Big Finish went to town, with actress Lisa Bowerman playing Summerfield, eventually through ninety audio dramas right up to the present day.

In 1999, based on their work on the Bernice Summerfield audios, the BBC licensed the rights to do original Doctor Who stories to Big Finish.

Why did Big Finish succeed where productions like the *Pescatons* or the *Ghosts of N-Space* failed? I think that these earlier efforts failed because they really didn't understand utilize the form of audio drama. The thing is that audio drama is a different thing than stage or television or movie drama, each of which has its own requirements. It's subtle, but without that visual aspect, you have to do things differently. You can do more; depict bigger and more awesome things. But you also have to find different ways of doing things. Sure, in an audio story, you can have bizarrely alien races, exploding worlds and epic scenes that simply couldn't be rendered visually. But as simple a thing as picking up a cup of coffee off a table needs to be expressed differently. Writing for audio is its own thing; it has its own rules, its own dramatic language and requirements.

So if you're writing audio drama, well, to some extent, all writing is the same. But still, if you're not familiar with the subtleties and nuances of writing audio drama, that's a little like crossing the street blindfolded. Malcolm Hulke, Victor Pemberton and Terrance Dicks were all credible television writers. But they were writing outside their medium.

On the other hand, Nicholas Briggs and the other Big Finish writers had started off with the Audio Visuals. They had spent six years and 26 adventures learning to write audio stories, and they'd gotten good at it long before they started Big Finish.

They knew and understood the format. They'd learned through twenty-six productions as the Audio-Visuals, and they learned with their Bernice Summerfield work, how to do it properly. They understood what the medium could and couldn't do and how to best use it. Audio drama was very mostly a lost art, but they'd mastered it. And more than that, they'd mastered it in the context of Doctor Who. They were able to put their finger on what worked in the television series, or in the novels, and capture that in an audio play.

Another handicap, of the earlier efforts: An audio series simply couldn't compete with the television show that was running at the same time. Take the *Pescatons or Journey into Time,* for example, they weren't ever going to be anything more than poor relations to a television show that was live, vital and on television every week. Big Finish, on the other hand, started back in 1996 and had years to establish itself and grow before Doctor Who returned to television. By the time Who relaunched in 2005, Big Finish's audio adventures were already an institution.

Critically, I think that both Big Finish and the BBV were able to tap into the niche network of fans and fan culture in ways that simply hadn't existed with the prior ventures. They weren't a general audience release at Target or Walmart. They were a specialty market that was plugged into a pre-existing network of fans, and of fan audio and video production and audience that had evolved through the 80s and 90s. That was a base, a loyal base, and as fan culture evolved and technology changed, they were able to build onto that base. That might be the most important.

There was one more critical factor: What separated Big Finish audios from most fan productions were the casts. The Big Finish people were fans. They went to conventions. Over the years, they'd all gotten to know and become friendly with people like Sylvester McCoy, Peter Davison, Colin Baker and other series actors who had guested at these conventions. The boundaries between fans and professionals were pretty blurred, particularly in England. And this was particularly so when the show was in the past. When Peter Davison or Colin Baker were attending a convention they weren't truly stars, they were unemployed actors, practically civilians like the rest of us, who had a unique connection to the show. That made them accessible.

So it was just a matter of asking them and being sufficiently credible.

It made a difference to have real Doctors coming back to their old roles. I don't think that they'd have had the same cachet if they'd started over with brand new Doctors, new actors taking on the role. Big Finish's first Doctor Who production in 1999 was the *Sirens of Time*, written by Nicholas Briggs and starring Peter Davison, Colin Baker and Sylvester McCoy. Having the actual Doctors from the television series coming back and reprising their roles gives their productions a unique authenticity, an identity with the show.

And on the whole, it's been mutually beneficial. Colin Baker's reputation as a Doctor rests as his sixty or so outings with Big Finish, as it does with his two difficult seasons on television. Paul McGann had one movie as the Doctor, and literally a mountain of audio adventures. Sylvester McCoy and Peter Davison both dramatically extended their bodies of work as the Doctor. Tom Baker, John and David Tennant have brought their Doctors into Big Finish. Just about every surviving actor who had ever played a Companion, and a great many who had played villains, came back.

And they've done it, mostly while competing with or complementing the actual show on television, which is remarkable. They really only had a four or five year window before the show came back on television. But their brand and their production didn't fade.

We're talking literally hundreds upon hundreds of audio adventures. The sheer sprawling volume of Big Finish adventures literally eclipses the actual television series. It's mind boggling. To be fair, they've done their share of crap, had their own misfires. In that sort of volume, there's bound to be some garbage. But there's equally an amount of sublime stuff.

They've done some interesting things, including re-mounting stage plays as audio adventures… with original actors, if available. They've issued a series of releases based on the lost scripts and story ideas of Colin Baker's original series 23, which was abandoned during the hiatus, in favour of *Trial of a Time Lord*.

They've done the same thing, albeit rather more farfetched, commissioning series 27 and 28 for Sylvester McCoy, based on Cartmel's ideas of the stories and writers he wanted to commission.

They've done series focusing on Companions. They've done alternate versions, in *Doctor Who Unbound*, including Arabella Weir as a female Doctor. They've done comic strip adaptations, novel adaptations. They've done official spin offs, like Torchwood, or their own spin offs, like the Paternoster Gang, Jago and Litefoot, or spin offs of their own creations.

Big Finish has branched out into other franchises, doing *Blake's 7, Sapphire and Steel, Judge Dredd, Dark Shadows, Captain Scarlet, Terrahawks, Sherlock Holmes* and *Stargate*.

Audiobooks are now a rising phenomenon, but audio books are basically just having someone a novel out loud. Yes, that's reductive, and there's a lot of production work that goes into an audio-book, but that's what it boils down to.

What Big Finish does, what the Audio Visuals, DWAD and other fan groups did, was take it up to the next level – not just read an audio book, but create an audio play – with different voice actors doing different characters, with sound effects, with background music.

The have literally found a way to reinvent Radio Drama, a form and format of the thirties and forties, and bring it into the 21st century, and make money at it. That's pretty amazing.

The worm has turned, nowadays it's likely that almost all of the fan-made audio adventures of the 21st century are inspired, not by the televised Doctor Who, but by Big Finish's audio universe.

And the cool thing is, unless you're in England, or a relatively hard core Doctor Who fan, you may not even realize that Big Finish exists, or appreciate how vast its library is.

The bottom line is that the story of the Audio Visuals and Big Finish and even the BBV, is the story of fans succeeding, creatively and commercially, where the professionals failed. Big Finish is now an Institution in its own right. Its stories are official and licensed, it uses the television Doctors, and its dramas have even aired on BBC Radio. The rebels have become an empire of their own, and their story is almost certainly worth a book in itself. This barely scratches the surface.

CHAPTER 15 - THE DVD STRIKES BACK

In 1996, Doctor Who finally came back to television.

And it failed.

That's about the size of it. It came, it went and that's all.

From 1989 to 1996, Doctor Who hadn't been a show but a soap opera, an unending succession of proposals and people, either to revive the show or make a movie out of it - Terry Nation and Gerry Davis, Steven Spielberg and Richard Leakey, Leonard Nimoy and Philip Segal. Doctor Who had lived in development hell, off the screens, out of sight, but in perpetual development. Proposals were made, scripts were written and then rewritten, and thrown out for new scripts, a series bible was prepared and abandoned.

All of this eventually culminated in a Fox/Universal/BBC co-production for a five million dollar television movie which was to serve as a backdoor pilot for a new American produced and financed series.

It aired on May 14, 1996, of Fox's Tuesday Night Movie series, and it bombed - Doctor Who garnered 5.5 million viewers – placing it 75th in the week's ratings -- and a 9 share. Segal had hoped for a 17 or 18, at least a 15 share would have been the minimal to convince Fox to go for further movies or a television series. It was below even the 11 share average for the Tuesday Night Movie slot. That was it, Fox closed the door and walked away. The rights reverted to Universal, and Universal let those rights expire and revert back to the BBC.

End of story. Seven years of backstage drama, of people in suits endlessly meeting with other people in suits in offices and boardrooms, of important people having lunches and writing memos. All that corporate stuff had all ended in a big fizzle.

The Doctor Who movie was successful in the UK, earning nine million viewers -- roughly double what the ratings had been for the show during its last four years, and well within the glory days of Jon Pertwee and Tom Baker. But this was still about three million shy of the BBC's goal.

The BBC wasn't interested in making the show. They were interested in selling it. What they saw was a merchandisable property that someone else ought to buy and make something with and give them money for. That's all. They didn't want to make it; it wasn't their kind of thing.

Since the series had been cancelled (put on 'hiatus'), there'd been a couple of times when the BBC had sort of dipped their toe into Sci Fi. *Bugs* in 1995, a sort of techno-thriller cop show, and *Crime Traveller*, a time-travel cop show - emphasis in both cases on police drama. The sort of thing that Doctor Who was seemed pretty foreign to the BBC's corporate culture, and it smelled expensive.

So the bottom line was, after 1997, so far as the men in suits were concerned, it was dead. There were no more meetings. The rounds of development wouldn't happen.

Revenge of the Grass Roots

Of course, Fans weren't men in suits. They didn't have a seat at the Boardroom tables. They weren't juggling complicated funding proposals or package deals. They just kept on liking the show. Fans were simply the audience.

Doctor Who was officially dead in 1997, but that was also the year of Rupert Booth in *Phase Four* and of Nick Scovell's *Millennium Trap*. Sharon Crooke's *Alliance* would be out the next year in 1998. 1999 would feature Dennis Kuhn's *Time and Again*, as well as with Sylvester McCoy and the Bill Baggs sticking their thumb into the Corporation's eye with *Do You Have a License to Save this Planet?* All of them far more ambitious and clever than they had any right to be.

Now arguably, all of these productions were just products of the creative momentum that had begun in 1990, catching fire in the crushing disappointment of 1993. But it also signified that corporate shenanigans, and the drama of men in suits was largely irrelevant. They didn't care, it didn't register. The BBC saw Doctor Who as a commercial property that they couldn't sell, and it was about as soulless as that. Fans saw something else.

Starting roughly around 1999, give or take, the fans relationship with the show, their perspective on it, was going to change, as would the productions of film makers, and eventually, the BBC itself would get dragged kicking and screaming.

Abandoned at the top, Doctor Who went back to grass roots. The show stopped being a merchandise property that men in suits were trying to dictate something from the top down.

Rather, it was percolating from the ground up, from the audience and fans. There was the next television production of Doctor Who - *Curse of Fatal Death*, a half hour 'Children in Need' charity spoof that aired in four parts in 1999. Rowan Atkinson was the Doctor, Jonathan Pryce was the Master, the Tardis console was back, the Police box was back and even an army of Daleks showed up. Everyone from Hugh Grant to Joanna Lumley, Richard E. Grant and Ed Broadbent, and

Julia Sawal volunteered their time. Written by Steven Moffatt, directed by Richard Curtis, this wasn't a corporate production; this was by fans, for fans.

How fannish was *Curse of Fatal Death*? The sets and Daleks were borrowed from fans and fan productions, notably *Devious*. It was a silly farce, made with the catering budget of the Doctor Who movie, but there was love and affection there.

Then there was BBCi. This was the online service of the BBC, which started out as equivalent to a company newsletter, or weekly schedule - essentially letting people know what was on, or where to find it. It wasn't really BBC mainstream corporate culture, but rather the province of nerds. These were people hired to put things up on websites and not rock the boat.

BBCi initially had little to do with Doctor Who. But, because they were nerds, they started a *Cult Television* subsite, which became quite popular and developed its own following. As an online audience coalesced, Doctor Who soon came to dominate its cult television pages.

BBCi started on to run the *Loose Cannon* Reconstructions of the lost stories - mergers of audio sound tracks of these serials with Tele-Snaps to recreate a version of these lost episodes, literally offering online programming. That was successful. So from there, the BBCi had gone on to work with Big Finish on a series of new semi-animated serials - Death Comes to Time, featuring Sylvester McCoy, Shada with Paul McGann and Lalla Ward, and Realtime, with Colin Baker. Again, grass roots. Here was a bunch of people whose job was just to maintain the web site, and they'd somehow gotten into producing original Doctor Who content.

This culminated in 2003, with BBCi relaunching Doctor Who officially as an ongoing animated web series starring Richard

E. Grant, as the official, canonical, new BBC Doctor, beginning with *Scream of the Shalka*.

Equally important, in 1999, Big Finish Productions, the descendant of a fan group called the Audio Visuals, obtained a non-exclusive license to the BBC-owned parts of Doctor Who - the Doctor, the Tardis, the Timelords, etc., to produce and distribute audio adventures of the Doctor. Big Finish recruited Davison, McCoy and Colin Baker as Doctors, and brought back many of the characters and actors from the original series. From this evolved a sprawling Doctor Who audio universe, as vast and voluminous as the original television series. Even BBC Radio itself would end up running some of Big Finish's Doctor Who stories as radio drama.

All of these developments were finding dedicated audiences. But none of this was coming from Corporate head offices. The BBC wasn't driving any of this as corporate policy or strategic decision making. They were letting it happen, certainly, but that was a permission borne of indifference. Some comedians want to use the property for a charity special? Sure why not. Big Finish wants to license it for an audio series? Whatever. Who listens to books on tape anyway. The online guys want to do a web series? Stop bothering us, we have important things to do. The fortieth Anniversary of the show was approaching, and the BBC was largely indifferent to that event. The property didn't seem to have a future, didn't seem to have value, so it didn't really matter, the door could be opened to all these little grass roots initiatives.

This wasn't Doctor Who as commodity, but rather, Doctor Who as community, from creators to audiences on shoestrings and good will. The thing was, these grass roots initiatives, they were finding an audience.

The Return

Even a blind dog can find a bone, though. Although the BBC in the late 90s really had no use for the property, all these grass roots initiatives kept manifesting on the radar. 'Perhaps there was life in the old commodity yet,' thought the men in suits.

In 1999, Russell T. Davies was briefly involved in an effort to revive the series - a project generally recalled as *Doctor Who 2000*, driven in part by BBC1 Controller Peter Salmon. This seems to have foundered because BBC Worldwide, another division of the BBC was still trying to flog a movie, even bringing in Paul Anderson.

Two years later, in 2001, Dan Freeman who had done the web series called *Death Comes to Time* with Sylvester McCoy, tried to launch a successor series. This one centered around a new Time Lord called the Minister of Chance. Unfortunately, it failed to take off.

There were concerns over rights issues. As we've seen, Doctor Who has a complicated rights situation, but these were resolved by BBCi's crew who did the homework for *Scream of the Shalka*, and proved that except for the Daleks, most of the key rights were pretty straightforward.

Finally, by 2003, BBC Worldwide had thrown in the towel. BBC1 under its new Controller, Lorraine Heggessy, had settled on bringing back the series, and Russell T. Davies was back on the project.

There was one unfortunate effect - the BBC was not going to have two Doctor Who series, and so the BBCi animated web series was shut down with the Scream of the Shalka. Its next serial, Blood of the Robots died on the operating table, and the BBCi Doctor was no longer canon. That's how the suits play.

Big Finish Audio already had its licenses, it had its classic Doctors and their followings, and it was sufficiently niche that it was left untouched by the BBC and their lawyers. It wasn't a threat; it was, for want of a better word, promotion.

But Doctor Who was coming back to television....

The Revolution will be Pre-recorded

There was something more. It had been ten years since the show had gone off the air. The BBC wasn't producing Doctor Who. Barring one-offs like the 1996 movie, there was no new Who. But there was a huge catalogue of classic serials - over a hundred of them. These had been released, beginning as early as the 1980s as a steady stream on VHS and then DVD.

Through the 1980s and 1990s, the video market was dominated by stores and rentals. This was just economics. Early on VHS releases were expensive. Even a mediocre movie would cost anywhere from 50 to 100 dollars. Way too expensive for most families. So stores bought and built up libraries of these things, and made their money back by renting them out. It was a system geared towards large, diverse libraries of tapes or DVD's and a steady stream of new releases to the audience

Of course, if you were making those investments in videotapes or DVD's, you wanted to be sure of renting them to a general audience, you wanted to diversify your library, have something for everyone. Cult items like Doctor Who might be good for one or two purchases, but not twenty or thirty - that made no economic sense. You weren't going to fill a section of your store with them.

Towards the end of the 1990s, and especially into the 2000s, the price of VHS and DVD began to drop dramatically. Suddenly it started to be feasible for people to start acquiring and owning a collection of DVD's or VHS. Suddenly, it was a lot easier to be a Doctor Who collector.

Of course, fans had been collecting Doctor Who on tape through the 1980s and 1990s, but these had been bootlegs - recorded off television, exchanged hand to hand through informal trading networks, dubbed and redubbed to the point of indecipherability. That culture of collecting, that potential market, that was already well established and waiting.

But now? Now we were seeing pristine product, crystal clear images and sound, glossy cases, fresh from the BBC, loaded with extras. Suddenly the home video market turned on its head and favoured collectors and collectables. Anyone with a credit card and patience could build a new Who collection, faster, easier and better than the laborious circuits of conventions and collector trading. People could discover the show, and then easily keep seeking it out.

The result was new waves of sales of Doctor Who by BBC Enterprises. Each new release or re-release became an event in and of itself, eagerly awaited, celebrated, pored over and reviewed in magazines and online. Doctor Who became accessible in a way it had never been before, and business boomed. People took notice. Certainly it was one of the things that BBC management were taking notice of.

Was this the entirety of what underlay the grass roots movements? No. It certainly helped. But in another sense, it was just another manifestation of the good will and affection the show had built through its 26 year span.

All of these developments had an effect on fan films. The renaissance and proliferation of the classic Doctors on official, high quality, DVD had a corrosive effect on the 90s trend of fans developing their own Doctors. The fan Doctors were generally cheaper productions, shot on inferior video, circulated on increasingly blurry generations of tapes, traded from hand to hand. They really couldn't compete with the much larger numbers and quality of classic serials and classic Doctors showing up on DVD. There were simply more of the Classics; their DVD's had better images and more extras. They simpler and were easier to obtain, a trip to a store and a credit card. The wave of audio stories from the 80s Classic Doctors at Big Finish also contributed to a revival of the Classics and to a decline in fan created Doctors.

It wasn't cut and dried, of course. The final appearances of Timebase's Rupert Booth Doctor were 2002 and 2003. The Harrald Doctor stories from Vortx begins in 2002. A fan production was always faced with the choice of whether to try and re-create classic Doctors they knew and liked, or come up with a unique version of the Doctor based on the actor they had.

But there is nostalgia, and the DVD's were reviving it. Fan film makers found themselves wanting to recreate the classic Doctors that they were seeing on their DVD's, people were dressing as Tom or Colin, as Patrick, Peter or Sylvester. The classic Doctors were coming back into fan film vogue, as we see with El Cheapo's productions. Ben Pocock, of El Cheapo, hadn't even been born in Troughton's era, but Troughton was his favourite Doctor.

There was something more, that was odd and interesting. The Classic Doctors, notably Colin Baker and Sylvester McCoy started appearing in fan films. Not regularly by any means. But they showed up. Other actors, Nicholas Courtney, Wendy Padbury, John Levene, Sophie Aldred also came back to recreate their roles decades later.

Why did it happen? For a lot of reasons, I think, not all of them well articulated. Partly between the revolution in the DVD market and the rise of Big Finish, they had experienced a renewed popularity. There had been the years of conventions, of meeting and interacting with fans, and familiarity bred affection. They were loved by fans, and they loved them right back. At the same time, it was increasingly clear that there would be a new series, the classic era would finally be at an end - there was going to be a new Doctor, new Doctors, and in a sense, their status would change. With the new show, nostalgia would fade. They would no longer be the current Doctors. So why not play the roles for fans one more time.

For Colin and Sylvester and the other classic series actors, there was a window opening for them, and they knew it might close soon enough. So we have Colin Baker and Sylvester McCoy, Nicholas Courtney and Wendy Padberry recreating their old characters in fan films, an affectionate return to their old roles. The future was becoming something to look forward to, and this lead, in a strange way, to looking back fondly, partly treasuring, partly seeking one last hurrah.

Review: Trident (2001)

Doctor Who Done as Tarantino's Pulp Fiction

STORY: *Episode One* - A mysterious figure is carrying a briefcase through London, as the Fifth Doctor hunts for a time anomaly, too late, the anomaly detonates, hurling the Doctor back three million years, where he finds a crashed spaceship and Cybermen.... *Episode Two* - Stan is the last surviving crew member of the star liner Trident, invaded by Cybermen and on a collision course with earth, when the Sixth Doctor Shows up.... *Episode Three* - the Seventh Doctor has been trapped by mysterious enemies who want his Tardis; can Ace save him in time? Episode four....

REVIEW: This is *Trident*, a serial of four full length episodes, featuring three different classic doctors, from El Cheapo Productions. Between 2001 and 2011, El Cheapo produced seven ambitious and interesting Doctor Who films.

El Cheapo originated around 1999 from two groups of young film makers - Chris and Ben Pocock and Craig Hurley on one side, and John Walker and James Copeland on the other, each with their respective groups of friends, each of whom were floundering, trying to do their own Who video. The Pocock/Hurley group had had some experience doing short films and had recently acquired a computer editing system. Their film would be basis of the third episode of Trident. The

Walker/Copeland group was working on a script which would eventually form the core of the second episode of Trident and had been acquiring props, including Cyberman heads. Eventually, they met up and over drinks in a pub, discussing where they'd gone wrong with their films; they decided to combine their talents.

Trident was their first and in many ways their most ambitious production. The first three episodes feature cold openings, catapulting each Doctor into a mystery. The last episode attempts to pull it all together. Interestingly, although they come close a few times, none of the Doctors ever quite meet. That little defiance of expectation is an example of the cleverness of the production.

Where *Trident* really stands out is in the sharp clever editing, crisp dialogue and the storytelling. This is a complicated story, weaving in and out of the lives of three Doctors in several time periods. The narrative is bold, even brilliant. There are things going on in the first episode, for instance, in the relationship between the Fifth Doctor and the Cybermen that we won't understand until we've seen the last episode.

Every episode has constant references, incidents, events, statements, that may not mean much at the time, but get filled in later. There's a sort of M. Night Shyamalan quality to it, Shyamalan from when he was good. But it goes beyond that, in that Shyamalan tends to have one payoff at the end, but here, it's a running thing, with the audience continually reappraising what has gone before as new information tilts it on its head. Perhaps a better allusion would be *Pulp Fiction*, with its three interlocking stories. But really, Trident is neither *Pulp Fiction* nor Shyamalan, but its own ambitious, somewhat lunatic work. It reminds me a bit of *Spectre From the Past*, multiple Doctors, an intricate story, and of course hungry things from beyond represented by coloured lights.

The tough part of *Trident* is that rather than fashioning their own Doctors, they've dressed up as existing Doctors - The Fifth, Sixth or Seventh. The trouble is it runs a risk. When you're playing an existing Doctor, you have to live up to that character, and it's a damned hard thing. You can't help but remind people of who you aren't.

Having said that, this is one of the few cases where it's unavoidable to play existing Doctors. In some other production, I could see doing an original Doctor. But the very structure of Trident requires that you have multiple Doctors bouncing around, and they have to be recognisable Doctors.

So, how does this bunch do? Well, we're not getting uncanny impersonations. None of the actors are physically their Doctors. But they each have moments where they manage to evoke the Doctor they're playing, particularly the sixth Doctor.

Chris Pocock as the Fifth Doctor is okay, but rather colourless. But then, that was kind of the trademark of the Fifth Doctor, he's colourless. Blandly handsome, dressed in muted colours, nothing striking or distinctive. Sincere and pleasant, but not passionate. He's a bit reminiscent of David Cullen in the role in Spectre From The Past. I'm surprised that we don't see more people playing the Fifth Doctor, his lack of distinctiveness should make him easy to do. But then again, it's not really a quality that people get excited to imitate. One of Chris's handicaps playing the Fifth Doctor is that he's in the first episode, which lays out events but doesn't tie them together. Both the Doctor and the audience are at sea, which is risky.

John Walker playing the Sixth Doctor has the toughest time. There's no resemblance obviously, he's just a heavy balding guy in an obnoxiously colourful costume. But he brings energy to the role. He's by far the most volatile Doctor - when I think of his character, he's always running or jumping about. There are times when his extravagance and energy feels like Colin Baker. He seems comfortable with the role, and he's got some of the most memorable lines.

Oddly, the best performance comes from Craig Hurley who plays the Seventh Doctor as a dual role. He has almost none of the frenetic bombast of a Sylvester McCoy. There are flashes of McCoy's performance, particularly when he's deadpan. The costume abandons McCoy's white suit and distinctive hat, for something dark and somber - all that's left of McCoy's outfit is the scarf and vest. It's distinctive without being showy, disciplined without being faint. Hurley plays it straight, bringing a dour intensity to the role that works very well. Unlike Pocock or Walker, we never get the impression of Sylvester McCoy in Hurley's performance. He's very serious about playing the role of the Seventh Doctor. He's just not bothering to play that role as Sylvester McCoy. It's an interesting take.

He's also creepy. I'm not sure why, but it's a running theme with fans who are trying to do their own versions of the Sylvester McCoy, Seventh Doctor. They come off creepy and untrustworthy. I've never seen a fan version of the Seventh Doctor that I'd want to leave my children alone with.

As to the rest of the principal cast, James Copeland, who has the writing credit for *Trident*, is thoroughly creepy as Ravensworth. Alicia Dickinson provides an excellent, if portly, Ace, a competent and energetic heroine. Steven Stansbridge provides light comedy as the hapless Stan, a computer programmer who accidentally deletes his ship's navigation software. Stan, by the way, was based loosely on the character of Stanley Tweedle from the *LEXX* television series. Fittingly, Stan's episode borrows the musical score from *LEXX*.

Truthfully though this isn't a film that's based around characterization. We don't have the sort of force of personality of a Benedetti, Booth or Scovell at work. Instead, *Trident* works on its intricate structure. There's way too much plot going on. The story, it's breakneck pace, and its meticulous developing intricacy tend to overwhelm the personalities. There's so much happening that everyone is just running as hard as they can trying to keep up. Only Copeland, as the menace, exudes a formidable presence.

Let's get the technical stuff out of the way. First up, compliments to the costumes. To start with, we have three different Doctor outfits, along with Ace's costume, UNIT operatives and even a hapless starship crewman. There are at least three Cybermen and a Cyber-leader. The

Cybermen look ratty, but it turns out that's deliberate, and they are well used - both dramatically, visually and in editing terms - they're good at making three Cybermen seem like a dozen.

Next - good locations and cinematography. *Trident* is almost uniformly well shot and visually interesting. The spaceship Trident's interiors, especially, mostly shot after hours at a London health club, have that clean, pristine, vaguely futuristic feel. The Sixth Doctor on the beach shot beneath the cliffs at Peacehaven, the Fifth Doctor in a primordial forest run riot as green, shot at Farthing Downs in Coulsdon, most of the London street scenes, all of these location scenes are visually striking and well composed.

It's not perfect, UNIT's storage room and the location and console for the time bomb that the Seventh Doctor confronts is pretty slack - but it's a matter of using the space you can get, in this case the warren of unused rooms above a video store. And for some reason, some of the starship corridors seem to be brickwork. But these are easy enough to overlook, and they do so many other things so well, they deserve to be overlooked. The production manages to consistently look far more expensive and professional than it is.

And as usual with fan films, the sound mix is sometimes wobbly. They're taking advantage of ambient locations, so depending on where they are; sometimes the dialogue is overwhelmed by room echo, outdoor wind, or other factors.

Overall, *Trident* doesn't quite manage to shake the impression of being a fan film, that's just the reality that very different people are playing recognizable Doctors. But it almost closes the gap in the way that the *Millennium Trap* or *Phase Four* or *Spectre From* the Past manage. Damned close indeed. It's the remarkable piece of work, and legitimately justifies watching a second or a third time.

El Cheapo's next video would be a direct sequel to *Trident*, *Asylum*, featuring the further adventure of the Sixth Doctor and the character of Stanley after they escaped from the crashing starship. Chris Pocock wrote in correspondence, *"It's the only one of our productions I'm not proud of. I won't bore you with the details. Suffice to say it was rushed and we weren't happy with it. We made some mistakes but learnt a lot from them!!"*

His brother, Ben Pocock was a little more forthcoming. *"Originally it was supposed to be a horror in homage to those 70s and 80s zombie films. The doctor and Stan arrive at an old mental asylum where a parasitic creature called "The Mind" was using people's fear as a channel to bring the dead back to life. We had Chris painted in blue face paint! That was supposed to be a homage to some zombie film; I'm not sure which one."*

Reminiscent of the Pertwee serial, *Mind of Evil*, it sounded like it had some potential. The asylum setting sounds creepy and intriguing and I would expect them to have found a suitable location. The zombies thing seems like fun.

"It was probably one of the worst scripts I've ever written. But there were a few problems on set too - as far as I know, the others had done another non-Who film on the same holiday so when it came to doing this one there was a lot of fatigue! I tried to write what I imagined at the time was a deep meaningful, emotional ending. The written ending saw the site

*manager killing himself as an act of defiance against the creature, which -
now powerless - was defeated. The guys just didn't want to do it so made
up an ending on the spot."*

To date, Asylum has never been released, and is unlikely to
be.

CAST: *Fifth Doctor - Chris Pocock; Sixth Doctor - John Walker:
Seventh Doctor - Craig Hurley; Ravensworth/The Entity - James
Copeland; Ace - Alicia Dickinson; Selby - Lynne Heaney; Stanley
Marsh (Stan) - Steven Stanbridge; Corporal Gonzo - Richard Pocock;
Receptionist - Linda Walker; The True Entity - Ben Pocock; Voice of
Trident - ? ; Cybermen - ?*

Reviews: The Holly Terror & The Ghost Pirates (2002)

A Blast to the Past, A Pair of Second Doctor Stories

STORY: *The Holly Terror:* After the Tardis materializes at the North Pole in the middle of a blizzard, the Second Doctor and his companions make their way to the estate of Lord Sant-A, where they discover a Christmas Wonderland gone mad, a demonic elf dolls, cheerful holiday themed deathtraps and an Ice Warrior plot to take over the earth....

The Ghost Pirates: The Second Doctor and Jamie land on a rocky beach, and encounter mysterious doings. A phantom pirate ship, a strange sailor who knows more than he lets on, nd unearthly events and objects out of time....

REVIEW: After *Trident* and *Asylum*, El Cheapo's next two productions, from 2002 and 2004 respectively turned the clock even further back, to the Troughton Era, for a couple of black and white adventures.

Both of them are divided into four parts - unnecessarily so in my opinion. *The Holly Terror* run together is about half an hour. *The Ghost Pirates* is close to fifty minutes. I think that rather than disconcertingly short segments, they could both have been run as single stories, or in the case of the *Ghost Pirates*, as a two-parter. But that may just my usual 'running time' hobby horse.

Ben Pocock plays the Second Doctor in both, and on the whole, it's not a bad impersonation. He's obviously a good 25 years younger than Patrick Troughton when he played the role, and he doesn't really resemble the man. But he gives it a decent go and he carries the audience. He's reminiscent of Nigel Peever's performances as the 2nd Doctor in *Spectre From the Past*. He's not as good as Peever, but Peever did Troughton for a Davison era type story, and Pocock does Troughton in the black and white era. Pocock is also assisted by Craig Hurley turning in a solid performance as a Jamie, again, no resemblance, but a real effort. The productions reproduce the look and feel of Troughton era Doctor Who in terms of cinematography and story pacing.

&&&

DOCTOR WHO AND THE HOLLY TERROR

The Holly Terror feels like a Patrick Troughton Christmas episode from 1968 or 1969. When I say this, I don't mean that it captures the look and style of the Patrick Troughton era. I'm saying that if Patrick Troughton had ever done a Christmas episode along the lines of Hartnell's *Feast of Stephen*, it would be exactly like this. It's crowded, it's frantic, the production design is low budget tosh, and it moves along with frantic pace. It's just about perfect.

"My younger brother Ben loved the Second Doctor," Chris Pocock wrote in an email, "*and we had recently acquired an Ice Warrior costume. It almost wrote itself! It was a lot of fun to film and after we finished it, we decided that in the future we would do further stories with the second Doctor as played by Ben.*"

Pocock's Doctor is a little broad in the *Holly Terror*, he bleats 'oh my' a little too much. But it resonates and it feels right, particularly for the kind of story. It's broad, but Patrick Troughton would have played this one broad. We're not talking nuance here. We're talking about being confronted by white-bearded gomers with Tinsel Tasers, Ice Warriors with Santa hats and beards, and a deathtrap that involves Christmas cookies. The crazy starts early and it never lets up, so complaining that Pocock's Doctor isn't quite there just misses the point. It's the right performance for the story. It's like complaining about the paint scheme on the Titanic. There are other things going on to pay attention to.

Where the *Holly Terror* excels is in its production design and its surreal sensibility. It really does capture the feel of 1960s low budget black and white television. The blizzard for instance, with its thick billowing flakes, as if a giant feather pillow exploded - perfect 60s television imagery. The cramped rooms, exploding with classic Christmas themed tosh everywhere, the overwrought kitchen - there's something endearingly cheap and thrown together about it all. You get the genuine feel of a 1967 BBC production crew getting a script landing on their desk and scrambling madly to put it together any way they can, grabbing whatever they get their hands on, and piling it higher and higher with a frenzied mix of desperation and delight. Even the stuff that's transparently tosh or fake seems authentically fake - the failures and shortcomings of a 60s production crew working with short notice and limited budgets.

Then there's the Ice Warriors, who are always a delight to see. They're supposed to be a surprise revelation during the episode. But what the hell - I subscribe to the theory that it's not a true spoiler if it makes you want to watch it even more. The Ice Warrior costumes are really quite well done. There's even a sort of rational reason for one of them to wear a hat and beard, and their scheme isn't any more lunatic than their usual schemes.

Bottom line, this is one of those pieces that replicate the feel of the series almost perfectly, while at the same time managing to be unique.

&&&

DOCTOR WHO AND THE GHOST PIRATES

If the *Holly Terror* is a Troughton Christmas episode that never was, the *Ghost Pirates* is a full-fledged story. In four short parts, but in terms of total running time, it's a match for a two part serial. Reproduced in black and white, begun in 2004 and completed in 2007, it's quite good at reproducing the feel of the old Troughton era stories.

In this one, the Second Doctor and Jaime drop in on a rocky beach where they find a mysterious message. Things get more mysterious when a ghostly galleon appears and disappears. As it turns out, the Meddling Monk is evolved, and the plot thickens. It reproduces a lot of the feel and pace of the Second Doctor episodes. It's not perfect. There are numerous small missteps or shortcomings that undercut the proceedings. But it's sometimes breezy, sometimes frantic enthusiasm, good performances, fun villains and impressive locations manage to carry it.

Ben Pocock, returning from the *Holly Terror* to play the Second Doctor again is much more confident in his performance. You can tell he's studied Troughton's tics and mannerisms. With more running time and a more conventional story, he has more room to develop his performance. Of course, if you watch carefully, you'll notice that sometimes Pocock is wearing old man makeup, to account for the fact that he's playing a late forties man, and sometimes he doesn't bother, from one scene to the next. It's there if you watch carefully. It didn't bother me all that much; I think not bothering with the make-up was a sign of Pocock's developing confidence in the role. Good for him, if not continuity, but it's not particularly distracting.

Craig Hurley also returns to play Jaime, carrying it off well. The rest of the cast is uniformly solid, with special notice to John Walker, who plays the Meddling Monk - a role originated by Peter Butterworth in two William Hartnell serials. Walker manages to capture the character's fey combination of amiability, incompetence and treachery, and makes you wish that the BBC series had done more with that character. Marina Mazzucchi, James Copeland and Rachael Wallis all stand out for well-defined characters that have real roles.

As usual with these fan films, we have yet another amazing location - this time, they somehow managed to get access to and shoot on the Cutty Sark. It's not just the label on a whisky bottle. The Cutty Sark is part of England's naval heritage from the age of sail. Built in 1869, it was one of the last, and one of the fastest of the clipper ships. It sailed for several years until 1922, eventually losing out to steamship competition. It was refurbished, and for a time was a nautical auxiliary training ship. In 1954 it was refurbished and put into permanent dry-dock as a sailing ship.

I have no idea how they got permission to use it. I lean towards blackmail. Which means that the Ghost Pirates takes place on, around and in an actual 19th century sailing ship. True, given that they're doing a story about 17th or 18th century pirates, that's a little bit anachronistic. Still, that's just impressive.

One downside of shooting on a museum ship is that you can't go 'dressing it up' with the clutter and disorder that you'd expect from a pirate ship is another. The Cutty Sark is just a little too clean and well ordered, but that's a small thing to forgive, and even within the story, there may be an explanation for it.

The rest of the locations - a rocky beach, a room dressed as a pirate's tavern, some landscaped outdoor grounds are all solid. Only a cave set is wobbly. They also manage some fairly impressive special effects.

Oddly, the use of the Cutty Sark and other outdoor locations may be too good. Troughton's Doctor Who is most remembered as a set based show. It did use some external locations, The War Games, Highlanders, the Invasion and Abominable Snowman, to name a few, all had some location shoots. But for the most part, when we think of the Troughton years, we really think of work on soundstages. To have so much of the action on locations is slightly jarring.

Props and costumes tend to be uneven. There are some very good pirate costumes and pistols. On the other hand, the 'cutlasses' seem way too small, they look like children's toys, which isn't good for the suspension of disbelief. There's a patently fake wig and beard that seriously distracts from the proceedings. This isn't BBC 1960s sort of tosh, this is just tosh in the 'we have no money and we're scraping the bottom of the barrel for props and costumes' sort of tosh. You have to make the choice to just move past it.

Bottom line, it's a flawed gem. There are things that need to be overlooked, and are kind of hard to overlook. But it does so much right: Good characters, good performances, an engaging story that works well, some amazing location. All considered it's well worth seeing, and an authentic and affectionate tribute to a bygone era.

&&&

AFTERWARDS

2004 was the cusp of the revival of Doctor Who. With the BBC series back on the air, the El Cheapo group moved on to further projects.

Samhain in 2005, was a two part serial, approximately 50 minutes, shot entirely in and around St. Margaret's Church at Rishangles, dating back to the 12th century. I'll repeat that for the record - their shooting location was a 900 year old medieval church, restored and renovated. Half gothic, half ghost story, Samhain involves three strangers - the Doctor, a ghost hunter and an atheist vicar, who come together at the church and encounter murderous secrets, ghostly beings and a mysterious shaft of glowing energy. The second part is set fifteen years later with the return of the survivors of that night for confrontations and revelations. John Walker returned to the role of the Doctor. Fifty/fifty as to whether he's playing a new Doctor, or just the Sixth with a bit of dress sense. John Copeland plays the ghost hunter.

The Time Machine, begun in 2009, was El Cheapo's strangest offering. A maid is killed when her head is baked into a pie, something that the rest of the household considers a minor inconvenience. Meanwhile a demonic clown roams the grounds. A tiny wizard leads medieval fantasy knights across dimensions in their battle against Cybermen. The lord of the manor is beyond squirrely, driven by childhood trauma to build a time machine. The Doctor shows up, played by Chris Pocock as either a new Doctor, or the Fifth Doctor in different clothes, as does an evil Time Lord with supernatural powers. Somehow, it all sort of comes together. It's pretty unique. This time they shot at a converted 'castle' in Wiltshire. Due to the sheer amount of effects shots, the film was only completed in 2015.

El Cheapo's final offering was *Fan Film Number 7*, which went all metafictional. The story involves a serial killer who specializes in hunting and murdering fan film Doctors.

Before, after and through this period, the members of El Cheapo were making non-Doctor Who films. This is a recurring thing, Ryan K. Johson at Seattle International, Graham Quince and Paul Vought at VortX, Nigel Peever at Planet Video, Marq English, the Constantescu brothers and the members of the Timebase crew all have extensive and diverse filmographies.

As to what happened to El Cheapo, like so many other groups... Life happens. People marry and move, they get jobs, they have families and careers, life takes them in different directions. It's harder and harder for the gang to get together and do a project. Slowly, it becomes a social thing, and mostly, fond memories. There's nothing wrong with that.

HOLLY TERROR CAST: Dr Who (2nd) - Ben Pocock; Jamie - Craig Hurley; Polly - Lynne Heaney; Ben - Chris Pocock; Sant-A - John Walker; Guard - James Copeland; Mr Jingle - Richard Pocock; Master Jingle - Josh Pocock; Commander Kralg - James Copeland; Ice Warrior - Ben Pocock;

HOLLY TERROR CREW: By Chris and Ben Pocock; Story Editor - Chris Pocock; Visual Effects - James Copeland, Chris Pocock; Snow Effect - John Walker; Camera - Chris Pocock, James Copeland; Designer - John Walker; Costume - John Walker, Linda Walker; Script - Ben Pocock; Editor - Chris Pocock; Producer - Ben Pocock; Director - Chris Pocock

GHOST PIRATES CAST: The Second Doctor - Ben Pocock; Jamie - Craig Hurley; Mary - Rachael Wallis; Blackbeard/Monk - John Walker; Jeake - Chris Pocock; Dante - Jonathan Fuget; Sapless Pete - James Copeland; Bloody Bonney - Marina Mazzocchi; Villainess Rectum - Ben Pocock; Goofy Giblet - John Walker; Pirates - Naomi Smith, Frank Sales, Matt Cordwell, Steven Stanbridge, Craig Hurley, Ben Pocock;

GHOST PIRATES CREW: By Ben Pocock; Producer - Chris Pocock; Script Editor - Ben Pocock; Designers - John Walker, Chris Pocock, Ben Pocock, James Copeland; Special Thanks to - The Cutty Sark Trust - Greenwich;

Review: Timestealers - The Three Masters (2004)

And the Monk and the Rani as Well

STORY: The Master's latest fiendish scheme is to go back in time, and fill his earlier regeneration in on all his mistakes, so that he can get it right. Being the Master, he screws it up and gets his earlier self killed, producing a new and distinctly terrifying regeneration. Now, the Master is running ahead of the time wave, having erased his current existence. Can anyone save him? How about the Meddling Monk! Guest starring the Rani.

REVIEW: There's this guy, Simon Williams, between 1999 and 2004, he got the idea to do a series of fan videos called *Timestealers*, about a renegade Time Lord: The Master. The fourth in the series, the *The Three Masters*, is the best in the bunch, and is dedicated to Anthony Ainley, who played The Master through the 1980s, and who had passed away in the same year of production.

The Three Masters is easily the most polished and fully realized of the series. For one thing, it's an actual story with a beginning, middle and end. With characters whose actions are driven by their personalities. It's also Williams's longest story by far, roughly 33 minutes, and with that time, they can actually tell a full story coherently.

But let's start with the character, because that's really the core of *The Three Masters*, and the *Timestealers* series. It's what makes it interesting and fun. Simon William's performance as and his version of The Master.

William's Master is not a good guy, except by accident. He reminds me most of George McDonald Fraser's character, *Harry Flashman*. The Master as played by Williams is a thorough villain. He would tie girls to railroad tracks on general principle. He's arrogant, treacherous, deceitful, brilliant, utterly unprincipled, a bit sadistic, fearless and oddly petty. He's the sort of guy who would find a way to urinate in the punch bowl at a mixer, just to sit back and watch everyone else drink it. At one point in the third story, without any provocation or reason, he destroys RTD2 with his tissue compressor... because it's fun. Basically, he's cheerful evil. He brings an infectious glee to the role. Mind you, his character is constantly doing this 'evil chuckle,' which is thoroughly annoying and gets on the nerves. But he's a watchable bad buy. He needs to lose a little weight, so he doesn't have the 'lean and hungry' quality of Delgado and Ainsley, but he brings a beefy thuggishness to the role which is engaging.

He's also not nearly as smart as he thinks he is. He's constantly screwing himself up, his treachery and dishonesty keep coming back to bite him on the ass. In short, he's only a slight exaggeration of the Delgado and Ainsley Masters, both of whom, despite their ruthlessness, having a decided penchant for shooting themselves in the foot. But their boundless self-confidence, their pride and utter certainty that nothing can go wrong prevents them from seeing it. They are their own worst enemies. There's just no self-awareness. It's this penchant for scheming his way into failure that makes the William's Master especially fun to watch. It's just entertaining as hell watching him scramble trying to cope with the messes he gets himself into, happily betraying everyone he meets.

It's an unusual take on the Master, not one you see with a lot of fan productions. Mostly, they go with the grim and dark scary Master, the dark side of the Doctor. That side is there definitely, with the incarnations of the Master. Williams does play that aspect – there are moments when his Master is almost menacing, when you think, *'hey this guy we've been laughing at, he's really dangerous.*

As engaging as William's Master is, Williams was smart enough to realize his character actually needed to have something to do, needs someone to do it to, and needs someplace to do it. So he manages to people his Master's adventures with enough characters and plot to keep it going. The previous stories in the series have a nice assortment of characters, from a group of late teens/twenty-somethings in the first, soldiers and Cybermen in the second, the Rani, Cybermen and Trekkies in the third.

For the fourth story, we have three different Masters, plus the Rani and the Monk; a hat trick of Time Lord villains! What more could anyone want?

The story of The Three Masters focuses on William's Master's diabolical plot to go back in time and fill his earlier incarnation in on a sort of cliff notes of evil. Basically, we start with the Monk minding his own business, when he gets recruited by the Time Lords to stop the Master's current scheme to mess with his own history so he can win a few this time. Unfortunately, the Monk, in the process of confronting the earlier Master and the Rani, accidentally gets the Master killed, triggering a premature regeneration. Because the Master has regenerated earlier in his previous lifetime, he becomes a completely new and much more dangerous version of the Master. The existing Master, Williams's version, is now in danger of fading away because his entire timeline has been changed.

So the result is three different versions of the Master: The earliest version, the premature regeneration version and William's version, throw in few more Time Lord villains and you have a story going. It's actually a premise that could have been stretched out across several episodes – I mean, you've got some impressive and untrustworthy personalities, all at odds with each other, and all natural schemers.

There's some very good camera work and editing. A standout scene is where two versions of the Master explain their evil scheme respectively to the Rani and the Monk separately as they walk along. The image cuts smoothly between the two versions back and forth. It's visually brilliant, and it makes what could have been a dull chunk of exposition lively. Generally, this production feels a lot more skilled and inventive technically than the previous *Timestealer*s.

As for the cast, apart from Genghis Khan, whose role is essentially a plot point, most of the characters acquit themselves reasonably well. By this time, Williams is very comfortable playing the Master. The characters of the Monk and the Rani are well done. Particularly so with the Monk, who is cast as the slightly unwilling, much put upon, hero of the piece. The Rani gets less to do, basically being a snarky sidekick.

The Rani, played by a different actress, also appeared in *Timestealers 3: Timetrap*. Both the Rani and the Monk have shown up as effective adversaries in other fan films - The Rani appeared in *Victimsight*, 2008, by Glass Planet Studios/Dream Out Loud Productions. The Monk was the villain du jour in Cheapo Productions Doctor Who and the *Ghost Pirates*, also 2008.

The new Master is absolutely ferocious - this guy really is lean and hungry, and he radiates malicious fury - he looks like he wants to go into a maternity ward and beat babies to death with a shovel, because somewhere, sometime, a baby annoyed him.

Nigel Peever, who you may remember from Planet Productions plays the Lord President of Gallifrey. Peever, and some of the other Planet Video alumni seem to be involved in the production, and Planet Video is credited for costumes and props. The world of these fan productions seems small, and you see all sorts of crossovers and borrowings.

Production values are very good. They do a lot of location shooting, and they do it quite well. The opening shot of the Monk wandering around some old ruins is amazing. The outdoor locations are consistently brilliant - including, remarkably, a scene in a boulder filled granite quarry.

There are a few shots of the Master in impressive locations which don't actually do anything for the story – it's just: 'Wow, this is a terrific location, we'll get a shot of Simon Williams being all Mastery here and just stick it in.' But having said that, there's some definitely nice bits, downtown London, some old castle or military installation, which actually do serve the story quite well.

One fun thing, particularly in The Three Masters, is very effective use of a Tardis' working chameleon circuit. At different points, the Masters or the Monk's Time-Space machine materializes as a boulder, part of the landscape, a stone house, or a doorway built into the side of a hill. It's a nice visual.

The Timestealers series never quite shakes its limitations. This isn't something you'll ever mistake for the BBC production. It's transparently no budget, no resources, tiny amateur crew. In the first couple of stories, the camera credit goes to 'whoever isn't in the shot at that moment' for instance. That tells you all you need to know about what the production was probably like.

On the other hand, they understand their limitations and work effectively to it. There isn't any point where you can say that their ideas or ambitions have outstripped so completely outstripped their abilities that they're crashing and burning like the Hindenburg as we watch. That counts for a lot.

On the whole, there's a charming earnestness to the entire Timestealers series, a good natured, naive quality that makes it watchable. It breaks down into four stories – the first two are connected by an overlapping cast, and might well be considered a single story. The third one is completely stand alone. The first three are quite short, averaging about fifteen minutes.

Fundamentally, they're amateur productions. On the other hand, they're genuinely entertaining amateur production – we're talking actual production value, locations, some sets and costumes that people put some effort into, scripts that mostly hold together, acting, and the whole nine yards. This isn't kids in the backyard with a camcorder, but people making an effort to tell a story. I'm happy to recommend them.

Bottom line, it's fun, particularly *The Three Masters*. I think the word is charming. There's a tongue in cheek quality that goes down real easy. There's nothing here that I would laugh out loud at. It's enjoyable without really tipping over into hilarity; it's not trying to be a spoof. Simon William's version of the Master is a watchable character. It's not a bad way to spend a little time.

CAST: *The Master - Merlin Norbury, Kevin Russell, Simon Williams; The Monk - Robert Angus McDonald; The Rani - Andrea Bamford; Lord President of Gallifrey - Nigel Peever; Genghis Khan - Choojo Tarrap; Mongolian Peasant - Dorj Tarrap; RAF Soldiers - Matt Gower, Dave Conway;*

CREW: *Tower Video Productions (2004); Producer - Simon Williams; Writer/Director - Kevin Russell; Camera - Merlin Norbury, Kevin Russell; Sound - Choojo Tarrap, Michael Herring; Editing - Kevin Russell, Simon Williams; Music - Mark Ayres; Costumes and Props - Tower Video Productions, Planet Video; Thanks to: The Tarrap Family, Nigel Peever, Philip Jackson, Cumbria Institute of the Arts; Filmed in Scotland; Dedicated to Anthony Ainley, 1932 - 2004;*

Reviews: Death Takes a Holiday (2004)

Filmed at an actual Mayan Temple

STORY: When a broken crystal in the Tardis accidentally ages everyone thirty years, the Sixth Doctor and Jamie must mind the Police Box, while sending the Brigadier and Zoe to retrieve a replacement crystal hidden in a Mayan Temple.

REVIEW: So, let's see. We have Colin Baker playing the Doctor. We have Frazier Hines playing Jamie McCrimmon. Nicholas Courtney plays Former Brigadier Alister Lethbridge-Cook. Wendy Padbury pays Zoe Herriot. Oh and by the way, the Production Consultants were Terrance Dicks and Barry Lets.

Now, if any of these names are unfamiliar to you, let me fill it in.

Barry Letts involvement with Doctor Who begins when he directed Patrick Troughton's Enemy of the World. He is best known as the Producer for Doctor Who during the Jon Pertwee years, and during this period, he directed *Terror of the Autons, Carnival of Monsters, Planet of the Spiders* and part of *Inferno*. During the Tom Baker era he directed the *Android Invasion*, and later was credited as the show's co-producer for the final year of Tom Baker's tenure, riding herd on a new John Nathan-Turner. He has credit for Jon Pertwee's two 1993 Doctor Who radio serials and several novelizations for the show.

Terrance Dicks – started out as a script editor for the Patrick Troughton era in 1968, co-wrote the *War Games*, and *Seeds of Death*. Partnered up with Letts as script editor for the Pertwee era. Also wrote for the Baker era – *Robot, Brain of Morbius, Horror of Fang Rock* and *State of Decay*. In the Davison era he wrote the *Five Doctors*. He wrote two Doctor Who stage plays – *Seven Keys to Doomsday* and *The Ultimate Adventure* (featuring Jon Pertwee and Colin Baker). He also wrote a lot of Doctor Who books.

Wendy Padberry is an actress who played Zoe Herriot, a 21st century astrophysicist and companion to Jamie and the second Doctor starting in season five, and throughout season six. She also reprised the role in the *Five Doctors*. She appeared on stage, as a different companion in the Doctor Who play *Seven Keys to Doomsday*.

Frazier Hines played the Troughton Doctor's most famous and popular companion, the highlander Jamie McCrimmon, through the fourth, fifth and sixth seasons, coming back for both the *Five Doctors* and the *Two Doctors*.

We'll just assume that Colin Baker as the Sixth Doctor and Nicholas Courtney as the Brigadier need no further introduction.

So, are we up to speed?

Oh, and I'll mention that part of it was shot on a cruise ship, and a significant part of it was shot in Belize on location among Mayan ruins and pyramids. You know, for production value.

So this is a fan film?

Amazingly yes!

This is Ryan K. Johnson's swan song (so far), with Doctor Who, sixteen years after the last Benedetti story. How the heck did it come about?

Apparently, since the *Love Boat* went off the air, cruise ships have had to be more inventive, and have adopted themes. There are now Seniors Cruises, Gay Cruises, Sports Cruises, and even a Sci Fi Cruise. In this case, Ryan and his buddies were off on a Sci Fi Cruise, with Courtney and Padberry as the celebrity guests, and part of the agenda for the cruise was to produce a little Sci Fi fan film.

Colin Baker and Frazier Hines only have a cameo role, introducing the proceedings with a bit of genial wordplay standing outside the Police Box. Their scenes were shot in Chicago, the week before, actually. Most of the short running time belongs to Nicholas Courtney and Wendy Padberry, who are sent off to a remote Mayan temple to retrieve a trinket that the Doctor needs.

As to the story: There's been an 'Oops' in the Police Box. Apparently some crystal cracked and in the backfire, everyone suddenly aged thirty years. The Doctor and Jamie stay back to mind the Tardis and the Brigadier and Zoey are sent to obtain a replacement crystal. Along the way, plot happens.

So, apart from the fact of cast and crew that would make a classic series fan go squee!, what can we say about this given that it has production values that would have made the first seven Doctors, who'd spent years in gravel quarries, uncontrollably jealous. They shot on location on a cruise ship and on the Mayan Riviera, at Mayan temples. Mayan frigging temples! They shot with an actual Mayan Pyramid! Doctor Who had been a show that was having a good day when it wasn't raining at the local gravel quarry. But here they shot in an actual Mayan temple!

Many of the best of the Doctor Who fan films have had the benefit of extraordinary locations. *The Persephone Complex* made use of an actual Roman Amphitheatre. El Cheapo's *Samhain* was shot in and around a 900 restored church. Who has that in their neighborhood? *Wrath of Eukor* shot in a temperate rain forest. *Ghost Pirates* used a classic sailing ship, the Cutty Sark. Shakedown used HMS Belfast, a retired navy destroyer. *The Hidden Face* used monastic ruins, *Phase Four* used a church for its Cyberman headquarters. Ruins, castles, towers, mansions, moors and cliffs show up a lot. England must be just lousy with the things. So many fan filmmakers, particularly the British ones, have been able to consistently find interesting and visually impressive locations to serve as spaceship interiors, historical places, futuristic settings, or whatever. And it's remarkable how much these locations, setting stories in these locations, add to the look and feel of a production. But a Mayan temple? Okay, they win; everyone else can go home now.

Did I mention that the opening titles, that whole psychedelic intro was great? Computer generated, rainbow coloured, consistent with the traditional intros, but a thing of beauty in and of itself.

It's a bit of fluff. I mean, it's seventeen minutes, so you're not going to get any kind of great or involved story. The plot is straightforward – retrieve a McGuffin, complicated by the fact that there are mysterious bad guys who occasionally shadow them. We're not talking Shakespearean dialogue, or kick ass action sequences, or even heavy duty acting full of nuance and by-play. It's not particularly fast paced. But then again, there's absolutely nothing wrong with it. This was just an amiable little lark by all involved.

The actors all do their stuff, don't get me wrong. They'd all had a lot of experience playing their characters, even if it had been decades ago. They're pretty comfortable slipping into the old skins, they're good sports, they enjoy themselves, and the story is fine. If not for the location and the names involved, I would have said, nice little piece of work and just gotten on with my day.

As it is, just for being what it is, it's kind of a small landmark. This wasn't Nicholas Courtney's final appearance as the Brigadier – he appeared in 2009 in Sarah Jane Adventures, and then in 2011, shot an 'in character interview' bit for one of the DVDs. However, for both Hines and Padberry, it was their last on-camera appearances as their characters. And while Colin Baker has been around, he was terrific in the *Five-ish Doctors*; I don't know that he's actually stepped into the role of the Sixth Doctor on screen since then.

In my reviews, I'm looking for Fan Films that in some way capture the spirit of Doctor Who, that are interesting additions or contribution to it. I want that Doctor Who feel. Like *Gene Genius*, this is a story that blurs the edges.

Shot in December, 2003, and completed in February, 2004, *Death Takes a Holiday* sits right at the edge of Who's revival. *Scream of the Shalka*, BBCi's effort to do an animated Doctor Who series, with Richard E. Grant, had been announced in July, 2003, and had aired in six fifteen minute installments through November and December, 2003. Literally on the heels of this came BBC's announcement that it would relaunch Doctor Who as a live action series back in September, 2003, with production starting in 2004.

In 2003 /2004, Doctor Who had suddenly begun to regenerate back into life, creating new waves of interest and enthusiasm. Fans were sitting up and paying attention. There was excitement in the air. I don't think it's really a coincidence that this project would rise up around this time. If nothing else, people were picking up the buzz and trying to get in on it, and maybe that wasn't restricted to fans, but included cruise ship directors looking for an angle, and old actors feeling the stir of fond memories.

If you want an angle on this…. call this a love letter to the old series, inspired by the birth of the new series.

And if you want to get your nerd on, let me offer you two thoughts:

First – on the *Two Doctors'* DVD, there is a seven minute thingy called *A Fix With Sontarans*. There's some historical interest here, because it may be Doctor Who's first 'minisode.' Basically, a youth dressed as a miniature 6th Doctor materializes on the Police Box, and helps the Doctor defeat a Sontaran invasion of the Police Box.

A Fix With the Sontarans came from a show called *Jim Will Fix It*. It was like the *'Make a Wish Foundation'* without the cancer. Kids wrote in to host Jimmy Saville, and he'd make it happen for them – whether this involved jumping out of an airplane, or starring in a Doctor Who skit.

Yeah, about that. Turns out that Jimmy Saville was a massive sexual predator and pedophile – we're talking hundreds of victims over a thirty year career. Saville used his celebrity to recruit endless victims, while shielding himself from the law. All this started to come out after Jimmy finally died. So for the next release of the *Two Doctors*, the BBC is removing *A Fix With Sontarans* from the DVD.

Death Takes a Holiday would be a perfect replacement, don't you think? Oh, and in case you're thinking, the BBC doesn't do that sort of thing… they already did. Check out the *War Games* DVD release and get back to me.

Second: When you think about it, it's easy enough to slip *Death Takes a Holiday* into the Colin Baker continuity following *The Two Doctors*.

Here's how I see it: The Troughton Doctor in Two Doctors is still travelling with Jamie. But Zoe was also his companion up to the *War Games*, and had appeared with Jamie in the Five Doctors (both of them illusions). So it's not unlikely that she'd still be travelling with the two of them.

So why isn't she in *The Two Doctors*? Because the 2nd Doctor, has been sent to a space station in the future to stop dangerous time-experiments from unravelling the fabric of reality. So the 2nd Doctor, before he goes into it, decides to drop Zoe off somewhere safe with someone he trusts.

Who would that be? Why the Brigadier, with whom he'd shared a couple of adventures, *Web of Fear* and the *Invasion*, and who Zoe had also met in the *Invasion*. Who better?

And when? Well, the perfect time would be during an incarnation where none of his future selves would be dropping in or out of the Brigadier's life. Which would make it the time of the Sixth Doctor.

Now, we don't know if the Doctor had something up his sleeve, or was just keeping her safe. But either way, he made a mistake – by dropping Zoe off with the Brigadier during the 6th's era, he had inadvertently appeared in a time where the 6th was also existing, and accidentally forged a temporal link.

Which is why, when things start going to hell for him with the Androgums and Zontarans and whatnot, it's the sixth Doctor in that specific time and place that feels the backlash!

After the *Two Doctors* all gets sorted out, the 2nd Doctor gets reluctant to cross the 6ths timeline again. So he sends Jamie to the 6th Doctor to retrieve Zoe. The 6th obliges, heads over to the Brigadiers to pick her up... And that's when the time crystal goes blooey – having already been weakened by the time experiments that the 2nd had been sent to stop – aging everyone thirty years (except for the 6th, who'd aged several hundred and so looks just as old).

Which brings us to *Death Takes a Holiday*. Simple, non? For my next trick, watch me pull a rabbit out of your ear.

Or just go watch the video – it's only seventeen minutes for God's sakes.

A final postscript, Sylvester McCoy himself would participate in a few of these cruises and plays the Doctor again, in substantially less polished projects - *The Crystal Conundrum* and *Twice Upon a Time Lord*. On the positive side, cruise ships and cameos from several companions. On the downside, McCoy clowns around a bit, and the scripts are a tad embarrassing, so we won't talk about it too much. McCoy turned in a much more compelling performance in *Gene Genius*. There were a few other cruise ship videos made featuring Who actors, notably John Levene. But *Death Takes a Holiday* is the most worthwhile, making the transition from home movie to a real story.

17 minutes, Mini-DV video, filmed December 2003, released February 2004.

CAST: *Nicholas Courtney as the Brigadier, Wendy Padbury as Zoe, Holly Swift as the Boss, Ron Daniels as the Henchman, Mike Leahy as the Goon, Dan Murphy and Jennifer Lowden as the Archeologists, Anne Sedell as the old boss, Brian Stearns as the Unlucky Tourist. Special Appearance by Colin Baker as the Doctor and Frazer Hines as Jamie MacCrimmon.*

CREW: *Written by Ron & Priscilla Daniels & Jennifer Lowden, Produced by Dan Harris, Cinematography and Editing by Ryan K. Johnson, Directed by Paul Scott Aldred.*

Review: Gene Genius (2004)

The Third Doctor Meets the
Seventh Doctor and Ace

STORY: The Seventh Doctor and Ace are attending a breakfast at an old friends place. The Doctor reminisces about how, the last time he was here, in the 1970s, things got quite sticky. As he flashes back, we see the Third Doctor, riding Bessie to his next adventure....

REVIEW: *Gene Genius* is credited to group or collective that goes by the name '*The Projection Room*' - the central person is Chris Hoyle, but the group includes or has included Robin Castle, Gordon England, Phil Newton, David Hobson – they seem to have formed around 1994, the same time as Timebase Productions, and their output is comparable in volume. I assume they started for the same reason – the aborted revival and implosion of 1993.

Gene Genius is one of their later era productions. But it is out of continuity with most of Hoyle's work – you don't miss anything by not having watched the previous adventures. It's a safe stand-alone.

But it's here because Sylvester McCoy plays the Doctor and Sophie Aldred reprises Ace in it. That's right: The real actors are playing their characters in a fan film. This isn't unique - Colin Baker appeared in *Death Takes a Holiday*. Jon Pertwee appeared in *Devious*. It's happened several times in some of the ambitious *Star Trek* fan films.

Sylvester McCoy has quite a history of these appearances - he has returned to play the Doctor in Ian Levine's productions - a re-edit of *Downtime*, and *Destiny of the Doctors,* and he participated in Sci Fi cruises himself at least twice, resulting in *Twice Upon a Time Lord* and the *Crystal Conundrum*. He's also appeared as the Doctor in non-canonical BBC authorized productions including *Death Comes to Time, Search Out Space,* and a Children in Need version of *The Weakest Link*.

There's also Colin Baker's early *'Doctor in all but name'* appearances in the Stranger series for the BBV, Sylvester McCoy's appearance as the *'Chiropodist... the Foot Doctor'* in *'Do You Have a License to Save the Planet'* and his audio role in The Professor and Ace. But although both Reeltime Pictures and the BBV re-used characters from Doctor Who, and occasionally skirted the issue, the explicit Doctor himself was off limits.

And of course, there's Big Finish Audio adventures, in which all the surviving classic Doctors have participated.

So, what to say about their appearances in *Gene Genius*? Well McCoy and Aldred have aged. This is most apparent with Sophie Aldred, who played Ace back as an adolescent when she was a very young woman. Well, now she's a mature woman, you can see the younger Ace in her, but she's clearly not the same person. Perhaps that's why she wears her Ace Jacket – the one with all the badges.

McCoy? A little grayer, a little more weathered, but he's the same. He was the last of the classic Doctors and he's weathered the passage of time the best. With a little hair dye and make up, he could pick up his old role tomorrow. In *The Fivish Doctors* he was the most unmarked by time. I saw him in 2015. Even then, he seemed barely aged, as if he could take up his old role the next day.

Aldred and McCoy are basically there for a framing sequence. They're visiting for breakfast at some friends, and McCoy starts to reminisce about some adventure he had the last time he was here, back in the 1970s. Cue flashback. At the end of the serial, the story returns to them, and they're back again, to join the action and help wrap things up.

In the main body of the story, doing most of the heavy lifting, we have John Field playing Jon Pertwee, playing the Third Doctor. Initially, I had no idea who John Field was, but I googled. He was known for dressing up as the Third Doctor, for the Doctor Who Experience in Llangollen. I had no idea what that was, so I looked it up. It turns out that the Doctor Who Experience in Llangollen was one of the largest exhibition of original props from the series, covering 6000 square feet. Open year round from 1995 to 2003, it averaged about 50,000 visitors a year.

So I imagine that John Field was dressing up as the Doctor because at least part of his work was as a host for the Exhibition. It was an actual paying gig – so he has some credit as a semi-professional Third Doctor. Field's connection to the Experience might explain some of the props seen in Gene Genius.

As I got further into this, I found that he had played the fourth Doctor in 'The Experiment', Shade of Death 2, the Dalek Invasion of Stockton, and the sixth Doctor in Shade of Death 1 and 2, the Labyrinth of the Blud Devils 2 and 3, played the Brigadier in Earthbank, and appeared in handful of other fan film roles, mostly with the Planet Video/Pacific-Uk/Ad Lib group back in the late 1980s and early 90s. By all accounts, he seems to be a charming fellow, nice guy and longtime fan.

And then he opens his mouth....

Okay, that's unfair of me. To be honest, the acting quality through the whole thing is variable, mostly tolerable. John Field does okay with his part. He's not really The Doctor for the most part – he doesn't inhabit the role of the Doctor in the way that Barbara Benedetti or Rupert Booth. He doesn't own it the way that Sylvester McCoy does so effortlessly.

There have been a lot of Doctors over the years, and a lot of approaches, both official and unauthorized. You have to give each actor some leeway to find the character. I think that some are more successful than others, particularly so when it comes to fan Doctors.

Field's problem is that he's not just playing a Doctor. He's playing a very specific Doctor. John Field is playing John Pertwee's version of the Doctor. I think that creates a certain expectation. It's one thing to create your own version of the Doctor. If you're going to do a specific Doctor, then you're going to be judged on how well you do that guy. That's the risk of deciding to channel a very specific character.

John Pertwee's Doctor was clipped and focused. Pertwee was playing an incredibly smart man, confident, a little impatient, and a bit frustrated. In a lot of Pertwee's scenes, he brings a kind of energy to it, even when he isn't necessarily doing all that much. He's stuck here on Earth and it's driving him up the wall, even as he resolves to make the best of it, and try not to lash out. There are occasions when Pertwee's Doctor gives the Brigadier a two barreled blast, and it's always clear that really, he's angry about something else. That may be why the Brigadier never quite takes it to heart, and why the two men formed a friendship.

John Field's performance is more laconic, especially at the front end. He drawls where Pertwee was clipped and seething. He's much more casual. He gets better at it in the second and third episodes, and he's helped a lot when things are moving fast and the pace of the story takes the pressure off him. Perhaps I'm being hard on Field.

Yes, John Field dresses up like Pertwee, and he wears a rather unconvincing wig to be like Pertwee, and he drives Pertwee's car… But I don't think he's entirely successful as Pertwee as the Third Doctor. At times, he manages to convey a certain irritability, and there are times he comes close, but that's about it. It's a shame, because I'm rooting for him.

One pet peeve – if you're going to play the recognized actor, maybe the script should have at least one line explaining why he looks different.

"Gee Doctor, it certainly is strange seeing you looking like that. Is that your new face from here on?"

"Oh no, Brigadier, this is just a time hiccup left over from my regeneration, it's like a spot of hay fever for you humans. It's very rare, and doesn't last. I'll be back to my regular features in a day or two."

Would that have been so hard?

But no, that never ever happens in Fan Films. Tom Baker is played by any teenager with a long enough scarf. The late middle aged Patrick Troughton is played by a twenty-something, Colin Baker is played by a strapping skinny lout or a fat, balding short man, and we are just supposed to accept it without explanation. I suppose, if you're a fan, that's cool. We do accept it. But hey, a little bit of reference and explanation wouldn't be amiss.

Come to think of it, remember *Time Crash*? That crossover minisode? Didn't the Tenant Doctor have some bafflegab to explain that crossing their timelines had caused the Davison Doctor to gain weight, lose hair and generally look thirty years older?

Might be the same effect here, with Pertwee knocked into Field by the fact that, unknown to him, McCoy's entered his timeline. For that matter, it might explain the slight differences between Hartnell and Hurndell in the Five Doctors.

Where was I? Oh yeah. Production quality and all that stuff.

So how does it stack up? Well, it's a three part serial, with episodes ranging in length from 16 to 13 to 24 minutes. The total thing runs 56 minutes.

Right off the bat, I can say that the production quality is remarkable. Image quality, as we're getting used to with 21st century video camera technology, is pristine. I'm assuming that they shot with a high end consumer digital camera, and mixed and edited on computer software.

John Field's opening scenes feature him driving around in a replica of Bessie, borrowed from the Llangollen Doctor Who experience. From the distance, it's an impressive shot, and as we flash straight back to the Pertwee era, it feels…right. In terms of Who elements, there's a nice Police Box shell exterior prop, and it's used with subtlety. They don't make a huge deal out of it, it's just there, reminding us that this is a Doctor story, but not blaring on over it

There's a nice moment when he waves at some cows as he drives by. It's a cute little throwaway gag reminding us that the Doctor is both alien and eccentric. The truth is that its little things like that, that often make or break it for us.

It's an earth-based story, and they've managed to find or obtain locations which look great and are actually pretty good at passing for what they're supposed to be in the story. So imposing brick buildings as research establishments, interiors that are quite clearly part of some large facility. There's a nice touch in that we see a lot of 70s era period vehicles and clothes. It's close enough to modern that we don't get our noses rubbed in it, but there's a decent sense of time and place.

There are very impressive costumes and some very nice props. In terms of production design or production content, I can't complain at all. I find myself wondering, in addition to the Bessie replica, how many other props they were able to borrow that were connected to the Exhibition. If they made them themselves, then kudos.

The actual story on the other hand, suffers from pacing problems. Pretty much nothing happens in the first episode. McCoy's Doctor makes small talk, then Field's Doctor drives Bessie, he visits the Brigadier and they make small talk, then he drives Bessie some more, then he visits the lab and makes small talk, then he drives Bessie some more. You have the impression they really wanted to show off Bessie. Then the episode climaxes when the Brigadier solves an anagram.

Okay, let me stop you right there: If your big cliff hanger-conclusion is solving an anagram… then you are in big trouble, storytelling-wise. What's the next big shocker? The Doctor opens his mail?

Look, if you're telling a story, you actually need things to happen, and you need a payoff. Solving an anagram? What the hell? At the best of times, that would be a tough sell. The only information that the word puzzle actually gives us is that it's probably the Master up to his old tricks. But the story has already established that the Doctor recognized the Master's picture, has poked around and found it suspicious, so the anagram adds precisely… nothing. And to add injury to the insult, it's presented in an uninspired way.

Luckily, the second episode moves along better. The Doctor and Brigadier have a row, and Fields manages to pick up some of Pertwee's fire. Remember when I said Pertwee was a pretty quick tempered Doctor? Well, getting fired up is when Field does him best. Events from there move swiftly in logical sequence and without padding. Phil Newton's version of the Master even manages to seem menacing at points. That's not easy when you're wearing a checkered tie. The story threads start to knit together, and it all culminates in the big reveal, which is genuinely well done as the Master's evil plot literally bursts into the screen and the alien monsters show up.

Pretty much everything they did wrong in the first episode, they did right in the second. Isn't that strange? You'd think that they'd be consistent one way or the other. Or that they would have merged the two, which would have allowed for better pacing.

The third episode starts with a bang, pretty much a replay of the climactic moment of the second episode. I don't mind, the classic series did that all the time. Developments proceed swiftly. After a bit of gloating, the Master's plan goes off the rails, as it usually does. The guy is like Wile E. Coyote, the plan always goes wrong. You'd think after all these times; he'd start to catch on. But no. The Master's fall from grace, or tumble for the worst, is very nicely done – spontaneous enough to catch you by surprise, but well played enough that you think 'yeah, he should have seen it coming.'

Most of the third episode features the monsters - alien menaces who have used the Master to culture a cure for their genetic weakness. Once they have that, they proceed to take names and kick ass. Their debut at the end of the second episode is impressive, and their arc through the third episode sustains that high note as they proceed, both implacable and impressive.

It's not perfect, there's an incidental music track that's just bemusing – do we need dramatic music to dial a phone number? But there's some witty bits, and monsters do their things and are photographed well, and the rest of the cast tries to keep up. Field's performance runs out of steam a little. But that's tolerable because the monsters are doing their thing and UNIT shows up.

Unfortunately, the battle between UNIT and the invaders is likely to provoke gales of laughter. But I'm inclined to be sympathetic. Here's the thing – you want to have a gun battle with invading monsters, you've got guns or at least realistic looking props, but you don't have pyrotechnics or blanks – what do you do?

Well, you shake your guns like you're firing them, and Foley in the sound effects. Good solution, I like it, no problem! There's just one thing. There's one thing, and only one thing to remember. If you want this to work, you have to keep in mind this critical thing: The barrel of the firearm has to extend off camera. If you do that, then you've got a decently convincing effect. I'll give them credit, a lot of the time, that's exactly how they do it.

But a lot of the time, they don't.

Ouch!

When the whole gun, including the tip of the barrel is in frame, then it's very clear that you're trying to fight off an invading alien horde by…. shaking your gun at them with furious intensity. That, my friends, is *MST3K*.

This is a shame, because apart from that unmissable boner, the UNIT scene feels really good. Everyone is wearing matching uniforms. The soldiers are visibly young, but soldiers often are, so that kind of feels right. The young actors approach their mission straight on with grim intensity. There's no winking or fooling around. They're focused and they act like soldiers. The weapons are mismatched but look authentic. When UNIT confronts the enemy, they don't go for a stand up fight, they're crouched in the ditch, behind bushes or cover, the way you would in a real firefight. The one pyrotechnic effect is well done. It's well executed and it looks good.

It's just that one thing… So if it strikes you, then go ahead and laugh, get it out of your system, and then appreciate the rest of it. Or dig into your pocket for a handful of forgiveness. Or just roll with it. Maybe you won't even notice.

After that, we return to McCoy and Aldred, who join up with the rest of the story and the rest of the cast in quite a clever and seamless way. Sylvester elevates the material with grumpy charm, and it all gets sorted out.

So how does it all work out? Good, but not great. This doesn't quite reach the level of matching the classic series – or if it does, it's scratching at the lower tiers. It's got things going for it – the locations are terrific, the props and costumes are great and they're used well, the 'money shots' are definitely impressive, McCoy and Aldred are charming, and even Field's performance picks up steam on its own. There's a story there, and it's competently told. It manages to weave all of its threads together, and to deliver several twists.

There's even a modicum of wit – the Field Doctor waving at cows, because, you know… they're all earthlings. It reminded me of the Pertwee Doctor trying to talk to a chicken in Carnival of Monsters. Then later when the Master explains his latest pointlessly complicated scheme, Field's Doctor deflates it with a dismissive 'I figured it was something like that.' Still later, there's a 'bully kicking sand in the face at the beach' moment. These are all nice little throwaway gags, well executed. They don't call attention to themselves, they don't drag the story down, but they're fun, and they're the sort of thing that makes Doctor Who what it is. They're things that are often lacking in many fan films.

Where does it fall down? Well, John Field struggles a bit with the Pertwee role. I've talked about that, I don't need to belabour it. He's not altogether a loss, and he definitely gets better as we go on. Stronger direction and a bit more focus would have helped him immensely. As it is, his performance is weakest in the first episode and that's a hard handicap to overcome. It lingers in our mind, even as he does so much better in the second and third episodes. I guess the consistent lesson is if you're going to stumble, don't do it in the beginning. Same problem with Utomu and their tosh wall flats, come to think of it. Bad starts are hard to overcome.

These are 'on the spot decisions' and we can't do much except choose to live with them. I'm not going to stop watching because of a few glitches here and there. Its little stuff, is what it is. But in this case, it subtracts. I've said that little things make a difference though, and they do for good or ill. Gene Genius has some terrific things working for it, but it's also got some little things working against it.

The script – mostly competent, but kind of pedestrian in some ways. As I've said, apart from a badly paced opening episode, the story structure is actually quite good. It lays out a lot of plot threads, and then manages to steadily weave them all together. The progression is logical. There are even some good lines. But the writing, the dialogue, that's somewhat flat at times. I feel bad saying that. Let me put it this way: Mark Twain said that the difference between the right word and the almost right word is like the difference between the lightning and the lightning bug. He was right. The dialogue is serviceable and competent and mostly lightning bugs.

Writing is a tricky thing, it's such a fine, filtered thing, and it can be hard to find the exact right word in the face of almost right words. I feel that they might have done better to have given the script a few read throughs, gotten some feedback and suggestions. But then, I'm not sure what conditions they were working on. And truthfully, the classic series has its fair share of thoroughly average or pedestrian writing. So… nothing too wrong with it, it just doesn't sparkle. But with a bit more work, it maybe could have sparkled. And that's such a shame, particularly getting McCoy and Aldred in, and getting some wonderful props and costumes and locations.

It's frustrating, because you can look at this and see unreached potential. A small handful of bad or sloppy decisions in an otherwise solid production process that undermines it. It could have been much better in the post-production process. Edit the first episode and then consolidate it into the second, so that instead of three uneven parts, you have two episode of roughly equal length. Tighten up some of the sag. Watch the incidental music. CGI in some muzzle flashes in post production. All that would improve it immensely. You can see the shape of a much better serial in there, a brilliant two-parter, perhaps still reachable.

But still, even with that, it's pretty good. I've said of Timebase that with just a little post production clean up, you could fit them right into the Classic Series. For *Gene Genius*, I think my verdict is that you'd need a lot more post production clean up, but if you did that and tweaked it just right, it too would fit into the classic series. I think that it just misses out, it could have been great. Greatness was within grasp. It could have been extraordinary. As it is…

Well worth watching.

In postscript (yes, the review part is over but I'm still writing, you can go home now if you wish) I have to say that I'm amazed that Sylvester McCoy and Sophie Aldred participated. How the hell did that happen? Blackmail? Threats? Huge piles of money? Or are they really just that nice? By all accounts, they actually do seem to be genuinely nice people.

I had the opportunity to ask Sylvester McCoy about Gene Genius in 2015. He had no recollection of it at all. Didn't remember it. Didn't especially care. For him, it was a few minutes of filming, at a garden party one afternoon, years ago.

Apparently, the driving force behind Gene Genius was David and Julie Banes, who wanted to do a Doctor Who fan film as a birthday present for their son Johnathan. If you watch the credits, the Banes show up a lot, props, costumes, production roles, and even onscreen. They knew John Field from the Llangollen Doctor Who Experience, and were friends or acquaintances with Phil Newton and Gordon England who seemed to be connected with the Projection Room group, and drew them all together. Then they got the idea of having Sylvester McCoy and Sophie Aldred attend their son's birthday party, and somehow talked them into doing a few scenes. Wow! I wish I had parents like that. That's one very well connected, very highly motivated, very talented family.

Ah well. I'm afraid this isn't my kindest review. But this is something unique and interesting in many ways, and if it doesn't reach the level of the series, you get a sense that it came very, very close. Its flaws we must forgive. If you're going to watch Doctor Who Fan Films, then this is a must see.

CAST *Seventh Doctor - Sylvester McCoy; Ace - Sophie Aldred; Third Doctor - John Field; Brigadier Lethbridge-Stewart - Gordon England; The Master - Phil Newton; Dr. Judith Kent - Susan Gibson; Professor Sid Topham - Chris Hoyle; Cyber-Leaders - Johnathan Banes and Alex Andreao; Cyber-Operators - Scott Buchanan, Jessica Bailey, Neil Edmonds, Philip Elliott, Tom Bawden and Gordon England; UNIT Soldiers - Johnathan Banes, Nadia House, Ashley Frame, Jamie Roberts, James Ferity, Tom Warren, Nicky Eckes, Neil Edmonds, Scott Buchanan,*

CREW: *By 'Kit Steels'; Produced, Directed and Edited by Chris Hoyle; Script Editor - Chris Hoyle; Camera Operator - Roy H. Schile; Visual Effects - Glen, Mabh & Conol Savage; Costumes and Properties - Cath Astell; Cyberman Costumes - David Banes & Billy Elliot; Tardis provided by Colin Jones; Incubation Cabinet Set - DJ Designs; Sound and Lighting - Ric Hoshley; Incidental Music - Tristram Cary/Dudley Simpson; Special Sound - Brian Hodgson; Hertfordshire Location Managers - Julie & David Banes; John Banes,Additional thanks to the Banes Family Friends.*

Reviews: Flight of the Daleks & Others (2004-2008)

Hark the Harrald Doctor Springs

STORY: *Plague of Lychwood* - in the isolated village of Lychwood, people are dying mysteriously. The Doctor discovers a rogue Cybermat. But there's something more going on.... *Flight of the Daleks* a war between Cybermen and Daleks puts the Earth at risk, can the Doctor sort things out... *Ghost* the Doctor investigates mysterious apparitions....

REVIEW: A.F. Harrold is a poet and children's entertainer, and from what I can tell, a very nice guy. He also turned in one of the most interesting performances as the Doctor through a trilogy of Doctor Who Fan Films, in *Plague of Lychwood, Flight of the Daleks* and *Ghost.*

Graham Quince and Paul Vought are a pair of independent film makers, or perhaps amateur film makers. They seem to have almost no presence in the Internet Movie Database. But if you look them up in YouTube, you'll find they've produced an impressive number of films under various banners – *Bikini Zombies from the Moon,* an *Australian Vampire in London,* a set *of James Bond* Fan Films, and so forth.

Quince and Vought are also assisted by what seems to be a loose group of friends or associates who are involved with their projects as they come and go. I'd really recommend you spend some time browsing through some of their other productions as well. It's clear from the breadth of their productions that they, like Ryan K. Johnson, or the Romanian brothers, are film makers first, and Doctor Who fans second.

The result is fairly polished productions. They'd picked up a fair amount of experience and technical competence, and they'd faced a broad array of challenges. That sort of breadth seems to make for generally competent productions. You can tell the difference. More importantly, you can enjoy the difference. These guys know how to compose a shot – I'll refer you to the genuinely stark and creepy opening scenes of *Plague of Lychwood*. They also know how to tell a story visually, to inject humour and action.

Now seeing as how we are reviewing the best of the Doctor Who Fan Films, I'll concentrate on their Who work, which is really only a part of their oeuvre. With or through a fan group called the Thames Valley Time Lords, they were involved with the *Persephone Complex* in 1995, followed by *Still Life* and *Assassin*. Years later, they'd release a re-edited, remastered version of the Persephone Complex. The original films revolved around the notion of a copy of the Doctor existing in and escaping from the Gallifreyan Matrix, they're kind of odd and interesting.

The Harrold films are Quince and Vought's second trilogy, apparently done on their own, the Thames Valley Time Lords being things of the past. For our purposes, I want to focus on the Harrold Doctor stories.

I want to emphasize this, because, although this review is about the Harrold Doctor Trilogy, and although I'm quite intrigued by Harrold's performance, film making is a collective work. It's not just about the star. Harrold has the benefit of a good script and he's got the benefit of people who know what to do with the camera, and who have been doing it for a while.

So what about A.F. Harrold? Well, basically, he's one of these ginger blokes, who likes to show off with facial hair. Born 1975, to apparently sensible parents, he went on to become a poet, a novelist, a children's entertainer and many other things in that vein. His biography on Bloomsbury notes "He writes and performs for adults and children, in cabaret and in schools, in bars and in basements, in fields and indoors. He was Glastonbury Festival Website's Poet-In-Residence in 2008, and Poet-In-Residence at Cheltenham Literature Festival in 2010. He won the Cheltenham All Stars Slam Championship in 2007 and has had his work on BBC Radio 4, Radio 3 and BBC7. He is active in schools work, running workshops and slams and doing performances at ungodly hours of the morning, and has published several collections of poetry. He is the owner of many books, a handful of hats, a few good ideas and one beard."

I think he may have written that himself.

He's also got a number of his own YouTube videos up, should you go looking for them. I don't see a lot of acting on his resume, but he's got an extensive background in performance, and he has evolved his own style of delivery which he brings to his version of the Doctor. Bottom line, this is an interesting, and likely, quite likeable guy.

I have no idea how he ended up becoming the Doctor in the Vought/Quince productions. Truthfully, I have no idea how he feels about his turn as Doctor Who. Proud? Chagrined? Frustrated? Embarrassed? I emailed him, but I never heard back. I'm hoping that it's a fond memory.

His take on the Doctor is interesting, and at first I wasn't quite sure what to make of it. He's got such a peculiar low key delivery. The only thing I can really compare it to is the sort of calm, unhurried monologue you might find on a cooking show, as they walk you through the recipe. Confident but not arrogant, in control, measured, knows exactly what he's doing. There's an almost weightless quality to it.

His Doctor conveys no sense of importance or gravity to situations, the Police Box is tumbling out of control, an alien ship is crash landing on Earth, the fate of the planet is at stake… and to him, it's basically small talk. Harrald's Doctor is informed and informative, calm, chatty. It's odd, and kind of interesting. And it makes a sort of sense. I mean for us, the end of the universe is a big deal, for the Doctor… its Tuesday.

Of course, we're used to bombastic over the top Doctors. Starting with Tom Baker, through Colin Baker, and then with Tenant, Smith and Capaldi, each has gone bigger and bigger to the point where Capaldi achieved somewhere between the stratosphere and low earth orbit.

We've had only a few relatively low key Doctors, mainly Davison and Ecclestone. Harrold is low key to the point of somnolence. When two of the Doctor's associates meet up unpleasantly in Flight of the Daleks, he's almost washed out of the room.

And yet, as a Doctor, he's entirely competent, he knows what he's doing, and more importantly, he knows what to do. He's just not pushy or boisterous about it. He's the smartest guy in the room, but very careful to not make a big deal out of it or to allow anyone to feel badly about it. He's never less than unfailingly polite, but he also never shows a drop of fear.

Indeed, his low key approach works, when confronting the enemy, whether Daleks or Cybermen or whatever, he's entirely disarming. You kind of believe he could walk into the middle of a Dalek base, and without any malice whatsoever, make them look stupid for trying to threaten him. It really is an engaging performance. Harrold manages to make the

Doctor his own, and to do it in a way that's entirely convincing, but which we haven't seen before.

&&&

THE PLAGUE OF LYCHWOOD (2002)

Opening: Stark 'point of view night' shots of a searcher in the woods, seeing through his camera, as he reports back to his controller. He finds the dead body of a woman. And then, an unseen something gets him. The camera falls. It's a terrific opening, a bit of Blair Witch, nicely shot, thoroughly creepy.

Daylight comes, the Doctor, dressed as the Shadow for some reason, long black coat, black fedora, flowing red scarf, arrives on scene. He wanders about the woods, stumbling first over a corpse and then across Captain Victory Holoway of UNIT.

Let's back up a bit. The Doctor literally stumbles over a corpse. Let me be clear. He doesn't find the body. He trips and falls over it. He literally falls over a dead body. Welcome to A.F. Harrold's Doctor. It's such a nicely done scene in every possible way. It's funny, but not overplayed, there's just a sly comic touch. Despite the pratfall, Harrold's Doctor never loses his cool, doesn't overreact, just kind of goes with it.

Dead bodies, it seems, are turning up pretty regularly. The Doctor traces the trouble to a single Cybermat. That in itself is peculiar, since cybermats generally run in groups. This leads him to a mad scientist and his unholy plot to build his own Cyberman from dead bodies and spare parts left over from previous Cyberman invasions. All this, of course, leads to a brilliant little twist, which we'll let you discover for yourself.

There's a lot to enjoy here. Apart from Harrold's pitch perfect performance, the story is fun, blending sly comedy and menace perfectly. The home-made Cyberman is excellent; it is exactly what you would expect from an untutored enthusiast haphazardly assembling his own Cyberman to look like. The locations are visually interesting and effective, the performances hit the mark. It's well shot and composed. It's Doctor Who with just a touch of Hammer films.

Holmes and Hinchcliffe, the writer and producer who were at the center of Tom Baker's gothic horror period, would have loved this little gem.

&&&

FLIGHT OF THE DALEKS (2004)

This is far and away the best of the trilogy, if for no other reason than the Dalek/Cyberman smackdown. But truthfully, it's probably Harrold's most confident performance, it's an effective story, and it's told with scope and panache... and a lot of impressive CGI work.

We start off with some decent amateur CGI of a space battle in some place called the Keyhole Nebula, and shots of some CGI Daleks. The Dalek ship gets blown up. A squadron of Daleks escapes in a Space Pod. It zips through a time warp, pursued by an enemy ship.

As they zip through the Time Warp, however, the encounter the Police Box, which gets dragged along for the ride. All three end up on Earth, with the Daleks crash landing just outside London. It turns out, that the Daleks have come up with an information package to wipe the Cybermen out of time and space. The Cybermen aren't putting up with that, and are prepared to sterilize a chunk of Earth with a mass driver to make sure that the Daleks don't escape.

It's up to the Doctor to sort things out, which he does by calmly talking things out with both the Cybermen and the

Daleks and giving the Daleks what they need to escape Earth, so the chase can continue, along with a bit of low key theft and sabotage. It's not a bad story at all, and remarkably, it runs only a little over twenty minutes, but somehow, it manages to feel like a complete story, neither simplistic, nor perfunctory, nor crowded.

A.F. Harrold is back, having shed 'The Shadow' outfit for a more pedestrian and less imposing wardrobe. This is probably his best performance as the Doctor; he's effortless in the role.

So what else works? The pace is genial, it moves along in an unhurried way, but things get done. It's a well constructed episode, which tells the story through cutaway scenes. The narrative is a lot more fractured than in Lychwood, which mostly followed a central character that the story orbited.

Here the Doctor is much less central. Information comes to us from all sorts of directions, including news broadcasts, bystanders, and the villains/monsters themselves. Everyone's got their own story, including a nice moment when the Doctor's companion, Sophie, locks horns with UNIT's Captain Halloway over some shared history.

A large part of the story is told through fake newscasts, which feels really authentic. It's got that local newscast channel feel, that same sort of delivery, the cutaways to whatever footage they manage to get. There's a bit of cleverness at work because the newscast is very unconscious. They're basically telling the story that the authorities are giving them, or based on what they know. Initially, they report the fall of the Dalek ship as an airplane crash, and then as video footage becomes available, they update it. But they don't know what's really going on. There's a sublime moment when a news-copter identifies a Dalek as some sort of bomb disposal robot, just before it blows them out of the sky.

Although *Plague of Lychwood* set us up for a Cyberman sequel story, this isn't a direct sequel. Nevertheless, there are plenty of linkages back to the earlier story. Captain Victory Halloway of UNIT is back, albeit played by a different actress, and the Doctor's companion, Sophie, references the events of the previous story.

The Cybermen are nifty. Unlike the Daleks who are entirely CGI, the Cybermen are men in costumes. It's a design of the Cybermen that I've never seen before, the headpieces are blocky, almost boxlike, the they have visor slits rather than eyes, but they're recognizable Cybermen. We glimpsed them in Plague of Lychwood, but they're full on here. They work well, being convincingly menacing, which isn't always something you can say about Cybermen.

The highlight of the story is a Cybermen/Dalek fight which, although brief, is really satisfying. It's a real fight. The Cybermen give as good as they get; until a special weapons Dalek shows up. It's peculiar, given that it's a battle between people in suits and CGI characters, it shouldn't work, but it does. Seriously, I loved it. This was the Dalek/Cybermen smackdown that we were promised in the Tenant era but didn't get. All by itself, it's worth watching the story for.

A huge part of this episode is CGI. The Daleks of course are CGI and well rendered. In scenes where they're composited onto the live action stuff, they manage to look very natural. They look like they belong, not like CGI at all for the most part. There's a lot of spaceship stuff, asteroids, energy screens. It's all very nicely done for what it was. We're not talking state of the art Hollywood stuff, but even that is a moving target. This is very very impressive stuff, particularly when you're considering it's done by people without a lot of resources and who did it back in 2004.

Finally, a huge shout out to the closing credits, which feature in most of the Vought/Quince Who films, a slow montage of shots of the Police Box parked in various locations, such as a next to a building with the Hindenburg blowing up, in the corner of crowd scenes, on alien landscapes, or in the middle of a herd of glyptodonts. It's intriguing, visually arresting and quite evocative. I want to see the episodes suggested by those images.

&&&

GHOSTS (2008)

This is the last, and perhaps the most perfunctory of the Harrold stories, at less than fifteen minutes.

Once again, A.F. Harrold is back to his black outfit, black fedora and red scarf. But this time, he sports a fairly outrageous goatee, so the effect is less 'the shadow' than a rabbi with a mission. That said, he turns in the same low key performance that we've come to appreciate.

This episode is linked to the previous ones by a reference to UNIT's Captain Victoria Halloway, although she doesn't appear. So, yes, it's a bona fide trilogy, despite the lack of true continuity between stories.

Unfortunately, his companion, Sadie Carter, played by Emily Kaye is kind of a weak spot. She tries, but she's no actress. She doesn't even walk convincingly, and she says most of her lines with a sort of clenched grin.

The story? Well, we never quite find out what the whole thing is about. There's a neighborhood plagued by ghosts, so the Doctor comes to investigate. Sadie goes door to door asking people if they've seen a ghost. The Doctor's searches turn up a mysterious secret buried military installation, a cell phone tower and a man with a girlfriend only he can see.

What does it all add up to? The Doctor makes a phone call, gets UNIT to fill in the buried military base, and tear down the cell phone tower. That should take care of the problem, whatever it is, and then it's off to the next adventure.

There's an incompleteness to the story which is sort of intriguing. We never get to know what's down in the military base, or what that story is. We don't learn how the cell phone tower is involved.

But there's a utilitarian practicality to Harrold's Doctor. He doesn't need to know these things. There's a problem, he fixes it, and then it's time to move on. All those background details, they'd be nice, but it's not really important. He did the same thing in *Plague of Lychwood* and *Flight of the Daleks*.

The other interesting thing is how he fixes the problem. He makes a phone call. That's it. No need to make things more complicated. He calls up UNIT, tells them what needs to be done, and that's it. Practical.

I'm not entirely sure this is what they set out to do. Most of the Vought/Quince Doctor Who productions run 20 to 26 minutes, so this is pretty short. They may well have had a longer script and more story that ended up cut out.

There are other signs that this was a bit of a rush – the image quality is the poor compared to Harrold's two previous outings, the effects and CGI are mostly absent, the gorgeous closing credits are missing. There was a four year gap between this and *Flight of the Daleks*. So maybe there's a story going on behind the scenes.

There's nothing actually wrong with this story. Apart from brevity and a bit of dodgy acting, it's perfectly serviceable and even interesting. A.F. Harrold turns in a fascinating performance. The cinematography is fairly good. They manage to find some interesting things in the woods to film. The story has some tension to it and the resolution is so unique and obvious that it makes you wonder why the Doctor doesn't do this more often – just figure it out, then make a phone call and tell UNIT what they need to do. By now they know enough to trust him when he calls in. That's cool.

The real handicap is simply that Plague of Lychwood and Flight of the Daleks are so well done that Ghost suffers for the comparison. But if that's the harshest thing we've got, that's not bad. Ultimately, we are gifted with a trilogy of very solid, very watchable films that provides us with a version of the Doctor which is a refreshing contrast, and interesting, quirky stories that are well told and well shot.

LYCHWOOD CAST: *The Doctor – A.F. Harrald; Captain Victory Holloway – Helen Whittaker; Reverend Cartwright – Graham Jones; Sam Smitter – Samuel Smitter; Radio Announcer – Allen Sinclair; Cindy Smitter-Smith – Helen Vought; Duncan Farrier – Matthew Edwards; The Master – Adrian Casjkowski;*

LYCHWOOD CREW: *S!H!P!Films (SHPFilms) & VortX Productions – 2002. By Graham Quince & Paul Vought; Visual Effects – Graham Quince; 3D Effects – Robin Edwards; 3D Meshes by Axeman 3D; Music Composed and Performed by Anne Marie Casjkowski; Theme by Paul Gooch; Cybercostumes and Props by Paul Vought; Written, Edited, Produced and Directed by Paul Vought; 2002; Run Time 23 minutes.*

FLIGHT CAST *Doctor – A.F. Harrold; Sophie Franks – Jess Plant; Captain Victory Holoway – Lee Niccols; Newsreader – Laura Holmes; Private Archer – Graham Jones;Jeff – Mikhail Franklin; Helen – Nancy Whittaker; Unit/Cybermen – Ben Hodson, Graham Jones, Chris Niccols, Graham Quince, Sam Smitter, Paul Vought.*

FLIGHT CREW: *S!H!P!Films (SHPFilms) & VortX Productions – 2004'; Graham Quince & Paul Vought. Written and Produced by Graham Quince and Paul Vought; Directed by Paul Vought; Visual Effects – Graham Quince; 3D Effects – Robin Edward; 3D Meshes by Axemen 3D; Editor – Amy Harris; Camera, Cybercostumes and Props – Paul Vought; Music – Anne-Marie Czajkowski; Theme performed by Joe Gooch, 2002; 23 minutes running time*

GHOSTS CAST: *The Doctor – A.F. Harrald; Maria – Roxanna Tohaneanu-Shields; Jane – Martina Draberova; Richard, Ghost – Charles McAlpin; Sadie Carter – Emily Kaye; Sgt Gorse – Martyn Harris*

GHOSTS CREW: *Special Thanks – Dana Radu, Tom Corrix; Theme Tune and Soundtrack – Joe Gooch; Title Sequence – Graham Quince; Camera, Producer, Director, Writer – Paul Vought; Run time 15 minutes.*

CHAPTER 16 – THE REVIVAL

The return of the series in 2005 and the emergence of the David Tennant Doctor in 2006, predictably, saw fan films transform once again.

Now, with David Tennant and Matt Smith, two attractive young men, both playing the role profoundly over the top, the Doctor was redefined once again for fans. The twenty foot scarves, multi-coloured coats, cricket outfits and porkpie hats were still around in the background. But now it was all tweeds and pinstripes, long coats, bow ties and fezzes. Fans now had Doctors closer to their own age and their own time period to emulate, and over the top performances that begged to be imitated.

Some people were still creating their own versions of a Doctor, like Matt Lucas. But most fan film makers were either dressing up as Smith and Tennant, or actively imitating their styles.

But underneath that, the real changes were in technology, which just kept moving and moving all along. Camcorders had been around since the 1980s, but year after year, they'd become better, providing higher resolutions, moving from VHS to high density cassettes, and then to digital, they became lightweight, the lenses were getting better and more adaptable. The camcorders themselves were getting steadily smarter, with automatic compensation for motion, glare, and colour balance. They were also getting cheaper.

In the 1980s, a camcorder was worth a small fortune and only a few families could afford them, it took real persuasion to be allowed to use them for a fan project. In the 21st century, pretty much every family had a camcorder of one sort or another. There were more accessories, tripods, microphones, etc.

This is all happening steadily, and you can mark it through the gradual progression of fan films from the 80s through the 21st century.

But beneath that, there were more fundamental changes. Computers, computer based video and sound editing, computer generated imagery, was steadily transforming the landscape. In the old days, fans worked to physically build a Police Box or a Police Box console. Now, someone like Josh Snares could capture images of the Police Box interior from television and insert himself into it. Instead of building props, it was about building green-screens. It was about sampling music or special effects directly from the show itself.

We saw this starting to develop in the late 1990s, with productions like *Millennium Trap* or the *Alliance* or *Time and Again* using extensive CGI backgrounds. The thing is, it was getting steadily better, more realistic, easier to use, until you start to have things like *Tyranny of the Daleks* where the Daleks are all CGI, or *Flight of the Daleks* and a fairly convincing battle between CGI Daleks and physical Cybermen.

Even distribution altered profoundly. It was no longer videotapes or DVDs traded or exchanged through conventions and mail order, collections painstakingly built up and shown at gatherings. Instead, bandwidth had steadily increased, to the point where videos, including fan videos could be posted on the internet. Traditional fan culture of the 80s and 90s, based around clubs and collections and zines, which had formed the substrate of the audience, gave way to an online culture and a web based audience.

Now, here's the thing with technology. It doesn't just make things easier. It changes the way we do things. A lot of Doctor Who fan film came out of formal and informal fan clubs, associations of people who loved the show, who gathered together to watch the videotapes at club meetings, who formed networks, who traded, who went to conventions.

In the 80s and 90s, even a modest film or television production was had. You needed an entire crew, you needed an arsenal of skills, a good fan film, or even a bad one, had to be a collective effort.

To be fair, we are still seeing those in the 21st century, no matter how easy computers make it, you still need actors... usually, you still need someone to build sets or props or costumes... usually. There are a number of those, Project Fifty, the Forgotten Doctor, Victimsight, the Ginger Chronicles. Now they tend to be almost crowdsourced, recruited more broadly - not so much the product of a close knit group, but now people united by an interest in the project.

And we're seeing the rise of 'one man shows' – Luke Newman, Bryan McCormack, Nathan Carter, etc. Small or almost negligible casts, very localized stories.

Review: Fire and Ice (2009)

And the Attempt at an Entire Season

STORY: Alice Hemingway is an ordinary young woman. But strange things are happening. She's having recurrent dreams of a flying child whispering about an oncoming storm. The army is having maneuvers near her home, and there are strange things in the woods. She meets a man...

REVIEW: Let's set our Wayback machine for 2009. 2009 was kind of a watershed year for the new Doctor Who. It was the year without a season. It was the year of 'David Tennant is Leaving' (cue ominous music). Actually, the word was out in late 2008, David Tennant had had three successful years, he'd done great, now he figured was time to move on. He already had other commitments, but the BBC didn't want to let him go.

The result was a series of four 'Specials' – starting in December, 2008, with *The Next Doctor* – tweaking the fans as it were, and concluding in December, 2009 and January, 2010, with *The End of Time*.

That might well have been the end of Doctor Who. With both David Tennant, the star, and Russell T. Davies, the producer leaving, the BBC brass were really unsure of what to do. Davies had almost singlehandedly resurrected the show, and Tennant had been an extraordinarily popular star.

With them gone, was there even a show? Did the Doctor have a future? BBC management was seriously thinking about cancelling it, although they had the sense to keep quiet about their thoughts.

So we had Schrodinger's Doctor. He was here, he wasn't here. He's leaving. Oh look, there's a special! Oh no, he's gone again! There was a lot of uncertainty in fandom. Tennant was definitely going, but we didn't know who the new guy was going to be. We didn't know if we'd like the new guy. Russell T. Davies was leaving, Steven Moffatt was taking over as producer, we didn't know what he'd do with the show.

It's in this context that a fan group decided to go for it, and produce their own Doctor Who.

The theme I keep coming back to is that the really great fan films, the interesting and important ones, seem to be called up by the gaps in the show. It's like these films are responses to a vacuum. It's as if there's a sort of dialogue going on. The empty places, where the show's future is a crossroads, the stories unmade, the gaps in the show, that's where we find the important fan films. Barbara Benedetti is the Doctor of the gap, 1984-86. *Spectre From the Past* is nostalgia manifested by the tribulations of the McCoy era, 87-89. Rupert Booth is the true Doctor of the 90s, a response to the disappointment of 1993. *Gene Genius* is the 21st century's fond nostalgia as we begin to look to the future.

So it fits that *Fire and Ice* should emerge from the gestalt in that period of uncertainty between the end of Tennant's last full formal series, and before the beginning of Matt Smith's. Here at least, we have the fan producers actually acknowledging it up front.

Fire and Ice has the distinction of being voted the greatest Doctor Who fan film of the 'Noughties' (the period 2000 to

2010), by YouTubers. It got real press coverage. The 'Den of Geek' an online sci fi news site gave it a feature.

It was going to be the launching pad of a fan based Doctor Who series that was intended to rival the new series in terms of ambition and quality. This wasn't going to be just, the Greatest Doctor Who Fan Film Ever! This was going to be The Greatest Doctor Who Fan Series ever, something to match and exceed the Female Doctor series of the 80s, or the Timebase series of the 90s.

So what happened? Well, according to some reports, they completed the first of the series, *Fire and Ice*. The second, *Guardian of the Solar System* was in production. *Fire and Ice* played and people laughed their asses off. And not in the good way. That was kind of the end.

These things take an immense amount of work, a lot of time, talent and dedication, and it's hard to sustain that in the best of times.

Apparently there was a hard drive crash, which wiped out the better part of *Guardian of the Solar System* which would be just heartbreaking. I can't imagine the amount of hard work that would have gone into that, to vanish in an instant.

I kind of have the impression that there may have been a falling out, and perhaps some hard feelings.

But really, the truth is that these things are just so difficult and require so much effort, it's hard to sustain. There are a few people who were involved who are still floating around, but I haven't seen much in the way of a production history or making of, from any of them. So I don't really have a window into what was going on behind the scenes.

Which leaves us with *Fire and Ice*, the fan film, the pilot and sole survivor of the planned fan season. The artifact itself, shorn of much of its history and context. How is it?

Well, first up – there's at least two or more versions out there. The full length version has been described as 75 minutes, although the long versions on YouTube is actually just under seventy 70. The broad consensus is that it's too long, but fair warning, I haven't watched it.

The version that I did watch on YouTube was 64 minutes. You know what? Still too long.

Technically that is. There's a danger that many film makers, even commercial ones, run into: Falling in love with your footage. The shot looks so good, the woman brushing her teeth or painting her toes, there's such poetry in it, yadda yadda. Let it stretch out for a bit. It's only five minutes! You could show it in five seconds, but it's so good how about ten or fifteen!

Sorry, you but you gots to kill your babies sometimes. There are a lot of shots that could have done with some shaving, and a few that needed some hacking.

The trouble is that we, the audience, have not fallen in love with your footage. We're okay with dating it for a while, but we don't want to make a commitment. We want to get on with the story, because we're looking for hotter sexier footage further on.

At this point, I'm going to step out of the review for a bit and have a digression. I figure if you're reading this, it's all right; you've got nothing better to do with your life anyway. So why not? Now, I might have said this before elsewhere in the books, but the thing is that audiences are trained to have certain expectations: Form, convention, the three act story structure. Some are overt, things that everyone knows. Some can be subtle.

Running times are a subtle expectation. We've all grown up with that. Basically, we've all grown up on television. Television divides its time up into half hour, one hour and two hour blocks. And of course, theatrical movies are generally structured as a two hour block.

Now, with television, they make way for commercials, announcements etc., so a television half hour – a self-contained, satisfying, television half hour story is actually about 22 to 28 minutes. The old classic Doctor Who ran about 25 minutes per serial episode. A television hour is actually about 45 to 55 minutes. A two hour television movie typically runs 90-100 minutes. In the movie theatres, the movie experience is generally about 90 to 120 minutes, not much longer.

The point is, this is what we expect. Go off those ranges, go into the gaps between those ranges people start getting uncomfortable. A two and a half hour movie? People are tapping their feet, checking their watches. A three hour movie, people are feigning death to get out. A four hour movie, and you start checking out your neighbors in case you have to kill them for food.

It's not just the length, a longer work is paced differently, the beats, the climaxes and plot points, they're in different places than we expect. So there's an accumulating feeling of discomfort. It's just stretching and stretching.

That same holds true for lesser lengths. Call it an uncanny valley, the place between two peaks of comfort or expectation, of things feeling right, where suddenly, the place between starts to feel wrong.

Significantly less than 20 minutes, the story starts to feel incomplete, unfinished. Past 30 minutes and but less than 45, there's a weird place where the story feels simultaneously too slow and too fast, it drags and seems padded but it feels rushed and incomplete at the same time. Between 80 to 85 minutes is roughly all people will tolerate for a short movie. Less than that, and you've got trouble. Hard to even call it a movie. On the other hand, 65 or 70 minutes... Way too long for a television hour.

Maybe this seems like crazy stuff. But trust me, it's the way people work. Used to be that we were all happy sitting through six hour productions in Elizabethan England.

Now? Our tastes are different, not better, not worse. It's just what we're accustomed to, what our comfort zone is.

So, Fire and Ice at 70 minutes, or 64 minutes? That's just harsh. The audience has some leeway, we're willing to go a few minutes long, a few minutes short, sixty minutes maybe, but not much longer. But geez. Sorry, that's how it is. Take it up with the entertainment industry.

Ah, you might say, but what about Day of the Doctor and Deep Breath, weren't they extra-long and in my so called 'uncanny valley'? Right you are. They did fall into that uncanny valley, and they felt simultaneously dragging and rushed. But then again, both of those had been building up goodwill and anticipation for eight years. We were going to watch them, no matter what. Fire and Ice didn't quite have that going for it.

Okay, back to the review...

The first five minutes ... smashing. There is a floating child thing screaming prophecy that is visually brilliant, and way creepy to boot. It sets up plot threads and raising questions intended for future episodes never produced.

Fire and Ice reminded me a lot of *Rose,* so much so that it invites comparisons. The feel and the progression of the stories are very similar. Both of them really are stories about the companions, not the Doctors. The Doctor is almost a secondary character, one who comes into the story, a force of chaos or change, an avatar of menace and possibility.

We get to know the Doctor through their eyes, as this mysterious, oddly quirky stranger who shows up and turns their orderly world around… Although more accurately, he doesn't turn it upside down. He just shows them that beneath the safe orderly world they thought they lived in, is another world strange and beautiful and dangerous, and he's a beacon of safety in it.

The two stories open the same way, basically with Alice and Rose, respectively, getting up in the morning and getting on with their day. *Rose* does it better – we see Rose's mum, her boyfriend, her job, we kind of get to see where she is in life, we get a very strong sense of who she is, and how rooted she is.

With Alice, not so much. She's a University student, but she's living alone in a huge house, no husband or parents around. She gets up, gets dressed, has her coffee, her actions are mundane and kind of aimless. Later on we'll be told that she's late for class, and then later that she's been late for classes a lot, and her grades are in trouble. But her earlier behaviour doesn't suggest she's concerned. Mostly, she seems to be drifting She's got a friend who seems to be hovering over her a lot. Then still later that she has a monologue about being frightened by life. The sense is that Alice isn't really as immersed in her life, not as connected or grounded as Rose was. I believe that deliberate, I think that they were presenting Alice as disconnected.

I'd guess if we had gotten to see more of Alice in future stories, we'd have learned that there was a reason for these disconnections. She's just suffered the loss of a husband, or of parents, which is why she's alone in the house and her friend is helicoptering and she just doesn't seem to care very much about things. That's just a guess. But they were planning a whole series, and it's likely that they were going to explore Alice in more detail.

There are several hints through the story that there might be a lot more going on with or around Alice than we're shown. She seems to be the one having these prophetic dreams of the coming storm. Alice may be a lot more important, and Alice may have more gifts, than she knows.

The stories continue to unfold similarly. Both Rose and Alice get dragged out of their regular lives by encounters with the monster – literally because in both cases, it grows under their feet. Because of their proximity, they keep running into both the Doctor and the monsters. Eventually they're deeply involved.

There are differences. Rose's episode is much more comedic, there's cool surreal and silly business. And it's a bit more baroque, the plot, while linear, has wiggles to it as Rose tries to figure out what's going on. In comparison, Alice's episode tends to emphasize drama or suspense, and there's more effort at a character arc than trying to put swerve into the plot.

Indeed, in both cases, the plot gets almost perfunctory – the Doctor confronts the monster, has a little chat; then Doctor gets in trouble, and it gets sorted out by a third party coming to the rescue. In Alice's episode, the conversation with the monster is real and has some depth, and when the Doctor sorts it out it's because the he had some tricks up his sleeve. In Rose's episode, the conversation with the monster is perfunctory, and he doesn't win, he just got lucky. In this sense, Fire and Ice is a little more satisfying, less deus ex machina and more plotting.

The point is that the two episodes are similar enough in terms of content and process that comparisons are almost inescapable. Is that a bad thing? Mmm maybe. *Fire and Ice* is going to suffer in comparison to Rose. But it's nowhere near one sided.

Take monsters, for instance. *Rose* gets Autons, which is sort of a silly-creepy monster, and kind of goes with the strong comedic touches of the episode. *Fire and Ice* gives us.... Ice Warriors.

Oops! Was that a spoiler! Did I just spoil something for you! Oh no!!! Actually, no, it's not a spoiler, it's an incentive.

Look, here's how I see it. Sometimes, in a piece of work, there are plot twists, or revelations, or characters, that you go 'wow' for. They change the whole direction of the story, they make you think new things, or realize something. Those are the things you have to watch out for. Those are spoilers.

Now, there's things which are part of the narrative, and which are things that may intrigue you in the narrative. It's the premise, or the information that draws you in, that sets the story in motion. You don't watch out for those. You actually talk about those. Those aren't spoilers, they're incentives.

Take the *Sixth Sense* as an example. Bruce Willis plays a sad psychologist in a bad marriage whose wife won't talk to him. Not a spoiler, kind of an incentive, who doesn't like Bruce Willis? He tries to help a kid who can see dead people. Also not a spoiler, actually, a really intriguing incentive. This sounds like a pretty weird kid, I bet Bruce and the kid are going to get into some wacky hijinks! These are not spoilers.

Bruce Willis was dead all along and didn't realize it. That's a spoiler! See the difference? Everything you thought you knew about the movie is turned on its head. It's a shock. It's the big payoff. Spoiler.

So anyway, I could say 'Fire and Ice has some monsters in it.' Well, big deal. Doctor Who always has monsters of one sort or another. But if I say 'Fire and Ice has the Ice Warriors in it.'

Whoa! Stop the presses!

I want to watch that! Ice Warriors are cool. You definitely want to watch an Ice Warriors episode a lot more than you want to watch a TBA monster. You see?

So Ice Warriors! Really well done too, in just about every sense. The build-up is gradual but effective. They're physically imposing; they contribute meaningfully to the action and sense of escalating menace. The costumes are great – very classic look, kind of inhuman, with a bulk that gives them genuine menace, despite being somewhat slow moving. Their lair has good visuals, they have some history, some motivation, they argue their case convincingly against the Doctor without ever losing the fact that they're the bad guys. They're really well done.

Some people have said that they handled the Ice Warriors better than the Matt Smith episode, *Cold War*. You know what? They're right. I give this one to *Fire and Ice*, fair and square. They win. Indeed, there's an arguable case to be made that the Ice Warriors were handled better here than the Classic series did, in either their Troughton serials, where they were simply monsters of the week, or the Pertwee serials where they were just part of an ensemble of aliens. Here, they've got a history, a point of view. So let me be radical, this may well be the best portrait of the Ice Warriors ever, at least on video.

There's a lot of really nice stuff here. There were a number of lines and images that stuck with me. There's a scene of snow in the forest, that's just beautifully done. The near car crash is terrific. The second encounter with the Doctor, as he listens to the ground outside Alice's house is pitch perfect - strange enough to intrigue her, not creepy enough to repel her. The initial encounter with the Ice Warrior is shocking. The conversation with the leader is striking. The opening, as I've said is amazing. The conclusion is simply... haunting.

Jennifer Richman who plays Alice may not be the actress that Billie Piper is. Or maybe she doesn't get as much to work with from her script. This might simply be the fact that they're playing a long game with her character, and they don't want to show too much too early. But her performance is serviceable, her character's actions and reactions are mostly believable. Overall, the acting and a lot of the writing is like that, serviceable, not extraordinary.

I guess now we come to the Doctor, played by Kevin Raymond Moore. Well, he's not a Rupert Booth or a Barbara Benedetti. He's not one of those actors that walks out and is The Doctor. Tom Baker had that. David Tennant and Matt Smith had it, from their first moment, they are The Doctor.

On the other hand, he's not a failure either. Some fan actors that play the role, they're not the Doctor, will never be the Doctor, it just ain't who they are. Sometimes they dress up for it in classic costumes, sometimes they don't, but either way, it doesn't matter - they just aren't the Doctor, it doesn't sell. Kevin Raymond Moore isn't one of those.

This guy falls in the middle. He's not the Doctor, at least not at first, but you could see him coming into the role. That's fair enough, I mean, you look at someone like Davison or maybe Pertwee… They started off slow, and kind of established themselves as The Doctor through the episode. They both started off their adventures flat on their backs. Come to think of it, so did Tennant.

Anyway, my initial impression was no. Too thin, too timid, too forced, trying to hard, not enough presence. He starts out a bit too slow and tentative. First glimpse, that's effective. Second appearance… he needed to be a lot stronger, he starts out quirky and then doesn't seem to have an idea where to go. Third appearance… sabotaged by a tweety bird. But the thing is, as he goes along, I tended to buy him more and more as the Doctor. At the end, was I completely sold? Not sure. But at the end of the episode, I was willing to keep buying in.

If they'd made more, I'd have watched, and I think it's likely that over time, he would have gotten it, filled out or inhabited the persona of The Doctor more fully. Does that make any sense? If there had been more episodes, I think… yes.

In fact, I know … yes.

Let me throw some spoilers at you.

The thing with *Fire and Ice* is that it is just the surviving fragment of a much larger, amazingly ambitious project – let's call it the Richman Master Plan. I suppose we could call it the Dinkins Master Plan… but let's not. The Moore Master Plan is just an invitation, and the Presswood Master Plan is a porn title.

So what was the Richman Master Plan? Let's take a look at the fragments we have. The operating monster in Fire and Ice are the Ice Warriors, who want to terraform (Mars-form?) Earth because their world is dying fast. There's a conversation where the Doctor tells the Ice Warriors that they have a great future, he's seen it. The Ice Warrior replies that the Prophets used to say that, but now everything is going to crap. Even more, the Ice Warrior puts it all up on the screen and the Doctor realizes it's true, the history that he has been to is not happening, the Ice Warriors really are dying.

I liked that whole encounter, the fact that the Doctor and the Ice Warriors were prepared to have a debate. It produced the most memorable line, and it centers the whole episode nicely. But it's not just filler. Something has gone seriously wrong with the Ice Warriors future. When I first watched it, it seemed like a dangling plot thread, intriguing enough that I wondered if the Doctor might be revisiting the Ice Warriors to save their future for them.

Of course, what it really said is that time has come out of joint – the future is unravelling. '*Side effect of the Time War*,' I wondered as I watched it.

Their second project, now survived only by some half recovered footage from a Hard Drive Crash and a series of trailers was going to be *Guardian of the Solar System*, written by Jeff Smith. This was going to be a loose prequel to William Hartnell's epic – *The Dalek Master Plan*.

Very quick rundown of *Masterplan*: 3rd season Doctor Who serial consisting of a record breaking twelve episodes. It's set 4000 years in the future when Earth is the center of an interstellar empire, ruled by the 'Guardian of the Solar System Mavic Chen. Mavic Chen is making a secret alliance with the Daleks, the time travelling variety of Dalek. There are encounters with the Meddling Monk, jaunts over the galaxy and a trip to ancient Egypt. It features first death of a Companion in Sarah Kingdom. The Masterplan is one of those 'lost classics' – only three of the twelve episodes survive.

Although *Guardian of the Solar System* died on the operating table with a hard drive crash, the script is available. It's set in the s same general era, and Mavic Chen appears as younger man rising to power. No Daleks, but there is a newly awakened Rogue AI which tries to take over, nearly engineering an interplanetary war before the Doctor stops it. It would have been a good story.

At least one other script for the planned series is still floating around, involving a visit to a planet of spiders.

That's the first three episodes. They planned thirteen. We don't know anything about the next ten. I don't know if they would have gotten them all. I think that there are decent odds they'd have had at least a few more over which the arc would have matured.

But we do have the final scenes of the final episode. The War in Heaven– test footage and a scroll crawl. What does that give us? It gives us the fall of Gallifrey, the final destruction of the Daleks at the hands of the Doctor, the imposition of the Time Lock on the Time War.... and a broken, exhausted Doctor's imminent death, cut away from the energies of Gallifrey.... which turns into a regeneration, into the Christopher Ecclestone Doctor, and a final word 'fantastic.'

Ladies and Gentlemen – this is the arc! This was what they wanted to do: They wanted to tell the story of the Time War! The whole story! Not just the final moment's passion play we saw in *Day of the Doctor*. They wanted to do an epic and give it an entire season.

I want to stand up and applaud at the very idea of it. What a mad, wonderful, brilliant, doomed quest. They were crazy to even think they could do it. But it's a fantastic, terrific, heroic crazy that I love.

This allows us to give *Fire and Ice* a second look, to reappraise it, not just as a work in and of itself, but as a part of a much larger, more ambitious work. *Fire and Ice* improves in that larger context. The plight of the Ice Warriors and the Doctor's apparent naiveté become more compelling and resonant. The storm that gathers, the floating prophet child, Alice's apparent fate at the end, it all works just a little bit better. The material is elevated.

It even leads us to take a second look at the Moore Doctor. I've criticized him for a sort of tentativeness, a kind of fainthearted quality. But in the context of the larger story arc, the Moore Doctor in *Fire and Ice* is a man unknowingly stumbling into deeper waters. He is in over his head, and only vaguely comprehending it. The Moore Doctor is a man who realizes that something is beginning to go badly wrong, but he doesn't know what it is or how to deal with it yet. He's the bridge between the confident and assured McGann and the shattered and recovering Ecclestone. It works. It's legitimate, and it's disappointing, because we never got to see the Moore Doctor go on his journey, we never got to see the rest of him.

It also goes a lot towards deepening the relationship between the Doctor and Alice. In *Rose,* Ecclestone's Doctor is pretty self-contained, and Rose seems happy and immersed in her life - it's a bit odd that they would go off together. But Richman's Alice and Moore's Doctor, are much more fractured characters, Moore is alone and lonely, out of his depth, and Alice is barely tethered to her life. They're both deeply unhappy beneath the surface; they need each other much more desperately than Rose and Ecclestone. They're drawn together, and that's got some genuineness to it.

There's a quiet pathos to the final scenes. The Doctor comes back; Alice happily goes off with him. But then there's a series of fast forwards of the empty house, abandoned, and a note that Alice never returned. Again, you get the sense of a long range plan at work.

One thing that strikes me is that it is remarkable how computer animation has become accessible. We see an entirely CGI rendered Tharsis lizard romping around, interacting with the cast. The larger part, perhaps all of the Ice Warriors base that the Doctor sneaks into is CGI and composited in quite nicely. It's perhaps a bit sub-par compared to things that they're doing in Hollywood with real money. But even as little as ten years before, the amount and quality of CGI that we see would be outside the budget of anything but a fairly well funded Hollywood production.

The amount of processing power available keeps doubling, and long with it, we see these quantum leaps in the sophistication of editing software of all sorts, storing and manipulating film files in digital format, and doing increasingly complex CGI, all of it more and more accessible to ordinary people.

Apart from that, there are some technical and structural problems. The sound mix has a few issues. That's one of probably one of the hardest things to work out, and it's often overlooked. When it goes wrong it kills you dead. If people's voices are muddy, or there's too much echo, or voice levels are too low, it takes you out of the experience. And then, Foley is just such an easy path off the cliff. The wrong incidental music in the wrong place, and it's 'WTF?' Or 'too loud?'

There's a crucial scene, the first real meeting of Alice and the Doctor, out in the woods after he rescues her from a Tharsis Lizard. You can barely make them out, because the world's loudest songbird is drowning them out with its tweets. Even worse, the tweety bird is a loop, so after a while, it gets visibly repetitive and annoying. Just a small tweak would have fixed it. But as it is, I'm sure that the incongruity had people howling with laughter.

It's maddening. Think about how hard they must have worked to pull that scene together. How much weight and passion went into it, what care they must have taken. Think of all the love and attention and commitment that got lavished on the scene, from shooting, all the way to post production. Think of the care and ingeniousness that went into thinking 'well, they're in the woods, some forest sounds in the background, a bird tweeting.' They must have felt so clever, and so proud of their attention to detail. And then, when it played, people laughed out loud at that point because the goddammed tweeting was so intrusive. I'm sure hearts broke at that moment.

Which is a shame, because generally the sound mix is pretty good. I actually like their music selections a lot. They do some David Bowie at the end, which in a commercial production, you'd never get the rights to.

There are also a few strange choices that drag down the script. The big one is a pivotal moment. A monster attacks, Alice runs home, then she has what feels like a five minute long life-crisis speech with her friend about how she's terrified by life and running away from her problems, before rushing back to help the doctor. Uh… what?

Two things: First, kills the momentum right stone dead. Second, if you stop to have a heart to heart with your girlfriend in a situation like that, well, when you get back, the Doctor will already be eaten.

I'm not saying she shouldn't have had that conversation. It's a good monologue, and it pulls the character together, it crystallizes Alice's lack of direction and lack of focus in life for us. It should just have taken place somewhere, else, earlier on, so that it didn't interrupt the flow of the crises, and it would have been more meaningful because we'd have had more time to integrate it with the character. Again, that's one of those things that people were probably laughing at. And again, I'd bet it really hurt, because it was an important moment for the creators, and it's an important moment in the story, it's just a little out of place.

But hey, this is a review not an autopsy. I don't propose to spend all my time reviewing every decision, good or bad. Those were the two most destructive boners. They made other mistakes, but most of the others didn't produce the level of sabotage that those two did. Had they managed to dodge those bullets, the production would have had a better reception, would have been stronger.

What's the bottom line? If you ask me, for a Doctor Who fan, is this worth watching? Yes! Definitely, yes. Totally! Is it the best Fan Film evah! Maybe. It's good, but it's got some problems that drag it down. Maybe a second pass in post-production could solve most of them, that's not unheard of in fan films. As it is, it's comfortably up there in the top tiers.

Is it a match for the new BBC series? I think yes. Somewhat.. Those problems I mentioned, it's hard to rise above them. But the boners aside – there's a critical weakness.

It's not the story or the effects. Here, we've got a story which is perfectly acceptable, even good. The writing's not Shakespeare, but it does the job. The Ice Warriors are terrific and they're well handled in almost every possible way. Ladies, gentlemen, we've had much worse.

But that operative word is 'somewhat.' It's not up there with the best of Ecclestone, Tenant and Smith. But it's far from easily dismissed. Is it damning with faint praise to say it is less than their best? That it has a respectable claim to being on par with the better than average or good? Or more than match for the more embarrassing outings of the revived series?

It does give us a treatment of the Ice Warriors better than their appearance in Matt Smith's *Cold War*. Richman and Moore, are far from disasters. It does a lot of good things. In the end, a few bad decisions do damage, well, perhaps it's worth looking past that.

Does it feel like authentic Doctor Who?

You want my advice? Go watch it. There are plenty of versions online to pick from.

Just do it, go watch.

Decide for yourself if I'm right.

What if I'm wrong, and it's stupendous! What if I'm right, but by god, it's still stupendous! Or what if I'm right about everything wrong, or it's even worse… stop watching. Some talented people put their blood sweat and tears into it, they put their hearts and souls, and the only reward they'll ever get is people like you and me watching it.

2009. Running time 75 to 64 minutes, depending.

CAST: *Kenneth Raymond Moore as the Doctor; Jennifer Richman as Alice Hemingway; Carmel Stowe as Marisa; Emily Richman as Captain Lynn Johnson; Matthew Johnson as Lord Slyzzar; Cody Presswood as Corporal Rothemid; Jonathan Davis as various Ice Warriors; Ben Patrick as Child of Prophecy.*

CREW: *Produced by Kenneth Dinkins, Jennifer Richman and Aron Presswood. Directed by Kenneth Dinkins and Aron Presswood. Written by Kenneth Dinkins; & lots of little Richmans, Dinkins and Presswoods pulling up the rear.*

Review: How to Stop a Time Lord (2012)

Sense and Sentiment from Romania

STORY: The Tenant and Smith Doctors end up materializing in at an empty school to solve a mystery and learn a thing or two about life

REVIEW: This is simply exquisite. Very well acted, great chemistry, well shot, well edited, the writing is terrific, and it captures both the humour and the sweetness that is at the heart of Doctor Who. It is an honest pleasure.

That's really all the review you need.

Go find it. Watch it.

Now.

Or if you'd like the rest….

One of the things that really impresses me with this production is the utter elegance of its simplicity. Two principal cast, two supporting cast, a single location which is a relatively nondescript high school and its grounds, no sets, almost no props to speak of, and only a few relatively simple CGI effects. The production is sparse to the point of being Spartan. At thirty three minutes, it's breathtakingly economical.

Production values are something I watch for in these things. I'm not impressed by a fan film shot in someone's living room, where they haven't even bothered to move the furniture and knick knacks. We tend to appreciate effort put in – whether it's the bother of finding and shooting in visually effective locations, or putting a set or props together, or knocking up an effective costume. A fan film, when it's really good, aspires to the visual complexity and richness of the original show, that's often the point.

Sometimes this leads straight off a cliff. There's nothing more jarring than ambition which stumbles. I'm thinking of *Fire and Ice* and the tweety bird scene, but I'm also thinking of the wall flats in *Visions of Utomu*, and god knows how many blown moments in *Gene Genius*, which undermine a potential for greatness.

What we have here is a very deliberate choice not to go that route, but rather, to make the production as simple and visually spare as possible.

It's a bit of a risk, because immediately, that constrains your storytelling and the sorts of places you can take your story. It also puts a great deal of weight on other aspects of the production, particularly the writing and acting. There's no gravel quarry, no Roman amphitheatre, no vast moors, no ruins of a church or castle or crowded London street, there's no time machine console – nothing to reflect what's going on in the story or in the protagonists' hearts, nothing to give a sense of place or progress. Nothing to do but watch the protagonists… It's working without a net.

They pull it off. Spectacularly well.

First up, let me say that this is a Transylvanian Doctor Who film. Well, Romanian. The thing is, due to Bram Stoker (an Englishman) and Bela Lugosi (a Hungarian), any time you say Romania we just automatically default to Transylvania, which is actually just one of the regions in Romania. But actually, they're based in Bucharest, the capitol, and that's not Transylvania either. By the way, not everyone in America wears a cowboy hat and speaks like a Texan. And not everyone in Canada lives in an igloo and fights polar bears (Actually, I do, but that's not all of us. Some of us are dentists.)

So: A Romanian Doctor Who film.

Everyone speaks English in it, and it's perfectly fine English, despite the Romanian accents. Completely understandable. But for some reason, they added subtitles. Okay.

I'm not really bothered by accents. Well, okay, sometimes I am. I'm bothered sometime by the fact that Hollywood seems to give every alien a British accent. I'm bothered by the fact that Captain Picard was a French man with a British accent (look, the occasional Merde doesn't cut it, okay). I'm annoyed by the fact that in Dracula Untold, all the Transylvanians had British accents and all the Turks had Hispanic accents. But mostly, I don't lose sleep over it. If it's a fan film, I'd rather that the actors try and speak comfortably and deliver a credible performance, than that they try to awkwardly flounder their way through a silly accent.

So we get Romanian accents. Which is kind of cool. I don't mind listening to them at all. It adds a nice, unplanned bit of quirkiness to it.

The heart of the story is about the Tennant Doctor, played by Andrei Constantinescu, and the Smith Doctor, played by Mihai Constantinescu, encountering each other. I assume by the surnames that Andrei and Mikal are brothers, or at least closely related. It may explain some things. They wrote the thing together, and Andrei seems to have done most of the Directing and a lot of the post production work.

My god, it's well written. Not just well written, but it captures the spirit and rhythm of both Tennant and Smith so well.

You can listen to it, you can watch their performance, their expressions, their pacing, and it's like they're channelling the actors. You can literally put Tennant and Smith in your head and project them onto the screen, give them the lines, the expressions, the body language... And it works. The minute they step out onto the screen together, it works. You're captivated.

I've talked about the difference between the right word and the almost right word, being, as Mark Twain said, like the difference between the lightning and the lightning bug. Well, I don't mind lightning bugs. Mostly it's a lightning bug world, and I'm pretty tolerant. But this stuff? This is the crackle and the flash.

This is a good script, it's fast paced, it's got a sense of humour, it moves steadily and quickly through the plot, and it gives the actors a chance to play.

The other thing that works is that Mikal and Andrei work together so well. They have excellent chemistry. That's such a hard thing to grasp, until you actually see it in action. Chemistry is the characters reacting to each other, interacting. It's not just reciting your lines in the same room, but this feeling that what comes out of an actor's mouth is not a line, but the natural response to whatever the other actor has just said or done. They play off each other, they bounce off each other. Somehow, in the two of them, there's more than just the sum of their individual performances.

It's a hard trick to master. Rupert Booth is probably the best actor to play a fan Doctor, but he never had that engaging chemistry with any of his companions or fellow cast members. Barbara Benedetti had that with Randy Rogel. Nick Scovell is a terrific actor, but he's never had a solid companion.

Even in mainstream films and television, sometimes it's there, sometimes it's not, and it it's not, you can tell. There can be a flatness to the performance, and you don't really buy the romance or friendship or whatever.

Andrei and Mihai have terrific chemistry. They play well together in a shot, and the editing is so tight that they play well together even when they're talking at each other across separate shots. That comes from just a really intimate level of knowledge and contact. They know each other, they can finish each other's sentences, they can pick up and toss ideas back and forth like a children's game of catch, they have an energy going on, they know each other's rhythms and pace and can play off against each other like a couple of skilled musicians.

Basically, you could watch those guys play anything – Holmes and Watson, Stallone and Schwarzenegger, Kirk and Spock, Sylvester and Tweety and they'd be compelling and interesting.

They play smart too. The Doctors as they play them are razor sharp, inquiring, incisive minds. There's a mystery to be solved and they unravel it very well.

There's a couple of other cast members – Alexandru Baicoana, who plays Lyle, the security guard for the empty school. He's not quite as good, but he manages to bounce off both Mihai and Andrei nicely, and his character works – his lines are plausible, natural, the sort of things a person in his position would say when confronted with two crazy men claiming to be Doctors, and his black moment is a window into his soul. Oana Lacramioara Berbec as Liz manages to keep up nicely.

Even the ending works, capturing the sentimental sweetness of the series at its best. There is literally nothing about this that I don't like.

For the record, the film was featured at two film festivals in the USA, respectively GalaxyFest in Colorado and the

Phoenix Comicon Film Festival 2012. At Phoenix Comic Con it won First Prize as Best Fan Film.

Some have called it the Best Doctor Who Fan Film Ever. Is it? It's damned good, first rank, certainly.

What do I think?

I think the BBC should hunt these guys down, throw money at them, and then go hire Tenant and Smith for a one off.

For the record, Doctor Who isn't their only production. If you go to Silverwolfpet.com and browse around, you'll find a lot of other short films and productions. I would recommend that. They've got a killer Lord of the Rings spoof, and a lot of terrifically fun and interesting stuff.

CAST: Andrei "Silverwolf" Constantinescu - The Doctor; Mihai Constantinescu - The Doctor; Oana Lacramioara; Alexandru Baicoana. Introducing Mihaela Veronica Stoica as Doctor River Song;

CREW: Andrei and Mihair Constantinescu - Writers, Andrei Constantinescu - Director, Editing, Special Effects, Some Music Here and there and Everything Else that is Cool; Verena Izoerski - Additional Audio; Constantin Copaceanu - Motion Cam / Special Action Cameraman; Albo Abourt, Pablo Scalo, Andrei Constantinescu and Murray Gold - Music rearranged and interpreted; ; Thanks to Principal Tonel Tunaru of Aexandru Ioan Cuza High School, Bucharest Romania; Mrs. Michael Drafta and her team; High School security force Chirila Dorel, Florea Ionel, Raduta Ioan, Dumitrescu Ion; Ship Images Simmo on Polycount.com; Ship model eRe3s3r on DeviantArt.com; Tardis model and pictures taken from various corners of the web belong to the respective owners; Silverwolfpet, 33 minutes.

Review: Project Fifty (2013)

An Anniversary Epic in Twelve Parts

STORY: Torchwood Glasgow has discovered that something is up at Universal Web Systems. The Earth is in Danger, the Universe in Peril, it's time to call in The Doctor.

REVIEW: Project Fifty is the brainchild of Bryan McCormack, inspired by the 50th Anniversary of Doctor Who, released as a twelve part between January and August, 2014.

McCormack, the writer, producer, director, editor and star, is a bit more mature than the average modern fan film maker, just under fifty himself. On the other hand, he has some chops. He's had an equity card since 1986, he's written a book on acting, taken a university degree in screen acting, and amassed a reasonable body of work as a public speaker, stage actor, voice actor, etc. It was while attending the University of the West of Scotland as a mature student to study screen acting, that he got the idea for this project.

In his own words, from his web site: *"It was only the second day of the Induction, back in September 2012, that I suddenly realised that UWS Ayr had all the facilities and equipment you could possibly need to enable you to actually make a fan film. And then, when I discovered that there were other students [and more than a few members of staff!] who were also fans…"*

That's right: Two days into University as a mature student and he's on it.

"Doctor Who – Project: Fifty started its production journey on Tuesday September the 18th 2012. That's when I had the initial conversation with a fellow student, who was also a Who Fan, that sparked of the whole idea."

That's the story behind the story, basically: Lifelong Doctor Who fan and actor wanders into the resources and people willing to join him on his mad venture to play the Doctor, and away we go.

How is McCormack as The Doctor? Not bad. He's a very restrained Doctor, he seldom smiles, his jokes are few and far between. He lacks the bombast we've come to associate with the Doctor through Tenant, Smith and now Capaldi, or for that matter, the Bakers or McCoy. If I had to find a BBC Doctor to compare him too, I'd say Ecclestone and maybe Davison. He has a quiet quality that he shares with them.

McCormack has large eyes and a grim set to his mouth and he uses that. His Doctor is a brooding man, radiating concern and sometimes a bit of trepidation. Even relaxed, the weight of the world is on his shoulders. In his first scene, when he pokes his head out of the Police Box to look around, he gives the impression of a man nervously checking to see if it's going to be shot off. In other scenes, McCormack is good at looking genuinely scared, which is actually a very good thing – it sells the seriousness of the situation to the audience. That's a considerable accomplishment.

McCormack's Doctor seems generally nervous, there's an air of uncertainty about him, a pensive quality. Confidence bordering on arrogance tends to be a hallmark of the Doctor, and mostly, he doesn't exhibit that. He's most assured when confronting menaces directly, then the nervousness and uncertainty goes away.

Put Zodin in front of him, or a Time Vampire, or a Dalek, and suddenly doubt resolves, he knows who they are, he knows who he is, and he knows what to do. He actually grins when told there's a monster on the loose, it's his best moment.

There's less wit and humour to this version of the Doctor. Not much in the way of fun or funny lines, very little of the playfulness. It's there, as when he casually discards an umbrella, or does department store announcements stepping into an elevator, but it's got a sardonic quality. He plays with a yo yo at one spot, but you can see he's thinking about something else.

McCormack's is a real Doctor however. He understands what makes the Doctor work, and he can express it, to the point of creating his interpretation. Not everyone gets that. So bottom line, a real Doctor.

I just wanted to mention the celebrity on the cast who was kind enough to volunteer for one day's shooting. That's Danny, the Black Dalek, property of a 'Mark and Julie.' Danny was actually a television Dalek, and had played the Dalek Supreme in the McCoy serial, *Remembrance of the Daleks*. Danny's last minute inclusion required a significant rewrite of the script, as did sourcing a couple of Cyberman costumes.

As to the rest of the cast – well, there's not many of them. Claire Mackie plays Helena Hamilton, chunky woman, Torchwood Agent, and de facto companion for most of the serial. She dies in the second episode, but then feels much better, and comes closest to having a realized personality. She's also, after McCormack himself, the most critical backstage person in the production, solving problems, sourcing the Dalek, and being generally essential.

Rebecca Skinner plays Bex, a more traditional companion in that her role is mostly to ask the Doctor questions, most of which she does via mobile videophone. Elidh Weir plays Becky, who seems to be an alternative version of Bex, who shows up in person.

Suzie Macari through the magic of superimposition, split screens and clever editing plays a legion of Time Vampires, she's a hot chick, wears black, looks menacing, and that's really all we need. Zodin, of course, is terrible (that's a joke, she's just fine).

Overall, with the exception of McCormack and Mackie, there's not a lot of deep characterization. But with a serial of a dozen, eleven minute long, episodes ending in cliff-hangers, you're not going to get Shakespearean characterizations. It's a matter of hitting your marks, getting your lines done competently, and keeping things moving.

This shouldn't be taken as disparaging. It's an entirely competent, polished script. McCormack took it through five drafts, and apparently was willing to take constructive criticism and it shows.

On the other hand – in its original form on Vimeo, it's a twelve part serial. Jesus H. Christ. Collectively the whole thing weighs in at an exhausting 160 minutes, or over two and a half hours, give or take. The original series itself in its 28 year run didn't dare to run 10 episodes or over more than a few times in its history, *Dalek Master Plan (12), War Games (10), Frontier in Space/Planet of the Daleks (12) Trial of a Time Lord (14),* that's about it. And those last two are pretty iffy.

Each episode of McCormack's serial runs on average 13 minutes. Now, there's some duplication – recap, titles, credit. But still, even dumping the surplus, you're still averaging maybe 11 minutes per. McCormack has released a more consolidated version in three parts to YouTube, and still collectively runs over two hours.

But really, a fan film running 12 episodes and two and a half hours, that's asking a lot of the audience.

That's impressive. That's epic. That's spectacular.

That's also brutal.

This is taking a risk

Paradoxically, even though I complain it's too long, I'm also complaining it's too short. Eleven minutes, give or take. That's not really much time to tell or develop your story and wedge a cliff hanger in. You may not get much more than a vignette. *The Forgotten Doctor* has this issue as well, but we'll get to that. And Luke Newman's *Fall of The Doctor* also has that massive length issue, but again, we'll get to it. (The point is, that there's no satisfying me).

So McCormack has chosen a certain format for his story, this twelve mini-episode mini-mega epic. That choice drives and shapes the sort of story he'll tell. Not a lot of characterization, not in eleven minute bites where you have to build to the next cliff-hanger. Not a lot of room for extraneous stuff.

But lots of corridors and the walking about of in, lots of plot twists and cliff hangers, lots of walking in corridors, lots of running about, oh and lots and lots and lots of wandering around corridors.

Does it succeed?

Yes, and handily so.. It moves along steadily, it's got a good pace to it, and the serial format means that even if the individual episodes are short, the story continually builds up to something. He manages to generate momentum and keep it building. It manages to surprise throughout. There's places where the plot kind of twists off in a radically different direction that threatens to lose the audience, but it never quite falters. There's nowhere that it actually drags.

Because the episodes are relatively, short they're easy to watch, and it's very easy to watch the next one. Kind of like eating potato chips. You find yourself not stopping, consuming the next one, and then the next one. It can end up going down far more easily and far less tiresome than you'd ever imagine a two and a half hour epic taking.

The story? I don't want to get too far into it. For one thing, there's a lot of plot going on, you need a lot of plot to sustain eleven cliff hangers, and there's huge spoiler issues.

Basically, Torchwood Glasgow is investigating strange goings on at Universal Web Systems, their first operative gets chased through the woods and killed in the opening scenes, the second operative decides to summon the Doctor, using a distress signal that they filched from UNIT. The Doctor arrives and in short order discovers that someone has been sucking chronal energy from the fabric of space and time, and it all has something to do with the fact that everyone has been implanted with internet access chips.

From there, we get Time Vampires, Cybermen, Daleks, Zodin, conspiracies, time vortexes, dead companions, live companions, a light saber battle, another Doctor, an alternate universe, the fate of the human race every which way. Like I said, it moves along.

The script is also loaded with 'Easter eggs' – it's just chock full of in jokes, references, allusions to the show's fifty year history. The target was fifty, but I think they went way past that.

It's heavy on expository dialogue, but it has to be, and McCormack is a good enough director that he keeps it visually interesting – no small challenge, given that something like 95% of it is shot inside the Ayr campus building of the University of West Scotland.

Physically, he's got a small palette to work with, and he's skillful creating his visuals. He's got a strong visual eye that lets him make the most of his location; I can see how another, less gifted director would just make a drudge of it.

Being visually interesting is a key part of Doctor Who, and it could have gone very wrong here. But it didn't. I'd like to offer compliments on the technical competence. That's often a hit or miss thing with fan films. Producing a film of any kind is a huge amount of work, and it demands competency and investment in literally hundreds of production areas – props, sets, set dressing, make up, lighting, locations, continuity, composition, focus, acting, costumes, and so on. There are a thousand details you need to get right, and if you mess up one… Well, that's the one that people notice.

Technically, this is amazingly polished. The image, as we've come to expect from 21st century technology is pristine, the sound mix is thoroughly professional, locations, lock offs. There's nothing that jars or intrudes. In the whole thing, I spotted maybe one scene where the sound was off – too much echo in a stairwell.

It's actually more polished than we realize – there's several instances of split-screen and superimpositions that are seamlessly edited and integrated into the narrative. We have the twins – Natasha and Natalya, Time Vampires, both played by Suzie Macari – who eventually morphs into a foursome. There are shots featuring a dozen Daleks moving in different directions on two levels, all splitscreens and superimpositions of a single prop. There's some nice morphing, a bit of digital enhancement here and there. I don't think ever I've seen this level of proficiency or camera trickery done so ambitiously or seamlessly in a fan film. Hell, it beats things I've seen even in a lot of commercial films. Again, a testament to McCormack's gifts.

Although almost entirely shot inside the campus building, he's done a minimal amount of location work, and used it effectively. The opening shots are of a man running through Craigie Woods, on the Ayr University grounds. A woman having a conversation inside a car in the rain, the Doctor's Police Box materializing outdoors and the Doctor strolling to the location. Very good choices, nice sense of place and transition, and by putting these scenes in at the start, he creates a wider world for the Doctor, even if he's going to spend most of his time indoors. It's always best to make a good impression on your audience early on, that carries you past a lot of flaws. Never lead with your chin, as boxers say.

The Ayr campus is a modern looking building. No ivy covered brickwork here. Instead lots of corridors, walkways and atriums, with those open interior spaces that Universities seem to be fond of. It's designed to handle large numbers of people moving from place to place, or simply hanging out for periods of time – in functional terms, it's half park, half mall, and half place of business. I think that this often gives University buildings a unique though consistent look and feel.

That's not necessarily a bad sort of space to work in, and you'll find a great many 'on campus' student and art films. It's clean, well maintained, vaguely futuristic and formal. It can do double duty for a lot of modernist locations – offices, laboratories, corporate or government quarters, alien bases, etc. It's usually close to your equipment, power outlets are close by, it's accessible to your cast and crew, you can usually book hours when you have the whole thing to yourself, the lighting is stable (which is not something you can rely on shooting outdoors), you have an amazing amount of control over the space.

On the other hand, it's a pretty sterile, formal space, and it's hard to shoot it in interesting ways. There's minimal dressing that you can do, there's a certain 'guerilla' film making quality, in that you only have the space for certain times, and you have to share it with others.

The result is that your student art film, or *Project Fifty*, takes on a certain look. Almost, but not quite, sterile; vaguely futuristic; striking in some ways – there's some nice vistas and geometries of imagery, but empty as well.

The hardest part is that it limits you – no matter where you go in there, mostly, it looks the same. You can try and jazz it up with different angles or locations, but there's no concealing the underlying uniformity of the location, the fact that it's all the same architecture and design.

Compare that, to the BBC show which makes a point of transitioning through different locations and sets, often several in an episode. Or compare that to the *Wrath of Eukor* where the lush Pacific rain forest is almost a character in the story itself, or the Timebase productions which consistently found impressive locations, or other productions which have employed a warship turned museum, a tall sailing ship turned museum, a Mayan pyramid, a Roman amphitheatre, etc.

Given that this was very nearly a one man project, I think he probably made the best choice available to him. Locations are grand and add a lot of production value, but schlepping an entire cast and crew and equipment around is a lot of extra work, and building sets can be a lot of extra work that can misfire so easily.

McCormack's well aware that endless university corridors would be dull, so he employs a number of cinematic techniques to keep things lively, such as changing the framework of the image. That's actually one of the best things about it - he consistently manages to find interesting ways to shoot hallways and corridors - it's like he wrote a textbook on how to do this right.

I can't stress this enough, McCormack practically has nothing but halls and hallways to work with, and he's able to take that and constantly make it visually interesting. That's incredibly hard to do, and McCormack does it smoothly and seamlessly, with practically no resources. McCormack writes that he thought he was an actor, but then realized he was really a writer who acts. I disagree, he's really a gifted director who writes and acts. He also wrote a script that would work to the specific location, a vaguely futuristic story of conspiracy and menace. Another smart move, he identifies what he has to work with, and tailors the script to it. That's subtle, but smart.

He sticks almost all his outdoor work at the front, as I've mentioned, hoping that will carry him (it does), and he plays with his timeline.

Oh, and he managed to talk people into building a perfectly serviceable Police Box shell and Tardis console, so good on him.

So what's it all add up to? It's a very disciplined, very polished, very ambitious project that lines its targets up carefully, and basically hits them. Is it brilliant? Very close to it. Exhausting perhaps, and well done. I have no hesitation in recommending it.

In the larger context, there's something a little sad. *Project Fifty* started off with a lot of ambition and high hopes. He set up a Facebook page to promote it, there's a web site. But the website is oddly incomplete, he was promising podcasts, a production diary, there's the promise of thing that never materialized. I think that it turned out to be a lot more work, a lot more difficult and time consuming than he expected, and perhaps that stole time and energy away from other things he'd planned.

I don't think he got the reception he was hoping for, it can be crushing to put so much work in and for people to not even notice, or to go 'mm hmm' for a moment and then move on. Since it's come out, McCormack seems to come to terms and feels better with the project. He's working on a Commentary, an edited compilation of the episodes appeared on YouTube, and he's also become involved with the *Altered Vistas* bunch doing voice work.

On the other hand, McCormack seems to have gotten it out of his system, with Project Fifty. McCormack has written a pair of books about his fan film experience, which amounts to a fairly biting chronicle of the frustrations and triumphs of both the experience of being a fan, and of the travails of low budget film making. The books are A *Fan Film Adventure In*

Space And Time! and *The Dalek Fan Film Invasion!* In addition to being worthy reads, the books provide links to 'extra content' including the online shooting script.

In addition, he's written a series of novels under the collective title, *The Paradox Club*, an *"epic time travel fantasy romance series, chronicling the adventures of Valentine and Milo across the twin dimensions of space & time and love & death."* Obviously inspired by Who, but also its own thing. Please feel free to seek out his work.

CAST: *Bryan McCormack - The Doctors; Claire Mackie - Helena; Rebecca Skinner - Bex; Eilidh Weir - Becky; Gordon Hunt - Alex; Suzie Macari - Natasha and Natalya, Time Vampires; Hugh Smith - Archie; John Dougan - Receptionist; Unknown – The Terrible Zodin; Mark McCreadie - Dalek Operator.*

CREW: *Bryan McCormack - Writer, Producer, Director; Toria Cassidy - Script Editor; Hugh Smith and Ian Horsburgh - Tardis Prop Builders; Mark McCreadie - Dalek Operator and Tardis Console Builder; Lisa Kuhni, Alex McCall, Mark McCormick, Joanna McKay, David Moyne, Mark McCreadie, Gabriel Malone, Martin Smith, Gordon Houston, Elsie Vekhanmeimi, Maximillian Neumann - Camera Crew; David Arnold, Mark Ayres, Don Harper, Paul Leonard-Morgan, Thomas Newman, Dudley Simpson, Ben Foster, John Debley, Atley Orvarsson, Edmund Butt, Murray Gold, Paul Dinletir, Michael Rix, Radiophonic Workshop - Music; Kiera Mackie - Runner; Lisa Kuhni - Production Assistant; Toria Cassidy; Claire Mackie - Line Producer; Gabriel Malone - Assistant Director; Keith Bird - Studio Manager; Jamie Hare - Studio Co-ordinator; Jamie Hare, Oliver Karaschewski, Gabriel Malone - Studio Lighting; Michael Mavor - Sound Supervisor; Alex McCall - Data Wrangler. With Thanks to Cameron Seaward - Alcam Precision Engineering. Featuring Music by David Arnold, Rob Duncan, Thomas Newman, James Newton-Howard, Chris Velasco; A UWS.DWS Fan Film.*

Review: The Forgotten Doctor (2013-2014)

The Black Doctor's Series

STORY: After the eighth Doctor defeats the Cybermen, he's forced to regenerate into a new incarnation, what will be the 'Forgotten Doctor' between eighth and ninth. Stepping out of the Police Box, this new Doctor finds a companion, encounters vampire slugs, visits a false paradise, helps out a friend, discovers a new menace and comes face to face with Torchwood in a series of eight episodes.

REVIEW: For me, Jevocas Green is the definitive black Doctor, preceding both Jo Martin and Ncuti Gatwa.

Technically, he's not the first, his *Forgotten Doctor* dates to May 28, 2013.

Approximately a six months earlier, August 16, 2012, Spencer Kennedy played the Doctor in Crow's Nest productions in two ambitious half hour fan films, The *Mystery of Rorrim* and *Untimely Death*. They're not reviewed here, but I have no hesitation in recommending you track them down.

And obviously, the original Black Doctor is *Lenny Henry*, who played the Doctor in a five minute sketch on his variety show, where he eviscerates the clichés of the 80's show, including screaming companions and endless hallways.

Despite this, it's Jevocas Green who stands out. Spencer Kennedy plays at the Doctor, but Green inhabits the character. Even more than that, Green's approach seems more personal and more comprehensive. He not only plays the Doctor, but writes, directs, produces and edits, it's very much his production. But even past that, it just feels more personal, as if he's telling stories that are important to him. Ultimately, what's critical is not that Jevocas Green is a black Doctor.

It's that he is the Doctor.

The Forgotten Doctor makes a good comparison to *Project Fifty*. They're both modern Doctors – released circa 2013/2014. Their timing is near identical. They're both full series – 12 episodes for Project Fifty, and eight for the Forgotten Doctor. They're both short episodes – *Project Fifty* runs 10 to 16 minutes, the Forgotten Doctor runs 5 to 21. Both average out about 13 minutes per episode.

Both revolve around the central personalities – Bryan McCormack and Jevocas Green produce, direct, star, you name it. They both seem to be the driving forces. They're both people who just want to be the Doctor.

Bryan's is the more polished and controlled work – he's got the better Tardis console, and he's very effective in his cinematography making maximum visual use of the very controlled environment of the campus. He uses a very limited setting and wrings every drop of visual effect out of it. Bryan gives every evidence of knowing every inch of the Ayr campus building like the back of his hand, he knows how to use the space cinematically, and he's good at making every shot visually effective. His editing, his sound, and particularly his computer image compositing is effective. It's like watching classical Violin virtuoso.

Jevocas is more freewheeling, he makes more use of different settings and locations, his intro is better. His locations include a park, an office complex, a warehouse, he tries to get sets built or at least dress up the warehouse. He puts more effort into costumes and make up. He seems to have a larger cast and crew. But because he's doing individual episode stories, it's hard to really master the spaces or the challenges of the moment. Still, taking more chances, despite imperfect outcomes, still gives you more results. He's like a terrific Jazz guitarist.

Both of them are using amazingly professional looking high end consumer or semi-commercial equipment, computer editing, CGI imaging and compositing. They're both accessing an identical level of technology and technological sophistication which is frankly astounding.

And they both make very sophisticated use of the modern media – they have Facebook, Websites, they produce trailers, there's teasers. Jevocas here has the edge. I have the sense Bryan was a bit burnt out by his experience, while Jevocas still had a lot of enthusiasm – his Facebook profile is very active, he seems to be tied into the American convention circuit. Of the two performances as Doctors, I'd have to say that they both have valid and credible interpretations, they're real Doctors.

Between the two of them, they're representative of a very significant movement in modern fan films, the 'Personal Quest.' Film is very had to do, even fan films, and as late as the 90's, it really needed to be a collective effort, as with Timebase and El Cheapo.

What we see with McCormack and Green, and for that matter with Luke Newman, Nathan Carter, even Crystal Moore & Chris Philips are what amounts to 'one person shows' where a single person (or at most, a couple of people) writes, directs, plays the Doctor, etc. They're the single driving force, for better or worse.

They still need help though, but it's getting closer and closer.

As a Doctor, Jevocas Green is a pleasure to watch. Confident, endlessly charming, the Jevocas Doctor exudes charisma and warmth. He might be challenged by Monsters, and if and when he is, you'll see his desperation and improvisation writ large, but he'll win through. Mainly, he's a Doctor that charms.

Oddly, Jevocas as an Actor or Director seemed to have less confidence in his character. He wastes a lot of his first episode having someone play the McGann Doctor and setting up the regeneration, and in his final episode, he's more insistent on trying to connect to the other Doctors. He doesn't need to, his Doctor stands perfectly well on its own. You do have a sense of him feeling out the character a little in the early episodes.

Then there's the companion. Jevocas' Doctor lucks out with a young woman named Sasha, played by Kylie Bara, who throws a mean right hook and has a few secrets of her own – there's the suggestion of an underlying arc to be found there. She strikes sparks off the Jevocas Doctor because she's not entirely a committed companion.

Her presence offers dynamism, chemistry and hints and story prospects.

The Forgotten Doctor is a series of individual adventures – the Doctor regenerates into his new form. He gets a companion.

He and his companion visit the Eloi of H.G. Wells.

Then they meet another Time Lord who is romantically and sexually involved with his humaniform Tardis.

He encounters the Weeping Angels for the first time.

There's a two-parter where they encounter Torchwood and Daleks, which ends on a cliff hanger.

As it is, it's like a book of short stories. A novel is perhaps better integrated, it's sprawling, but you'd better like it, because you are in it to the end – the characters, the situation, the style are all going to be the same all the way through. A novel in its way, is an ambitious unified work. A collection of short stories may be the same word count, may represent the same creative investment, but you get a diversity of styles, characters, approaches and that's it's strength, short stories take more chances and run more risks, but at the same time, their briefer meter means that they've got less room to develop. Both approaches are worthwhile, they produce very different things.

Here, there's not really a larger story. But we still have these relatively short segments don't allow a lot of time to develop. A good example is *Marnal's Error*, the fourth episode, at sixteen minutes. This is the one about the Time Lord who's romantically involved with his humaniform Tardis. (In *Keeper of Traken*, the Master's Tardis took the shape of a statue that could walk around and interact with its environment. Subsequent Doctor Who novels extended this further, coming up with Tardises whose chameleon circuit allowed them to take human forms and who could walk, talk and interact). It turns out the Police Box is stolen, so the Doctor goes there, there's resistance, its overcome. No sooner is the problem posed, than it's immediately solved. It doesn't feel like so much as a story, as the idea or outline of a story. But then, there's more to it – Jevocas is meditating on true love in all its forms, alternative lifestyles. The story's just a frame, it's about Marnal's relationship.

But then, there's a freedom to do different things. *Weeping* depicts the first encounter with the Weeping Angels, before the Doctor knows what they are. He's forced to figure them out and cobble a defense together on the fly. Does it work effectively? I dunno. It's tough to build an origin story like that from the ground up in the time available.

There's a downside, because the stories are self-contained, taking place in different locations, with different casts, the production suffers – This story, for instance, features those Nun-Catwomen, but the make-up and applications are a bit half assed, you can tell what they were going for, but they didn't quite get there.

On the other hand, this episode featured people attending a religious service and clearly being shown receiving comfort and enlightenment from their worship, and then later having a feast together, and again showing pleasure and assurance from these communal activities. That's a very interesting thing, because it's taking minutes from a story which is perhaps not told as well as it could be, and it serves no real purpose in terms of plot. But you know what, there's something real going on there, there's something profound and meaningful, and I can't fault that decision. It works.

With the Eloi episode, you have some of the same things. There are some beautiful moments in the stories, and Jevocas as a director is patient enough to let his shots linger as long as they need to. That's a rare thing these days. There's a tendency for Directors to fall in love with their footage and let it drag, and there's the opposite trait, cutting too fast. Jevocas seems to know how long to let something last, even if he's not always leaving himself enough room for the story. The story is slight, but in the end, it's not really about the story. There's a sweetness to the episode.

Jevocas shifts in format that makes it harder to tell a full or proper story, but he's willing to accept that, and willing to do other things. It's that willingness, that interest in doing more than telling a linear story, the fact that he'll try for something and he's prepared to allow himself to follow that something, that makes it interesting.

It looked like Jevocas Green's *Forgotten Doctor* was going to go for a second season, which was a good thing overall. Sadly, that second season never materialized – technical difficulties, hard drive crash, that sort of thing. It's a shame, because from the trailers and stills we see, including Jevocas' Doctor in an elevator with analogues of the Smith, Tennant and McGann Doctor's, I think it could have been brilliant.

In the end, Jevocas Green's version of Doctor Who, like McCormack's is a success. It is a pleasure to watch.

As with *Project Fifty*, there's a lot of temptation having watched an episode to go onto the next one.

CAST: *Jevocas Green – Doctor, Cyber Controller, Dalek Voices, Kylie Bara – Sasha Princeton; Benjamin Bryant – Previous Doctor; Robert Vardaros – 11th Doctor; Zachary Vaudo – Agent Stanley; Thomas Dooley – Agent Jones; Morgan Daniel – Susan Foreman; Vara – Haviland Forrister; Matt Siano – Tietamaton; Richard Hempton – Marnal; Gale Skipworth – Hope; Agent Pyke – Eric Green; Paul Carter – The Master; Edward DeGruy – Lord Tserma; Erica Underdown – Reverend Mother; Richard Burke – Priest; Tyler Sutherland – Weeping Angels; Amber Gay – Yvonne Hartman; Rishik Patel – Agent Peresh; Evan Barger – Agent Keeper; Vernon Deckstrom – Torchwood Agent; Emily Ramos – Cynthia; Rachel Marie Howell – Alix Grant (partial cast listing)*

CREW: *Inspired/Based on DW Graphic Novel – The Flood, written by Scott Gray & Gareth Roberts, Piani Books Publishing; Jevocas Green – Exec Producer, Writer, Director, Art Director, Wardrobe, Makeup Supervisor, VFX, Foley; Robert Vardaros – Exec Producer, Editor, Score, Wardrobe, Sound Mixer, Foley Artist, VFX; Richard Hempton, – Exec Producer, Writer, Director, Editor, Set Design and Construction; Elijah Gleason – Asst Director; Jessica Gartland – Art Director; DOP – Eric Gartland; Sean Gartland, Emily Ramos, Eric Green, David Cook,, Kurt Bergeron (partial crew listing)*

Reviews: The Ginger Chronicles (2014-2015)

A DAME TO KILL FOR and A LOUD HUSH

STORY: A Dame to Kill For - The Doctor's enemies have caught up with her, and as the Tardis goes down in flames, regeneration begins. The new Doctor is finally ginger... and female? A Loud Hush - The Doctor makes a friend of a firefly, and encounters the voice stealing Gentlemen from Buffy the Vampire Slayer.

REVIEW: We have Lilly Nelson as another female incarnation of the Doctor. How did that come about? Well, Matt Smith was leaving the role of the Doctor, and Peter Capaldi hadn't been announced yet. So there was a gap, a period of uncertainty, where no one was quite sure where the show was, or where it was going to go. Anyone could be the next Doctor. The next Doctor could be black. Or a woman. Anything really.

Lilly Nelson decided that she really, really wanted to play the Doctor. It was that simple. I don't think that there was any deep feminist statement. She loved the show, she wanted to be the Doctor, and there didn't seem to be any good reason why she couldn't.... Legalities aside.

So what's the Nelson Doctor like?

What I'll say for Nelson is that she dominates the screen easily. Actually, she bludgeons it into smithereens.

In A Dame to Kill For she approaches the role of the Doctor like a hummingbird on amphetamines driving a stolen car fleeing from a high speed police chase. It's just barely possible that she might be slightly over the top. It's a little bit too influenced by the frantic excesses of the David Tennant and especially the Matt Smith Doctor's. It's allowable I guess. Fresh regeneration and all. She tries too hard and needs to slow down, but when she allows herself to relax a little, she does slip into the role and allows her own Doctor to evolve.

In her second outing, A *Loud Hush*, Lilly Nelson's Doctor has gelled a bit. She's still definitely flighty and hyper, but her character has settled a bit. Nevertheless, her character retains the cheerful and animated and effortlessly buoyant.

But there's steel under all that froth. Nelson's Doctor, for all her frivolity and animation, misses nothing, is surprised by nothing, she's relentless and always one step ahead. Underneath the airheaded cheer there is something utterly implacable to Nelson's Doctor. For all her clowning and playfulness, she's like a freight train with a happy face painted on it. All that bright and smiley is just cover for the fact that her Doctor is an unstoppable force. She's one step away from being terrifying.

Nelson's Doctor reminds me a little of Groucho Marx in this. Someone blindingly intelligent and fast, who creates and perhaps inhabits this flighty, flaky persona. The fool who is actually several steps ahead. Partly because it's her, partly because it's fun, and partly because it disarms people and makes it easier for her to do her things. There's a sense at points that she's play acting, when she boxes with the Hush zombies, for instance, there's a careful exaggeration in the movements - her fists rotate like a comedian in a 1920s silent reel. She's like a sped up version of the Troughton Doctor.

Which makes her interesting and compelling? Fundamentally, this is what makes a Doctor. That eccentric force of personality. Benedetti has it, Booth has it, Bennett, Scovell, Harald have it, and Nelson has it. It's expressed differently with each actor, but it's there.

&&&

A DAME TO KILL FOR

As the story goes, the Tardis crashes in flames and the Doctor is forced to regenerate once more. Waking up on a couch, the Doctor discovers that this time she's a dashing, frenetic young redhead. And a woman. A lot of the episode is taken up with getting over the shock and awe of regeneration.

All this is witnessed by a hapless, bemused couple Jim and Liz Baker, who came along to rescue her, and whose couch she woke up on. Played by Rebecca Larken and Monte Hampton, they handle the fish out of water situation engagingly. They're everypeople, decent, normal, humdrum who find themselves completely out of their depth in dealing with this strange being who has come into their life.

After introductions are made, she demands to be taken back to the Tardis, and her bemused rescuers accede. Instead, they discover a park full of people trapped in blue force fields. It's nicely done effect. Then the Master shows up.

Miles Dwight Snow gives us the most restrained version of the Master that we've seen. In pretty much every incarnation, Delgado, Ainsley, Roberts, Simms, or among fans, Williams and Christopher, the Master is usually vaulting over the top.

But here Nelson's performance as the Doctor is so hummingbird intense, there's really no place for him to go. Instead of trying to match her, he plays the Master as a silent plotter, watching the Doctor flit around with calm, even benevolent amusement.

Did I say benevolent? He's still the Master, and he's still up to no good, with an evil trap for the Doctor. It kind of sneaks up on you that he is a truly bad guy. While the Doctor is distracted by the euphoria of regeneration he springs it. And fails, because Nelson's Doctor, despite her frenzy, is clear thinking and sneaky.

In the end, the Baker's, not entirely sure what they've gotten into, go off with her, setting the stage for further adventures.

So what's the bottom line on *A Dame to Kill For*? It's only half an hour so it feels kind of brief, and yet, oddly it feels slow as well. I think that the plot is a bit too straightforward.. Way too much time is taken up with Nelson's Doctor dealing with regeneration euphoria, and it undermines the story somewhat. But there is a real story here, even if a little slight, and it works.

Technically the production values are straight up comparable to the modern BBC series. The production strikes me as careful. There's a small cast, a fairly limited number of locations. Overall, it's a good looking production which doesn't quite manage to be completely satisfying, but leaves you wanting to see what they do next. *The Ginger Chronicles* have been crowd funded through a kickstarter program, and so what you get is a highly professional product.

&&&

A LOUD HUSH

The Gentlemen are utterly silent, perpetually grinning, well dressed ghouls who float around, carving people's hearts out. They're assisted by minions; loping, straightjacketed, thuggish ghouls who are equally silent. The Gentlemen's shtick is that they steal voices from everyone in the community so that they can carry on their business without all that bothersome shrieking.

If the Gentlemen sound familiar, it's because they're from the *Buffy the Vampire Slayer* episode, *Hush,* one of the creepier episodes from that series. In fact, this film actually references the events in Buffy's Sunnydale at one point.

I'm assuming that the original episode must have been a favourite for Lilly Nelson, or Steven Hancock, or Rebecca Larken or all of them. The evil plot and visuals of the Gentlemen, their origins and actions, dominate the episode. I'd have to go check, but I'm pretty sure that the Gentlemen get as much screen time as the Doctor. You're not seeing a lot of plot, nuance, characterization. But that's okay. Nelson, Larken and Hancock know what they want to do, and they do it.

This might be influenced by the style of the story. *A Loud Hush,* like its inspiration, is essentially a silent film. Sometimes this is very obvious - when the Doctor fights the Gentlemen, her fists are pin-wheeling like a Buster Keaton character. The silence may be a plot point, but it's there, and in terms of having to shoot it and having the characters interact, inevitably, it reproduces some of the feel and physicality of the old silent films of the 1920s. That definitely shades the performance. But that's not all of it.

I think it also plays to something very mannered and old fashioned in Nelson's Doctor. I've said she plays like a speeded up Troughton, and I'll stand by that. What's interesting is how out of place her companions, the Baker's feel in this story, and how comfortable her Doctor is.

Rebecca Larken returns as Liz Baker. Monte Hampton's been replaced by Michael Ray Williams and they've made a plot point out of it, good for them. Their performances are fine, although truthfully, the creepiness and omnipresence of the Gentlemen and their minions tends to overwhelm everyone else.

We get to see the Tardis Interior, which is kind of cramped - the backgrounds are liberally sprinkled with gauze and Christmas tree lights. Interestingly, the Tardis console bears a vague resemblance to the one from Time and the Doctor. The locations work, a combination of homey and gothic. Ultimately, the big effect, the dominating image and situation is the Gentlemen themselves. Nelson's Doctor holds her own; but it's the Gentlemen's story.

Ultimately, I don't think that either the A Dame to Kill for or *A Loud Hush* are the defining stories for the Nelson Doctor. They both feel like warm ups for the big story. We'll have to wait and see.

A DAME TO KILL FOR

CAST: *The Doctor - Lilly Nelson; Liz Baker - Rebecca Larken; Jim Baker - Monte Hampton; The Master - Miles Dwight Snow; Victim - Melissa Eastwood; Drunken Night Watchman - Steven Hancock;*

CREW: Producer/Director - Steven Hancock; Writers - Steven Hancock & Lila Wilde; Co-Executive Producer - Vince Barnett; Director of Photography - Alethea Delmage; Co-Cinematographers - Tom Gore & Christine Parker; UK Unit Director - Christine Parker; Title Sequence - Anthony Kiely; Camera Operators - Alethea Delmage, Tom Gore, Joey Martin, Christine Parker; Camera Assistant - Jesse Latham; Sound Technicians - Jesse Latham & Phl Blattengerger; Editor - Joey Martin; Sound Mixer - Joey Martin; Colour Correction - Joey Martin; Visual Effects - That Endless Horizon Productions; Music - Kevin Macleod; Behind the Scenes - JD Mayo; Makeup Assistant - Angela Pritchett; Props - Steven Hancock, Mick Heckl, Drew Neill & Lilly Nelson; Catering Assistant - Dan Black; Extras - Chris Brewer, Angela Pritchett & Mike Zuchick; Special Thanks to - Adam Hancock, Jacquie Hancock, Megan Hancock, the Hancock Family, the Nelson Family, Mayo Films, Incompetech, Old Salem Museum & Gardens in Winston Salem, King Recreational Acres in King NC, Reddragonmovies. Filmed on location in North Carolina. 2014 Lightspeed Productions.

A LOUD HUSH

CAST: *Lilly Nelson - The Doctor; Rebecca Larken - Liz Baker; Michael Ray Williams - Jim Baker; Jaysen - Buterin - Gentlemen 1; Preston Edgar Campbell - Gentleman 2; Miles Dwight Snow - Gentleman 3; Tanner Lagasca - Gentleman 4; Steven Hancock - Gentleman 5; Tom Gore - Minion 1; Jon Dietz - Minion 2; Will Garret Davis - Gentleman's Boy; Erin Dea Bell - Neighbor Kathy; Tim Bell - News Reporter; Keith Kittrelle - EMS Medic 1; Jenny Maas - EMS Medic 2; Robert Gordon - Neighbor; Libby Seymour - Tardis Voice.*

CREW: *Written by Lila Wilde, Steven Hancock & Rebecca Larken; Produced by Rebecca Larken; Directed by Rebecca Larken & Steven Hancock; Assistant Director - Tom Gore; Editor - Konrad Arnold; Assistant Producers - Steven Hancock & Lilly Nelson; Sound Design - Alex 'AJ' McDonald; ADR Technician - Kevin Darbro; Directors of Photography - Tim Bell & Sean Pollock; Post Production Supervisor - Rebecca Larken; Visual Effects - Bill Mulligan, Dean Garris & Konrad Arnold; Animation - Lilly Nelson; Titles Designer - Callum Trevitt; Make-Up and Hair - Anthony Shelton & Evelyn Putnam; Special Effects Makeup Supervisor - Jennifer McCollom; Special Effects Makeup - Bill Mulligan; Costumes - Kimberly Wills-Starin; Set Design & Construction - Jon Dietz; Series Photographer - Paul Cory; Series Graphic Artist - Kimberly Wills-Starin; Music - Steven Grove; 'Somebody Call the Doctor' written by Kat Robichaud, performed by Kat Robichaud and the Darling Misfits, 2015, used with permission; Special Thanks - Steven Pender, Tamara Hipp, Jeff Campaign, Don Butto, Maple Wood Cemetery; Ambulance Footage - 'I remember Hannah' Team; Donors.*

Mini-Reviews: Some Interesting Projects

These two volumes are about the Greatest Doctor Stories Ever. By and large, I've tried to highlight the stuff that I think is most important. The films and videos with historical significance, that are most relevant to the history of the show, to culture and technology, the performances and productions that stand out. By and large, I think my choices are justified. But they are intensely subjective. Someone else might have made different choices.

But there's a lot of works out there. *Time Rift, Tyranny of the Daleks, the Persephone Complex, Theta G, Masterplan or Deadly Alliance*, didn't make it onto my list. It wasn't that the people involved didn't work extraordinarily hard, they did, they poured their heart and soul in. And perhaps someone else might have included some or all of them. At the end of the day, space is limited; I had to choose who to leave in, and who to leave out.

Beyond these, there are some very interesting modern productions worth a look. *Plastic Treachery*, high school level production, featuring the Master and the Autons; *Zeeland Breeze* about an invasive sentient fungus, shot in Amsterdam; *Gene Pool*, shot in New Zealand, featuring the Goald from *Stargate* and reformed benign Daleks, *Doctor Vu* an Italian version of Doctor Who, Doctor What featuring the Doctor as an amoral slacker.

But obviously, there's an element of subjectivity to this. In the last decade in particular, there have been a number of very impressive productions. Choosing one over another becomes a very personal matter, perhaps if I'd watched in a different mood, or chose to focus on different things, or chosen to forgive different things, or simply had more space, I might have selected differently, or selected more.

For what it's worth, here are a handful of productions that are remarkable and interesting, but that I didn't select. For one reason or another, they weren't my cup of tea. Perhaps they should have been.

Perhaps they're worth your taking a chance on....

&&&

2008 - VICTIMSIGHT (35 minutes, British Colombia, Canada)

This Canadian production features a Tennant style Doctor, a cyberspace theme, witty script, a government conspiracy vs law and order angle, and the Rani. What's not to love?

It's smart and full of ideas, and yet, somehow it feels incomplete to me. This is one of those stories where the plot just feels too linear, the progression too straight line. The story feels like a slender reed, and the Doctor never seems to be in real danger.

Although it resolves with the Rani defeated and withdrawing, it feels incomplete and inconclusive, as if this was simply the first round in a duel between the Doctor and the Rani.

Overall, it's a fairly polished production. The opening scenes are the best, particularly where the Doctor comes on the scene and embroils himself in the mess. There's a real effort to capture the peculiar charisma of the Tennant Doctor, and he does manage to get it now and then. The frame-up of the Doctor isn't particularly convincing. It's the Doctor; we know he's been framed. On the other hand, we've got an interesting take on the Rani that avoids the arch excess of Kate O'Mara, and gives us a more clinical, genuinely dangerous personality.

CAST: *Graham Steeksma - The Doctor; Aurora Buchanan - Anna Thomas; Jay Danziger - John Wells; Andrea Brown - Veronical (The Rani) Smith; Waylon Klix - Robert Shane; David Waltho - McGill; Philip Westendorp - Security Operator; Shawn Greek - Judge; Shelley Picard - Sue; Eldon Letkeman - Suit; Robert Westendorp - Guard; Brendan Greek - Security Operator #2; Ashton Bannister, Brian Steeksma, David Collie, Liam Field, Robert Spaulding - Victims.*

CREW: *Written and Directed by Eldon Letkeman; Story by Eldon Letkeman & Robert Westendorp; Executive Producers - Eldon Letkeman & Robert Westendorp; Producers - Marie Tate & Michael Alderking; Original Score - Bryan Steeksma; Casting - Marie Tate; Key Makeup - Lindsay Jang; Makeup - Bonnie Lowen & Denise Douglas; Boom Operators - Jordan Block & Waylon Klix; Craft Services - Greg Letkeman; Camera Operator - Harry Sullivan; Editor & Sound Effects - Robert Westendorp; Special Effects - Mike Yates; Costume - Marie Tate & Eldon Letkeman; Documentary Footage - Brendan Greek; Still Photography - David Fuchs; Special Thanks to Allena Letkeman, Lisa Westendorp, Larry Clark, Websmart Solutions, Elbert Pater, Rien and Katherine Westendorp, Michael Alderking, Infinite Possibilities Media, Grace Bennett, Global Harvest Centre, David Waltho and Greg Letkeman, Lower Mainland Urban Streetwear, Michael Hinger, Global Healing & Restoration Centre, Ben Kuker, Virtuousi Media, Patricia Braun, Sevenoaks Alliance Church, City of Abbotsford BC, Overwaitea Food Group Ltd., Ian Stewart, Danny Stewart, Peter O'Rourke,*

&&&

2009 - THE OTHER SIDE (48 minutes, Plymouth Productions, England)

Plymouth Who Productions first video starts out very strong. The Doctor wandering into the production of a 'ghost chasers' reality show and its investigation of a creepy old orphanage which it turns out, really is haunted.

There's a lot to like, the locations are visually impressive. The cast manages to capture the feel of a low budget cable paranormal show, going through the mundane operations of trying to get an episode in the can. Mark Humphries stands out as a bored, sarcastic tech, just putting in his time. The show's resident psychic is downright entertaining.

Unfortunately, after that strong start, the production loses focus and direction, as if, having established their premise, they're not quite sure what to do with it, or how to do it. The pacing slows down, the Doctor eventually has to explain the plot to people, and it all seems to wrap up on its own, without actually needing to do much. There's a psychic who starts off as interesting, but this thread fails to add to proceedings. The plot is too straightforward, and would have benefited from some twists.

Steve Green plays the Doctor, and unfortunately, his performance is mostly underwhelming. Green does manage to convey a certain underlying sadness to the character, that I could see growing on me. But overall, he doesn't really convey the charm or eccentricity, the force of personality that defines the Doctor for me. Perhaps the script or direction doesn't give him room to do the character justice. But then again, he wrote and directed, so that's a problem.

One of the really interesting things here is the resemblance to episodes of the new BBC series, both made and unmade. The Doctor intruding on a paranormal investigation show is very similar to plans for *Century House*, a Tennant episode planned and abandoned for 2007 and 2008. It also anticipates Matt

Smith's premiere episode, The *Eleventh Hour* in 2010, where the Doctor encounters a prisoner escaping through a crack between dimensions. Finally, there's some resemblance to *Hide,* a Matt Smith 'ghost story' from 2013.

Apart from that, the major technical flaw is the sound mix. Due to the locations, there's way too much echo. Nevertheless, it's worth watching.

CAST: *Steve Green - the Doctor; Jemma Bassett - Macey Furguson; Melanie Hack - Jo Atkins; Lawrence Duncalf - Alexai Rochenco; Mark Humpries - Mark; Andrew Hack - Julz; Zoe Collins - Izzi; Jamie Trace, Katie Rafton, Jessica Rafton & Zoe Evans - Ghost Children; Kriss Ellis-Stansfield, Gina Brown, Chris Nicholls - Film Extras; Alison Trace, Steve and Joanna Rafton, Sharon and John Evans - Child Wranglers.*

CREW: *Produced by Steve Green, Mark Humphries, Jemma Bassett & Chris Nichols; Written by Steve Green; Idea by Steve Green & Chris Nicholls; Directed by Chris Nicholls; Assistant Director - Steve Green; Camera - Everyone; CGI - Graham Quince; Video FX - Mark Humphries; Story Board - Chris Nicholls; Edited by Mark Humhries; Special thanks to Woodland Fort Community Centre, Whiteway Wilkinson at Eggbuckland Keep, Symon Sweet; 2009.*

&&&

2010 - INCURSION (43 minutes, Plymouth Productions, England)

The fourth story, and second video from Plymouth Who Productions (the other stories were audio). Steve Green writes, directs, produces and stars as the Doctor.

This time the Doctor is confronting the Hydra, a race of alien battle-armor suits which control their wearers. It's actually a brilliantly cool idea: An evil, alien, networked battle-suit that wears you. It's a nice twist on the idea of possession, and it seems to have so much potential. Mostly here it's used for a runaround. But seriously it's the sort of high concept that begs to be explored. But then this was a problem for the Other Side as well - really interesting idea that just doesn't get exploited fully.

On the positive side, its set outdoors, has good locations, good computer effects, nice design, a good story with a plot. There are some very nice moments, a UNIT Agent driving along and passing by the Tardis, and stopping with shock. A flashback sequence involving the Doctor and an alien spaceship. A scene on a park bench.

On the downside, I find it hard to be engaged with Green's version of the Doctor, who seems to lack the eccentricity that makes the character compelling. Green seems more comfortable with the role here than in the *Other Side*. But Green's version of the Doctor is just a regular bloke. Which is fine, I guess, but it's not the Doctor. Perhaps, though, that's just me.

The plot is just a little too linear; it could have done with some curves and complications. There's nothing wrong with complications, hell, without complications, Hamlet would be only fifteen minutes long.

The Hydra battle suit and space pod interior are just barely tolerable, but the operative word is tolerable. You can tell the pod interior is a shed, and the battle suits are obviously cobbled together. But they're good enough, that if you get into the story, they serve. I've certainly seen worse, even in professional productions.

Overall, this is more than competent enough to be worth watching.

CAST: *Steve Green - The Doctor; Jemma Nicholls - Macy Furguson; Gina Brown - Ellie Parker; Alison Trace - Caroline Parker; Chris Nicholls - Alec Pentacost; Cheryl Boxall - Sylvia Pentacost; Jeff Boxall - Jedd Pentacost; Andrew Kelly - Dave Villiers; Penelope Masters - Jane Villiers; Kriss Ellis-Stansfield & Chris Mugridge - Hydras;*

David Trace - Colonel Francesco; Kriss Ellis-Stansfield & Steve Williams - UNIT Soldiers; Mark Humpries & Ian Paul Cliffe - Voice Over Artists;

CREW: *Written by Steve Green, Directed by Steve Green & Mark Humpries; Script Editor - Melanie Hack; Camera - Anyone not in shot; 3D Visual Effects - Graham Quince; Video Effects - Mark Humphries; Edited by Mark Humpries; Music by Pigorey Productions, Jack Wall & Sam Hulick; Filmed on location at Long Ash, Clearbrooke & Dartmoor, Devon; Thanks to Plymouth Off Road Vehicle Society, Laurence Duncalf, Mrs D Green, Curtis Solicitors, 2010. Hydra Costumes - Lawrence Duncalf & Steve Green; Car Stunt Driver - Gina brown,*

&&&&

2010 - DOCTOR WHO: A TREK THROUGH TIME
(28 minutes, ...) - *Captain Kirk and Mr. Spock meet the 9th and 10th Doctors and their companions on the Enterprise. Literally.*

this is what's called a mash up, William Shatner, Leonard Nimoy, Christopher Ecclestone and David Tennant appear from the original footage of their original series, cleverly edited together to give the impression that the two casts are actually interacting. At points, there's a bit of CGI composition used to place the Tardis on the Enterprise, or make it appear that *Star Trek* and Who characters are in the same room together. It mostly works, though it feels a bit disjointed at times. Things don't quite match up, particularly dialogue and eye lines, there's an odd feeling of disconnect. But considering how difficult it is, the fact that this exists and is as coherent as it is, is amazing. 70 episodes of *Star Trek* and 40 episodes of Doctor Who were used as editing source material for this, the hours that went into this production are incredible.

The story is the Tardis comes under fire from the Enterprise. Kirk beams the Tardis onboard, and while they're interrogating the Doctor, the Enterprise comes under attack. Somehow, Kirk gets catapulted into an empty Enterprise in a mirror universe where he meets the Ecclestone Doctor, Davros and Daleks on an empty Enterprise. Meanwhile, Spock is stuck with the Tenant Doctor, trying to figure things out, which eventually takes them to the Next Generation crew, and to the older version of Kirk....

The story doesn't entirely hold together, it feels like too much incident happening, without enough connections, the pace is too frantic, the music seems to be perpetually in climax. There's just way too much going on for the 28 minute running time. It feels like the edited highlights of a really amazing crossover. You find yourself wanting it to slow down so you can catch up. But there's a lot of cool stuff - Scotty trying to break into the Tardis, the Enterprise ramming a Dalek Saucer, or the Enterprise in hot pursuit of the Tardis. It is consistently inventive and surprising.

Another well known Mashup is *Wholock*, the Matt Smith Doctor gets together with the Benedict Cumberbatch Sherlock. It's only a few minutes, but quite well done. There's a lot of mashups out there, using various media and properties. Most of them are short: music videos and fake trailers are particularly friendly to Mashups, because the emphasis is on imagery, not narrative coherence. Typically, mashups aren't terribly long, it's one thing to improvise a conversation from snippets of dialogue, but it gets tougher the more extensive you get.

Mashups are a tough genre, dating back to the VCR era in the 80s and 90s. They're major editing projects, but they're getting easier with the availability of DVD and electronic media as sources, and computer generated imaging which allows you synch and balance sound and dialogue, and even lift and place moving images against different backgrounds, or edit figures together. Basically the more of a library you have, the more you can do things with it.

CREW: *Produced by Rick Kelvington and Paul Sibard, Directed by Rick Kelvington.*

&&&

2011 - A SURVIVOR'S TRIANGLE, (108 minutes, FanRant Productions, Florida)

The first major effort from FanRant Productions. Originally released as ten minute segments, and then later compiled into a full film. It starts off prosaically with a mother, Margaret, and daughter, Jessica arguing. It seems that the daughter, Jessica, doesn't like the man, Robert, in her mother's life. She's got a point, he's creepy and dangerous, and there's something very, very wrong about him and his influence over Margaret.

Robert turns out to be the Master, played by Jeffrey Breslauer. Breslauer doesn't bother with an accent. He plays the Master low key and disturbing. His version of the Master is a competent, respected professional, who, once the work day is done, goes home and calmly beats his wife. Regularly. The overtones of a domestic violence household, the hanging tension, the sense of menace and brutality just waiting to happen, add to the proceedings.

Unfortunately, it's one of those things where you strike a chord, but aren't quite sure where to go with it. Having established a seriously disturbing Master, the character doesn't really seem to have any particular ambition. Sure, eventually he springs some sort of plot, but it feels almost perfunctory.

The Doctor shows up, played by John Reid Adams. He connects with Jessica played by Kara Saadet Shwarz. Then he and the Master make speeches at each other, and nothing much happens. Later on, there are zombies, sort of, but they're still making speeches at each other.

Too much 'serious dialogue' and not enough stuff happening. John Reid Adams, who plays the Doctor, is stiff in this one. His performance in *Theosilv Burning* is much better. It may be the melodramatic quality of the script that constrains him, or maybe he hasn't quite found the character.

There's some genuine effort at production design, and a very nice Tardis console. One of the highlights was shooting and editing various locations for the Tardis interior which give a sense of how immense the Tardis interior is. This is something the original show, in its classic or new version, often had difficulty conveying.

Overall, the whole seemed slightly less than the sum of its parts. Breslauer's Master is strong, Adam's Doctor is tolerable, and the rest of the cast are solid. It's entirely competently done. It's possible that it's just not clicking for me.

The end credits suggested that it would be followed up by a story called Infestation, but as nearly as I can tell, the sequel was actually Theosilv Burning.

CAST: John Reid Adams - The Doctor; Kara Saadet Schwarz - Jessica Ridgemond; Jeffrey Breslauer - The Master; Margaret Ledford - Gwen Ridgemond; Robert Cervera - Manny the Janitor; Darryl Baldwin, Mary Penate, Danielle Schuchman, Beatrice Allen, Amber Crawford, Ryan Donaldson, Natasha Gilreath, Dominick Pfefferkorn, Bunny Foofoo, Shu Shu Sanders - Crazies.

CREW: John Reid Adams - Script; John Reid Adams & Peter Gould - Executive Producers; Harrison Biswas & Brian Zazzara - Producers; Brian Zazzara - Director of Photography; Peter Gould - Second Unit Director, Editor; Darryl Baldwin - Stunt Coordinator; Floyd Adams & John Reid Adams - Set Pieces; Jake Black - Boom Operator; Daniel 'Shade' Seiser - Location Lighting; Danielle

Schuchman & Tammy Bowman - Make Up; Ashley Lyons & David Weise - 3D Tardis Opening Sequence modelers; Baffour Annor - Composition/Rendering; 3D Title Credits modeling and rendering - Jackson Tejada; Special Visual Effects - Capeda Digital, a Capeda Productions Company; Russell Cardinal - Location Manager; Lyn Cherowbrier - Production Assistant; Special thanks to Lyn, Kara, Jeff, Pete, Robert, Margaret, Darryl, Harry, Brian, Dad, Mom, Greg, Russell, Paul McGann, Sydney, Verity, RTD, Toby, James, Tony, Rob, Steve Moffat, Murray, Fans, G-Star School of the Arts, Filmed on location in Southwest Ranches, Florida.

&&&

2012 – THE MYSTERY OF RORRIM (25 minutes, Lincolnshire, UK)

Spencer Kennedy is the first black actor to play a fan Doctor, preceding Jevocas Green by about six months. They Mystery of Rorrim is a near meta-adventure. The Doctor has this feeling he's being watched all his life. This leads to a pursuit and interrogation of a Dalek, which gives up the name Rorrim. With this clue, the Doctor follows the name through time and space, meeting a strange man on an odd planet and trading a small mirror for a small mirror. The mirror contains coordinates to a house the Doctor's future self bought for him, which contains a room full of mirrors, and a surprising discovery.

The Kennedy Doctor is probably the most flamboyant ever, his hairstyle and wardrobe beating Colin Baker's senseless. The production values are impressive. The performances aren't bad, they have a police box and Tardis console. But the story feels kind of slight, and it feels like it ends too soon. But it's not clear where it could go after the final scene. Produced by Crow's Eye Productions, which seems to specialize in period costume videos.

CAST: Spencer Kennedy – The Doctor; Bryony Roberts – Alice Almond; Peter Halse – Dalek; Charlie Massey – Dalek Voice; Neil

Parker – *Beachcomber; Estella Platts – Abigail; Nick Loven – Surprised camera man.*

CREW: *Nick Loven – Director; Rick Everson – Script; Pauline Loven – Producer &Costumes; Jo Read – Additional Costume; Emma Kennedy – Doctor's Wardrobe; Luke Maxwell & Oliver White – Sound; Tim Walker & Annie Walker – Music; Set Design and Construction – Peter Halse; Toni Foley – Graphic Desig.*

&&&

2013 –UNTIMELY DEATH (35 minutes, Lincolnshire, UK)

The second outing of Spence Kennedy as the Doctor for Crow's Eye Productions. This is a more conventional adventure, although the Kennedy Doctor's wardrobe and hairstyle is outre as ever. The Doctor detects tears in space and time, and seeks out the source. This leads him to a 19th century fancy ball, which is invaded by UNIT forces and The Master. It seems that the Master has escaped prison with a Time Scoop, a crude time manipulation device. Now he wants the Doctor's Tardis.

This time the companion, Alice, played by Bryony Roberts actually has a role and dialogue beyond following the Doctor and asking questions. There's space allowed for other characters to perform, including the Master, William and the beachcomber from the previous episode.

Once again, very high production values, very good costumes and solid performances, with 32 credited extras. The visuals range from space-scapes, to scenes in the Tardis, a futuristic prison, the 19th century ball and mansion grounds.

The most interesting part is a five minute post credit scene with Alice, six months after departure as she reflects on her time with the Doctor –equal parts trauma and adventure, which leaves her feeling dislocated from normal life, and ends with her deciding to find and travel with the Doctor again.

CAST: *Spencer Kennedy – the Doctor; Bryony Roberts – Alice Almond; Ben Poole – The Master; Neil Parker – Beachcomber; Ad Snow – William; Sophie Kamal – Lady Augusta;.*

CREW: *Nick Loven – Director & Music; Rick Everson – Script; Pauline Loven – Producer/Costumes; Jo Sullivan – Dresser; Lindsay Martin, Sophie Eagle, Jess Tandy and Anita Cudbertson – 18th century hair, make-up and wigs; Lucia Staniaszek, Luke Maxwell, Reuben Furlong – Music & Sound; Peter Halse – Set Design and Cosntruction; Avril Sanderson – Period Set Dressing;*

&&&

2013 - BESIEGED (95 minutes, Scotland)

Doctor Who meets *Aliens* in an extraordinarily ambitious and polished ninety-five minute production, available as either a two television hour episodes, or a single feature film. In addition, there are no less than four prequel shorts, and a couple of half hour 'making of' documentaries.

Perhaps too fast paced, things get lost in the headlong rush. Such as the Doctor. This one is much more *Aliens* than Doctor Who. Perhaps with a dash of species 462 from *Star Trek: Voyager*. It seems that in the far future, a mad scientist on an interstellar research vessel manages to pierce the dimensional barrier, catapulting them into an organic universe of evil. The Doctor gets caught up in things of course. It turns out that this organic universe treats the interlopers as an infection, and so the human crew begins to be infested with 'Alien' monsters, as the Doctor and his companions try to find their way out of the situation. It moves fast, it's fairly gripping, and there are genuine moments of claustrophobia and tension.

On the positive side, excellent production values, notably the locations, spaceship sets, the costumes, the alien planet. Excellent CGI for the Aliens, who are pretty much straight out of the Ridley Scott/James Cameron movies. The cinematography is effective. It's fast paced, and frantic. There are genuine sets, and if some of it looks sparse and bare bones, I've seen worse in commercial productions.

There was apparently an impressive monster costume, but sadly, it wasn't used as effectively as it could have been. That's the problem sometimes when you're basically running on a shoestring, there isn't the time or the money or the energy or maybe just the creativity to get that extra bit that moves you from good enough to brilliant. This was good enough to be a commercial direct to video B-movie. Strip out the copyright infringements and elements, and you could see this showing up on DVD or Netflix or some streaming channel

Where it breaks down for me is with the character of the Doctor, and I think that's both in the script and the actor. Essentially, the Doctor is an eccentric, a charismatic, unconventional personality. That doesn't come through here, Hendries Doctor is too low key; he doesn't really stand out. That's a problem, because, these sorts of films, or the official series for that matter, stands or falls on the character of the Doctor. The Aliens elements and story pacing really overwhelm the Doctor, he gets a bit lost in the unfolding crisis. That's tough. There's always the risk of the adversary running away with the story.

Oddly enough, in the prequel shorts, Hendries does much better at developing his Doctor and his relationship with his companion. The scenes of Hendries Doctor wandering through a convention are sublime and funny. It may be that Hendries Doctor, like Davison, is a bit too low key for the story, a different story might have allowed him to shine. The shorts are worth watching. Indeed, the sheer volume of material surrounding Besieged, the prequel shorts, the trailers, the making of documentaries, actually adds to the watchability of the production. You get drawn into it all in a way that a simple standalone movie doesn't. *Besieged* isn't just an adventure, but a kind of conglomeration.

Still at the end of the day, it's Doctor Who versus *Aliens*. That's just cool.

CAST: *Ryan Hendrick – The Doctor; Jennifer Byrne – Lydia; Natalie Clark – Ade; Stephen Clyde – Cooper; Calum Cormack – Captain Mulgrew, Frankie MacEachen – Lt Ryder; Andrew Forest – Lambert; John Love – Brett Jones; Robert Radcliffe & Bill Murdoch – Professor Erobus; Karen Bartke – Jessica Myles; Vivien Taylor – Nurse Brown; Hamish Willson – Dr Hiller; David Newman, Neil Holmes, Urszula Kocol, Chris Pickering, David McKeitch, Mark Boggis; Charlie McGarry & Will Carlyle – Marines; Evonne Beardsworth, Hayley Rankine, John McShane, Marie McCallum & Gary Cullen – Scientists; Bri McEnroe – Xenomorphs; Fletcher Mathers – Computer Voice.*

CREW: *Ryan Hendrick – Writer/Producer; Lauren Lamarr – Director; Neil Meffan – Associate Producer; Stephen J Sinclair, Pete Harper & Iain Thompson – Directors of Photography; Ryan Hendrick & Urszula Kocol – Editors; Jacki Clark – Art Director; Evonne Beardsworth – Production Coordinator; Heather Jane Winship – 1ˢᵗ AD; Elizabeth McCann – Costumes; David Newman – Set Builder; Paul Reeves & Vanessa May Dolphin & Joe Gibson – Visual Effects; Richard Brookes & Jon Gransden – Title Sequence; David McKeitch & Ryan Lindsay – Sound; Gary Somerville, Nina Blake, Debbie Harper, Ashley Thomson & Rachel Gallacher – Make-Up Artists; Joanne Ferrie, Davie Green, Neil Foulis, Gary Cullen & Christianne MacArthur – Art Assistants; Colin Nicolson & Campbell McLeod – Unit Drivers; Suki McGregor, James Fry, Kristian Andrews, Matt & Bracher – Special Thanks.*

&&&

2014 - THILOSIV BURNING (38 minutes, FanRant Productions, Florida)

Also from FanRant Productions (John Reid Adams and David Zuckerman) is a more modest production than a *Survivor's Triangle*, but also a more effective piece.

They've toned down the portentousness, and have just focused on telling a good story. It opens with the Doctor running through an alien forest, ranting at unseen beings. Entities from another universe are wedging into ours, leaving the Doctor with a memories of worlds simultaneously dead and alive. It's a shorter story, smaller cast, smaller overall. It's less ambitious in production, no hordes of zombies for instance. Yet it works better.

Its strengths are a much faster pace, a more intriguing story and a much more confident performance by John Reid Adams as the Doctor. I wasn't thrilled with Adam's performance in a *Survivor's Triangle*, but here Adam's version of the Doctor comes into his own here, passionate, quirky and confident. His Doctor is a bit rumpled, with a five o'clock shadow and wrinkled overcoat. But he's intense, witty, eccentric and compassionate by turns.

What may be pulling John Reid Adams performance together is his companion, Chelsea Taylor Leach, played by Jessica Ridgemond. Her character is smart, fast and sometimes sarcastic. Leach and Adams have excellent rapport and they bounce off each other nicely

The Tardis console is still intact, but it's been visibly wedged into someone's garage. It's not at all terrible, but if you're watching for it, it's obvious. Still, there's enough of a set, the actors commit strongly, and the shots are focused enough that it works. Beyond that it seems to have been shot in local parks and woods. This is enhanced by 'in computer' effects - the alien world is depicted by changing the colour balance on the woods. Reverb adds menace to the invaders from another dimension. This really is a textbook for telling a good story with limited resources. It's carried by a good script and good performances.

The end credits indicated that there would be a third, but it doesn't seem to have materialized, which is disappointing, because I would have liked to see more from Adams and Leach.

CAST: *John Reid Adams - The Doctor; Chelsea Taylor Leach - Jessica Ridgemond; Sam Waters - The White Guardian; Lyn Adams, Alicia Ferrell, Alison Spruill - The Entities.*

CREW: *Producers & Directors - John Reid Adams and David Zuckerman; Written by John Reid Adams; Director of Photography, Editor - David Zuckerman; Lighting - Kaiel Eytle & Allen Cheesman; Props - John Reid Adams; Audio - Chelsea Taylor Leach; Visual Effects - Brandon Dorn; Tardis Console - Michael Mills, John Reid Adams, Peter Gould, Alison Ferrell, Nolan Moon, Sam Falco and Edward John Foeller.*

&&&

2015 - LUCKY THIRTEEN: EYE TO EYE (30 minutes, South Carolina)

This is a thoroughly American version of Doctor Who. This version of the Doctor, played by Jon Dondero speaks with a laconic North Carolina accent, and a laid back, untroubled attitude. It's an odd portrait of the Doctor, since we're used to a more overt eccentricity. Dondero's Doctor isn't really overt with his eccentricity, he's just quietly strange.

Unlike a lot of fan films, this one has a genuine sense of humour. Garret Mooneyham plays Richard Morgan, an everyman, a regular guy, a bit husky, a bit hairy, but fundamentally ordinary, and comfortably seated in his own life. Indeed, the film is really shown from his perspective. We meet him having a good time at a bar, and then just wandering home along deserted streets. It's a really nice sequence of shots that grounds the character.

Then the Doctor shows up, and his life starts to get steadily crazier as thing move from 'dealing with a weird but harmless guy' to 'inflicted with a really annoying eccentric' to 'Hey, this is a real alien invasion.'

The alien invasion is represented by some fairly decent CGI Robots.

I found it a bit slow, and I could have lived without the shower scene. But, as I've said, genuine sense of humour, and it successfully transplants the sensibilities of the British show into American culture. They were working on a second episode, Artificial Insanity, but it's not clear if it was ever released.

CAST: *John Dondero - The Doctor; Garret Mooneyham - Robert Morgan; Nev Kelly - The Preist; Jon Kingsley, Carolyn Kingsley, Rebecca Sweet, Erica Meares, Nick Hartley, Michael Davis, Shield Brakker, Chauntal McCoy, Melanie Burton, Sarea Kelly, Maggy DePersin, Danny Phoenix & Jordyn Kirkland - Atraxi #1 13;*

CREW: *Directed by Charles 'Torch' Baldwin; Written by Garret Mooneyham; Produced by Dave Harlequin; Executive Producer - Dave Harlequin; Associate Producer - Chris Baldwin; Digital/Visual Effects by 13th Floor EFX; Visual Effects Coordinataor - John Dondero; Director of Photography - Jordan Bradley; Assistant Director - Dave Harlenquein, 2nd Unit Director - John Dondero, 1st Unit Camera - Jordan Bradley, Earnest P. Eich IV & Nev Kelly; 2nd Unit Camera - John Dondero, Jon Kingsley, Emily Gilbert; Lighting Technician - Jordan Bradley & Tommy Hines; Production Sound Mixer - Tommy Hines; Utility Sound Technician - Dave Harlequein; Utility Sound - David Largeteau; Boom Operators - Tommy Hines, Dave Harlequein & David Largeteau; Film Editor - John Dondero, Story Editor - Dave Harlequin; Set Decoration - Hannah Scott & Jon Kingsley; Production Drivers - Adam York, Nev Kelly & Chris Baldwin; Craft/Location - Ricky McWaters; Production Assistants -*

Nev Kelly, Emily Gilbert, Adam York, Erica Meares, Hannah Scott, Jordyn Kirkland, Mike Mayew & Ryan Reese. Special Thanks to Jada & Everone with ConCarolinas, Ashley Bell & Everyone with ValhallaCon, Tod Patton and Everyone with ConNooga; Jade Woodruff and Everone with AmeliaCon; Valentine Wolfe and Everyone with Gaslight Fantasia; Nev Kelly, the 'Real MVP' of this production; Santiago Cirilo, Daphne Reeder, Angela Pritchett, Ricky McWaters, Jaysen Buterin, Marius Riley, Manny Mac, Gallifrey Pirate Radio, Cinema Slasher dot-com, Sun & Moon Studios, the Rabbit Hole, Zoe's Coffee House, Freeman's Pub.

CHAPTER 17 – WHERE TO FROM HERE

THE GREENSCREEN KIDS

Whoville is a different world, nowadays. For the BBC's Doctor Who, the wilderness years are over, at least for now. For over fifteen years now, the Doctor has been a certifiable hit, despite a few ups and downs, a worldwide phenomenon, with spin offs, merchandise, and bona fide theatrical events. I watched Capaldi's debut, *Deep Breath* on an IMAX screen surrounded by adoring fellow fans.

It's a different world for fan films, too. Many of the great fan films were driven by the fact that the show was off the air, or in some kind of limbo. They were inspired by the gaps in the show, by the empty spaces and the missing pieces.

Now there's a new generation of fan films that are driven by the fact that the show is now alive and famous. Hell, there's a generation of fans coming up, for whom the new Who has been on the air and in production their entire life, or most of it. They have no idea the Wilderness years were even a thing. A lot of them weren't even born. That just blows me away.

Today you can watch entire seasons on streaming services, collect the DVDs or Blu-Rays. You can assemble a complete collection of Doctor Who going back to an Unearthly Child and complete your collection with no less than five full spin off series.

You can assemble a set of sonic screwdrivers, and hang your Christmas tree with Daleks, or buy a Tom Baker scarf. Back in the day, you had to knit your own scarf and build your own merchandise. Now, you can fill a department store with stuff.

The Doctor isn't just big, it's available in an unheard of way. There's more Who around in more ways than there ever was before.

There are more fans; there are more fanatical fans, and more platforms and opportunities for fannishness.

And there are more people more willing to make fan films for a live show, lots more.

A hell of a lot more.

It's not the absence that inspires, but the presence. It's the immediacy and urgency that motivates.

Some of the old motivations are still there. Every time there's a changing of the guard, as one well established Doctor starts to leave, there are a lot of people who think "Wouldn't it be fun to play the next Doctor?" That's inspired a lot of films. And fan films have inspired more film makers.

But there are new motivations, new opportunities.

We talked about how Audio recording and Super 8 film opened doors, or how Camcorders and Videocassette players shaped fans and fandom and birthed the fan film movement. But that wasn't the end, not by a long shot.

The technological revolution that underlies production has been gathering momentum all along. Cameras have gotten better and cheaper, more versatile, smaller and easier to handle. The gap between professional and semi-professional equipment gets narrower and narrower. Editing software has become computerized; it's gotten more user friendly. There's no more working with little snippets of film. Now the professionals are all editing online on their desk tops, and there are commercial and even free versions of their software available to any user, even to precocious kids with laptops.

Computer generated imagery and effects have undergone revolutions. It used to be that you had to build a Dalek or a Police Box, that there had to be research to find the specifications, an investment of time and work, and materials to have your Tardis console and control room.

You can still do it physically, but it's easier now that all the specifications are online, there are YouTube Tutorials, builders groups sharing tips and information. It's a hell of a lot easier.

But you don't even have to, not anymore.

Now? All you need now is a laptop and a greenscreen.

Teenagers literally have their own greenscreens now, they do compositing and 3D animation, and superimpositions and everything else. People set up greenscreens in their living rooms and garages. It's amazing.

Music? You can compose on your laptop. Or access, sample and arrange from an internet of music. You can rip music now straight from the television show, and rearrange it to your heart's content.

Hell, you can even borrow visual effects from the television show. You can incorporate a hell of a lot of apparent production value with very little effort, or actual new material.

Something that twenty or thirty, something that even ten years ago, took a small army of people working together.... Now it can be done by one sufficiently obsessive kid with a good computer deck and some cheap software, and access to the original material.

It used to be that even doing one was a herculean effort. A lot of fan films existed as single productions, people working their ass off and in the end deciding that one is enough. It was a minority that did more than one. And a tiny minority that created a body of work.

Now, once you've invested in the software, the set up, the learning curve and work to do one, it just gets easier. You can do a series. It's still an incredible amount of work, but the landscape has been rearranged.

Meanwhile, the very environment has changed. YouTube, Dailymotion, Vimeo all date back to only 2005. That's barely fifteen years ago, the same time that the show relaunched. When you think about it, the new Doctor Who and YouTube have literally grown up together.

These streaming sites have become giant clearinghouses for video. They're accessible, they're searchable. The bandwidth has increased to astonishing levels, you can watch entire movies and television series on YouTube. Legal and illegal downloads in the fast five or six years have grown exponentially.

In the old days, there was an entire culture of copying by hand, trading or video tapes from person to person, or having to travel to conventions where films were shown or available to buy or borrow. It was a laborious process.

Now, with these it's all but instantaneous and massive.

It's also interactive in a way that we never really saw before. Not only do these fan films come together quickly, they're posted quickly. They're seen as soon as they're completed, and they can be seen by a worldwide audience. They're watched. The level of access is astonishing.

If you look at Barbara Benedetti's *Wrath of Eukor*, it's been around thirty years? How many people have seen it – ten thousand? Luke Newman's fan film, *Dawn of the Doctor,* has been seen by almost 200,000 people in less than three years. Even a run of the mill fan film might be seen by hundreds or thousands or tens of thousands of people. And if it's viral in any way, potentially the audience could be millions.

And they're not just releasing fan films. They're curating them. It used to be just the fan film itself, but if you look at Josh Snares, of DW2021, or Velocity, any number of current fan film productions, there are trailers, there are teasers, little documentaries, interviews, production or effects footage, making of snippets. You can literally see them get put together.

People comment. Historically, Art has always stood as a barrier between the artist and the audience, but with this world of instant access, that barrier can be a thin one. There's more feedback, and more positive feedback, faster and even instantaneously. That has to have an effect.

Literally, every single thing about the way that fan films have been made, have been seen, have been experienced in the last ten years or so, has changed in utterly astonishing ways, has changed profoundly.

I find that amazing.

The result is an utter explosion of '*Young Doctor Who.*'

Suddenly there is this wave these films by young adults, teenagers or even pre-teens in some cases. Some are not old enough to drive, some are not old enough to shave, but there they are, waving around department store Sonic Screwdrivers like Harry Potter's wands, regenerating in flashes of light, dashing around CGI sets.

The way fans come together has changed – with El Cheapo and Timebase, it was groups of fans, little fan clubs and film enthusiasts, meeting physically, deciding to work together to accomplish something collectively that they couldn't on their own. That's not really valid any more.

A lot of old fan films started because someone brought a camcorder to a meeting and people got enthusiastic. That's not really valid.

The network of fan clubs, of tape trading, that community doesn't exist in the same way.

That becomes a challenge. Film making was always a collective thing, you need, or you used to need a lot of people to come together to make a film.

Except you don't any more. One, or one or two, sufficiently precocious and driven teenagers or young adults could to it.

But here's the thing, the way they'll do it has changed.

As always, productions are defined as much by their by their limitations as by their opportunities.

You can do a lot with CGI and editing software, but there are things they can't do. They can't build physical props. They can't build sets, or consoles, or police boxes. That takes time and money and labour.

You can pose in front of a greenscreen and act all you want. You can even composit people to be there with you. But you can't interact with it. Even Hollywood films find they need a few physical objects in greenscreen world for the actors to touch, pick up, move towards or away from or around. You can CGI a Tardis console, but you can't actually operate it, or move around it.

The new productions often suffer from lack of locations - we don't usually see impressive ruins, 900 year old churches, submarine museums. Mostly it's just the local neighborhood - which makes sense if you don't have a driver's license. Or if your crew is basically just you.

We don't see elaborate props or costumes. Casts are restricted to a few friends who couldn't get away fast enough.

The acting, the writing are typically meh. CGI and computer editing allows you to do amazing things quickly, accomplishing what it would have taken a bunch of technicians a long time. But it doesn't create or facilitate certain kinds of skills.

What we have is a situation where technology makes it incredibly easy to do certain things which were once incredibly hard and time consuming, and makes it easy to get their films out there. But doesn't necessarily help them to do anything else, with the result that things often don't get done. Or they don't get done very well.

That actually hurts. You end up having to shoot around your limitations. No good locations, you shoot around the back yard, or composit in CGI. If you can't do a good or even poor monster costume, you work around that. No choreography, no real capacity for action, well then you get a lot of people standing around talking about feelings, having very serious conversations and being important and portentous. Or you have ridiculously low-fidelity runarounds. What you often have is a desire, and the software, to tell a Doctor Who story, but not the actual ability. They try anywhere.

There's a young YouTuber, Jerry Within, B.I.G. productions, who has created DW Fan Film Bingo, a chart of the endless clichés that fan films fall into. Well, he's got a point, and the clichés are there.

There are a lot of films out there that maybe shouldn't have been made, or perhaps shouldn't be circulated. But then, that's always been the case.

I sound like I'm about to shake my fist and tell those damned kids to stop horsing around and get off my lawn. Kids these days dammit, it's all easy, we had to work hard, so we made good films in my day. Yeah right.

I'm honestly not sure what to make of it all, this explosion of young talent. I'm not sure what they make of it, whether it will lead anywhere, or what they'll do with it.

But my point is that technology and culture shaped the way we made and experienced fan films at any stage, and right now, technology and culture are reshaping fan films, introducing opportunities which offer possibilities and limitations that have to be overcome.

The truth is that nobody starts out as experts or professionals, no matter what field you're in, everyone has to learn, everyone stumbles as they learn, and early efforts are usually embarrassing. That's just life.

The reality is that commercial productions will inevitably be much more polished, because they have tens or hundreds of millions of dollars, and literal armies of technicians to throw at a project.

And yet, commercial productions fail all the time, they end up being insultingly stupid, or lazy or uninspired or unoriginal, and we walk out of movie theatres or shut off the television feeling uninspired or let down.

Well you know what, if they're going to swallow a hundred million dollars and drop a steaming load, for sure, hold them to account.

Some teens or twenty-somethings put on a video with wooden acting, or awkward papier mache, or a dodgy home computer CGI effect, I'm inclined to look past these flaws and missteps to see if there's something interesting or worthwhile, and often there is.

And sometimes, the fact that a bunch of young people with no money and no resources can somehow create something that is far closer to the quality of a BBC Doctor Who production, or might even exceed it, that's something to be impressed by, something to celebrate and something to search out.

So the greenscreen kids are out there, these new generations of fan films and fan film makers. There'll be a lot of garbage. There'll be a lot of monologues, endless, tedious, portentous monologues. There'll be multi-doctor stories with legions of teenagers waving sonic screwdrivers at each other. Angst over lost companions and the tragic fate of being immortal and being able to travel anywhere in time and space.

But perhaps something more?

Still, there's a lot of potential here, and it's worth canvassing a few representatives of this brave new generation.

Josh Snares is a young fan Doctor with approximately forty videos of varying length to his credit. Snare's video output is immense, he plays the Doctor in fan films, but he also does animations and reconstructions, lately he's doing a lot of fan documentaries. He's obsessed with Who, talented, and follows his star.

As a Doctor, he has too much baby fat in his face, so his features aren't really distinctive, and his acting style is to just step on and draw out every word. When he's on, he's on. When he's not, he's like a little boy trying on grown up clothes. Snares seems to lack the single mindedness of Newman, which suggests that he might be a bit better socialized. A much less effective Doctor, but perhaps more unpredictable.

Unlike Newman, Snares didn't build himself a Tardis console. Instead he built a greenscreen, and has shown remarkable technical sophistication in compositing himself onto the Tardis bridge, and convincingly fakes the operation of a nonexistent console. A CGI console goes all the way back to the Alliance, but Snares ramps it up to the next level. It's actually convincing, and you have to look carefully to realize he's not on the actual bridge of the Tardis.

Another fascinating hat trick that Snares pulls off is SuperWhoLock. A series of relatively short videos in which Doctor Who, Sherlock and Supernatural cross over with each other, with Snares taking the roles of the Doctor, Sherlock Holmes and Sam Winchester, all composited in the room and arguing with each other. Credibly, despite taking on all three roles, Snares manages to give each character something of a distinctive voice, and his editing is sharp enough that it feels like they're all in the same room arguing with each other at the same time.

Snares is also notable for animating some of the lost episodes, notably Evil of the Daleks, and the Daleks Masterplan. This isn't conventional animation, but rather, what Snares does is take elements from within the telesnaps, such as people, and move them around the screen. It doesn't really simulate live action, but it creates a more lively story.

Currently, he seems to be deeply involved in a series of fan documentaries of particular serials and particularly lost episodes, that are compelling.

All in all, there's much more of a sense of Snares experimenting and having fun with his obsession, he seems to explore more.

Another change of pace is the work of Thomas Rees-Kay. Rees-Kay is another technical whiz, with his own greenscreen and computer wizardry. He manages to composit himself nicely into the bridge of the Tardis. He often uses quite good visual effects. And like Newman and Snares, he's fairly cunning about ripping the music from the actual series to add production value. He also seems to own a real police box shell.

Thomas' thing seems to be an at times uncanny rendition of Matt Smith. He's got Smith's erratic twitchiness as the Doctor down pat. Rees-Kay, like Newman and Snares, tends to overdue the melodrama and bombast in his stories. The limitations of being largely a one man show tend to show up again and again. But he also has more humour, or capacity for humour. His short, *Baking With the Doctor* is brilliant. Rees-Kay's body of work consists of a several dozen pieces. Most of them are short. His longest stories are probably no more than ten or twenty minutes.

Even then, these barely scratch the surface. There's a world, even a community out there of adult, teen and even pre-teen Doctor Who creators. There's Rob Baines with Robcam productions, Rob Banks with Johny Who Productions, DDK productions, the DoctorofWho with William Yates, Not-so-Amazing studios, Tricorum Productions, checkm8productions, the Time Agent series, Nathan Carter and his NTC pictures, Confused Adipose with Jack Street productions and many more. A collection of young men and women who are astonishingly prolific and polished.

The landscape has changed profoundly, in terms of what can be done and is done, and it will almost certainly continue to change. This new generation of adolescent Doctor Who fans and film makers often falls short but, but perhaps that's not the point. It's their world now.

They're doing something they love, producing something meaningful to them and others. They've crossed that barrier from being a passive audience, to active creators trying to tell their own stories, and they've found a community that supports them.

Reviews: The Little Red Doctor (2013-2022)

Dynamic Works 2012 – Series 1 to 4

If you go to YouTube and type in *"Doctor Who fan films"* or any variation on that, one of the first places it will take you to is DW2012, the Little Red Doctor, Luke Newman, and his gargantuan body of work.

Back in the day, Stalin said *"Quantity has a quality all its own."* His point was sheer numbers, sheer volume and intensity can be decisive in and of itself. That applies here, with DW2012, the total amount of production is simply stunning 'five seasons,' 36 episodes mostly from 20 to 60 minutes, (including remastered and double and a triple length episodes) - effectively 39 episodes, plus 14 minisodes. Plus a series of at least ten short audio stories. Taken all together, this is a unique body of work, comparable to any of the modern Doctors. There you have Stalin's 'quality.'

But it's not just quantity, it's a good series overall. There are many episodes that are watchable, some episodes that are brilliant, and even in weak spots there's usually something interesting. The series is bolstered by excellent performances by Dokka Chapman, Megan Shirley, Jay McGuinness and Luke Newman himself. Despite lack of resources and missteps, the series is consistently ambitious.

Add to that literally dozens of teasers, trailers, previews, production diaries, video-logs, bonuses, documentary pieces, set builds and demolishings, prop manufactures and regular social media updates, all of which basically amount to curating all of this in detail. This is a just stunning body of work.

Even with all the advantages of modern technology, camcorders, computers editing and visual effects software, this is still an astonishing achievement. When you think about it - in the 80s, Barbara Benedetti made four stories, in the 90s, Nick Scovell and Rupert Booth both managed roughly half a dozen stories in episodes or stage plays. The Professor What adventures got to nineteen, but they were mainly short, and produced over a twenty-year period.

Each in turn were utterly remarkable for their time, but now, almost commonplace. There are a lot of modern fan film series that go several episodes that are framed and run as actual series, or amount to epic feature film length.

But even by these modern standards which have become quite prolific, Luke Newman's body of work is amazing, both in terms of sheer volume, of persistence over time and quality.

Look, making even one fan film is extraordinarily hard. It's not just clowning around in front of a camera for twenty minutes (well some are).

But an ambitious production involves writing a script, recruiting actors, accessing camcorders and microphones, rehearsals, lighting, finding and moving to locations, or building sets, sourcing or building props and costumes, coordinating complex shoots, editing the footage, fixing sound, adding music, titles and visual effects. Doing one really good film can be challenging.

Doing a few full length ones or a series of shorter ones, is damned near herculean. Luke Newman built a legacy that can go toe to toe with the Classic 80s Doctors, or their 21st century counterparts. You should be in awe, I am.

It's doubly impressive when you consider that this isn't just a huge volume, but by and large, it is far better than it has any right to be.

Certainly there are shortcomings and no shortage of them. There are some laughably bad monsters or costumes, most of the cast are clearly late teens or young adults of the same age range, there are wooden performances, weak meandering episodes and dialogue that just runs on and on. DW2012 is not at the level of the professional BBC series.

But at the same time, it comes close enough often enough that the BBC with its millions of pounds and armies of trained professional should really be embarrassed at how narrow the gap is. The gulf is not nearly as wide as the disparity of resources should make it. That's a testament to Newman.

And while DW2012 isn't Doctor Who prime-time level, it would work fit in nicely on BBC2 Saturday morning children's and teen viewing content as *"Young Doctor Who"* on the same level as *"Young Sherlock"* or *"Young Indiana."* It would give *Sarah Jane Adventures* a run for its money.

This is triply impressive when you consider that Newman has done this very nearly single-handedly. In addition to starring as the Doctor, he often did double duty playing Sontarans, Sea Devils, Cybermen, evil Doppelgangers or steampunk alternate selves. There have been episodes where there were literally only two characters and he was both of them.

He's written the entire series, except for one episode by Megan Shirley, and some of the short tales. He's directed or co-directed most, done almost all the editing throughout, been camera operator, built sets, props and costumes, video effects and music.

He hasn't been entirely alone of course. Daniel J. Patton has been involved from the start, mostly credited with titles, intro and visual effects, but also providing the voice of K9 and occasionally appearing on screen.

Megan Shirley and Chloe Naughton have been key figures, both on camera and behind the scenes. Over time, he's accumulated a recurring list of contributors, actors who help out on set, production people who appear on camera. Elizabeth Kirk, Jay McGuinness, Dokka Chapman, Dominic G Martin, and so forth. An ensemble team has slowly assembled around him, on screen and off.

But when you look at the credits, or just watch the screen, it's very apparent just how much Luke Newman is the driving force for the series. This was not a bunch of fans coming together, this is Newman wanting to do it, and somehow managing to drag other people into his obsession. In terms of sheer omni-commitment, he's literally on the level of a Russell T. Davies or Steven Moffatt, a J. Michael Straczynski of *Babylon 5,* or Paul Donovan of *LEXX.* Even after handing over the role of the Doctor to Dominic G. Martin, and backing off a little in other departments, he's still pervasive in his presence and influence.

So who is Luke Newman?

He's a young man from Birmingham, who seems to have been obsessed with Doctor Who for much of his life. Fortunately, he's not been shy about his obsessions on YouTube and Social Media, so we know a bit about him.

This is a young man who built a succession of miniature playset Tardis consoles growing up, culminating in a full sized version out of cardboard. He eventually built an entire Tardis control room, complete with functioning console and electric wiring in a shed in the family back yard, tore it down and built another one. Supportive parents, definitely, but also a hell of a lot of dedication. And yes, the console and room was for his films, but no one puts that kind of work in unless they really really want to do the thing. In one of the video clips, he talks about the console room like a home away from home, a place he's clearly invested a lot of emotion in.

The console's instrument panel is extremely detailed, the switches actually switch, the levers yank, the drawer works and the rotor lights up and moves. That in itself is impressive. The space is cramped obviously; it's a good sized shed but still a shed.

Mainly though, it's a real physical space, for Newman and other actors to move around in and interact with, levers to pull, switches to flick, lights to glow, it's a thing you have to negotiate with, something that casts shadows and reflects light; not a greenscreen artifact where they have to remain in place. That's impressive, and it's a subtle but effective asset for the episodes.

Sometimes I wonder what inspires a person to decide to make a fan film or to play the Doctor, but in Newman's case, it seems inevitable. His path was a railroad track long before Dawn of the Doctor, although I suspect he never intended the journey to be so long or the ride to be so bumpy.

Hell, even before *Dawn of the Doctor*, he'd spent at least three or four years, back to 2008-2009, collecting action figures, building miniature sets, and eventually teaching himself limited stop motion to create Action Figure Adventures. These went up on YouTube, earning a following with stories like *The Lost Cyberman*, the *Redemption of Davros*, *Power of Ice* and *Night of the Doctor*.

They're mostly gone now, but I was able to track down a few. Some of the stop motion isn't too bad, it's the sort of thing you'd expect from an obsessed twelve year old, full of youthful fixation and persistence. I found other shots more interesting, like a tracking shot down a cardboard hallway, or a perspective shift. The films were amateurish of course, but the point was that I was watching a learning experience, Newman literally teaching himself cinematography on his play sets, learning how to frame a picture, learning how to do an establishing shot. Learning how to shake the camera for a dramatic scene, what angles worked, how to build tension and tell a story visually. In a sense, it was an education process that no one, perhaps not even Newman, noticed.

After a lot of action figure stories, he experimented with live action, doing a few shorts playing the Matt Smith Doctor. He came of age in the Matt Smith era, so Matt Smith's definitely his Doctor. Capaldi somewhat, but definitely Smith. You can hear Smith's voice in a lot of his early dialogue, and his shorts where he does a Smith co-splay mimic the body language.

Somewhere around 2013, all this youthful obsession coagulated into an idea for a Doctor Who fan film, *The Fall of the Doctor*.

It was an epic, which needed a preamble, a lot of backstory, before you got to it, so he in order to work out the Fall of the Doctor, he also had to work backwards, creating a framework of ideas, arcs and plot threads, until he got to a beginning, *Dawn of the Doctor*.

Basically, in 2013, Newman got the idea for, and worked out, what would essentially become a television novel, and he stuck with it from 2013 through 2018, producing four series and a movie. That's just a stunning accomplishment, more so because it was well done.

It's this giant television novel that really makes DW2012 stand out as an accomplishment.

The current incarnation of Doctor Who has seen a handful of Doctors, but mainly they operate on seasonal arcs. A bunch of individual one and two part stories, some of which have connecting threads culminating in a season finish, spanning anywhere from six to thirteen episodes. Newman's series have that quality. But they whole work collectively transcends it.

But Newman is also telling a much bigger story over his first four series and his movie, and it works. Wobbly episodes, rubbish costumes, weak sets, they just don't matter, because the overall story is so big. There's a massive investment in the Doctor, in all these continuing characters, these plot threads. This is the whole being far larger than the sum of its parts. In this sense it manages to go beyond the original series, to tell a bigger more engaging story, an epic that runs from *Dawn of the Doctor* to the *Fall of the Doctor.*

This scale and scope actually allows DW2012 to hold its own against the BBC Doctors. This is a body of work you could put alongside the real thing.

I often have to remind myself that a fan film is a team effort and that it's not just the Doctor. But it's also true that show and the fan films stand or fall on how effectively the actor inhabits that role, and not everyone manages it.

Newman makes a good Doctor, he's not the greatest fan Doctor, but he's capable and he knows what he's doing. Relatively slender in frame, Luke has a gaunt quality with well-defined bone structure. It gives his features a degree of maturity that is often missing in youth.

As an actor, he's serious and careful, so he manages to give his version of the Doctor some weight. And he is an actor, he knows his lines, delivers his dialogue, reflects it with his physicality and body language, and he works off the other actors in the scene. In this respect he's well ahead of a lot of his peers.

His range as an actor is limited; he's not nearly as fluid as his inspirations, Matt Smith, not as forceful as Capaldi. But he's smart enough to work within his range, and he can convey emotion - in the second series opener Days of Forgotten Past, he becomes increasingly despondent listening to messages from his friend Jess, doing no more than sitting quietly. You can see genuine pain growing as he listens to each voicemail. It's actually a hell of a performance, and conveyed simply sitting in a chair not saying a word. Mostly, he goes for deadpan, with side order of sarcasm.

The critical thing, though, is that he's got the gravitas for the role, he's not a kid playing at being the Doctor, he is "The Doctor." He's very much a Doctor, and his Doctor is a distinct character, both somber and mischievous.

On the production side, Newman knows what he's doing. The writing is generally competent within the boundaries of fan films, and you can see him developing as a writer as he goes along. He could have used a script editor, and perhaps some more time in the oven with some stories, but it's tolerable.

The stories don't have the flair or diversity of something like *Velocity* or the Booth or Benedetti adventures. In DW2012, I don't think I'm seeing the subtexts of *Velocity*, or the social commentary the BBC series was known for. There's nothing I'd call truly experimental or challenging, this is mainstream Doctor Who, heavily influenced by the Smith and Capaldi years, but drawing widely from both the new and classic series, but it's mostly delivered effectively. Basically, DW2012 is about telling stories, telling good stories and ultimately telling a very big story.

Newman makes good use of his Tardis set as a platform for dramatic effect, whether that's frantically flipping switches, arguing with people in the room, or the old classic, flinging yourself about while the camera shakes (don't knock it, it works). He makes an effort to find good locations to shoot in, and thanks to Daniel J. Patton, he's got some very good CGI. Very, very good CGI, as we'll see.

Technically, he's got it down. All those years of watching the Doctor on BBC, and doing action figure adventures, has paid off, as has working literally from the ground up, he was paying attention. He knows how to frame a shot, when to do close ups, how to keep the microphone out of the frame, mostly manages his sound.

In the first couple of series, he had a tendency to rip off Murray Gold's 'big damned hero' musical riffs. I can't say that's a bad decision, there's something bombastic to that scoring which can make something as prosaic as opening your mail seem like a gripping adventure. But I suspect that the BBC may have eventually started to make some noises, and in any case, eventually it wears out - people realize "Hey, this isn't really exciting, he's just opening his mail." The series shifted to a more custom, less blatant scoring as time went on.

These are blanket generalizations. Newman's body of work and his episodes span a decade and a huge number of productions.

That's hard to generalize. When your body of work runs almost forty stories over five or six years, it's hard to make a sweeping statement. He got steadily better over time, in literally every facet of film making. But even some of the earliest work is quite polished. He has some failures scattered through, but also some brilliant episodes like Glitch.

In all that time, he's going to evolve, his Doctor evolved, the productions and episodes evolved. Almost any criticism based on any episode can be rebutted in another episode.

The first series was Newman almost as a one man band, enlisting only one or two other people, at most, a little naive, but surprisingly efficient and competent through *Dawn of the Doctor*, *Whispers in the Woods*, *Blood Hunter* and *Nightmare Within*. Originally, the plan was eight episodes, but that turned out to be overwhelming. The only real collaboration was *Eternal Darkness*. The series ended as four episodes, with a late entry, *Nightmare Within* as a kind of bonus. But overall, it was clearly a success, or at least an accomplishment.

The second series did not go nearly as well. Newman had opted to go with a 'two doctor' set up - basically, his Doctor would find himself travelling with his own predecessor, played by Jay McGuinness, who had misplaced his Tardis. Together with a new companion, Lily Roberts played by Jessica Prestage, the three of them would bop through the Universe, having adventures, bantering and bickering. The Sea Devils, Cybermen and ultimately the Daleks would be back in increasingly big episodes, while in the background, there'd be an accumulating through line that something was terribly wrong with time.

It should have worked - the three body set-up had real potential, Jay McGuinness was a charismatic presence and he and Newman struck sparks off each other. Too many sparks unfortunately, there was a falling out, McGuinness left suddenly after the second episode. Jessica Prestage turned out to be a lovely person, but an utterly dire actress and also departed on the second episode. To salvage the season, Newman jettisoned some planned episodes, notably *Curse of the Mummy*, wrote a filler, *Dark Night of the Scarecrow*, brought back Chloe Naughton who seemed to have been a loyal friend, and enlisted Ryan Hennessy, who had appeared as a Doctor in *Eternal Darkness*, as the second Doctor to fill out the arc, and finished out with six episodes. I'm not sure if the plan was eight, or if the first series had lowered his ambitions. In the end, despite problems, it got done.

Newman came out of it all pretty dispirited, almost ready to quit, but soldiered on, intending to do one more season and then retire, passing the torch to the next Doctor.

In the first and second series, Newman was mostly influenced by the Matt Smith era, and that influence remained strong throughout in dialogue and story development. Capaldi didn't start to air as the Doctor until August 2014, when the second series was well under way, but there are signs, perhaps as early as *Scarecrow* of Capaldi's approach being influential. But equally clearly, as time went on, Newman and his Doctor evolved their own style.

In the third series, he was joined by Megan Shirley, who played the new companion, Megan Williams. Shirley turned out to be a formidable actress onscreen and a major presence, off, and her character developed rapidly in the third series, and fully matured in the fourth.

Kai Nelson also started participating in the shoots. Gradually, more people were getting involved both in front of and behind the camera. The third series tried for and managed eight full episodes and four minisodes, with a successful underlying arc. I think it's the first fully mature series, and perhaps the first one that went fully according to plan.

Bolstered by this, and his developing arcs, Newman continued to play the Doctor for a fourth series of eight episodes. The series arcs moved to the background, the ultimate villain had already been revealed. Instead stories moved back toward stand-alone episodes, with the Doctor and Megan confronting Daleks, Cybermen, the Silence, a rogue AI.

Megan Shirley steadily became a key player in production, and her character, Megan Williams grew from companion to partner, a force and personality in her own right And that lead to the movie in 2018, and beyond.

Following this, Newman decided to take down the first two series and redo them. I can understand this. You tend to be embarrassed by your early work, wincing at the mistakes you made before you knew better, the lost opportunities and frustrations of the things that went wrong. Writers are often tempted to fix their early work. I understand the temptation.

Considering how much work and aggravation is involved in doing these things, the idea that Newman would even consider literally re-making his first two series to be... insane, pathological, demented. This is being a glutton for punishment, or a lunatic, obsessive perfectionist.

So far, he only re-made and released four of the five episodes of the first series in 2019, and nothing since. Maybe he's still working on the rest, or maybe he woke up one day and went *"What am I doing?"*

But you know what this means? DW2012 has lore! It has an entire missing season, seven lost adventures and a missing component to the overall series narrative arc. For the record, here are the *"Lost Episodes"* -

Eternal Darkness, the Fiftieth Anniversary Special (November 23, 2013, 95 minutes) - *the original fourth episode of the first series. Technically, this was remade and remastered, but the original was a ninety minute epic that incorporated a lot of major fan Doctors who were active around 2013, so I think it qualifies. The story is essentially the same though.*

The Nightmare Within (March 22, 2014, 18 minutes) - *the fifth, final and shortest episode of the first series. An economical two-hander where the Doctor meets a little boy with supernatural gifts, an effectively creepy, oddly poignant episode.*

Days of Forgotten Past (August 16, 2014 - 49 minutes) - *the first episode of the second series. Featuring the death of Jess; the introduction of the new companion, Lilly, played by Jessica Prestage;*

the 'other' Doctor played by Jay McGuinness; and introduction of the Mirror Demon. The story is a bit meandering. The Demon is resolved too easily, the other Doctor shows up suddenly, it's like two smaller stories sandwiched together. Apart from that, excellent performances by Newman and McGuinness bouncing off each other, and a good sense of momentum.

Peril of the Unknown (August 30, 2014, 41 minutes) - The return of the Brigadier, a plot by the Sea Devils, the departure of Lily and the Other Doctor, all together in an engaging, fast moving, slightly flawed story. The principal weakness are the Sea Devils themselves, who are poorly rendered papier mache. The key incident – workers being killed when they find a mysterious hive, happens offscreen and is simply discussed later, robbing dramatic momentum. Apart from that, a lot to like, the big strength being the actions and interplay between Sarah Naughton and the two Doctors, and the antics of Jay McGuinness Doctor when left on his own.

Dark Night of the Scarecrow (October 15, 2014, 33 minutes) - The Doctor by himself in a cornfield, talking to a scarecrow, also played by Newman. Despite nothing much happening, it's authentically creepy and that moodiness almost carries it off. It's extremely reminiscent of the Capaldi episode, "Listen" which aired September 13, 2014. Overall, a failure, but better than it has a right to be Concludes with the return of Jess.

Destiny in Metal (April 18, 2015, 43 minutes) – A decaying Cyberman sends an unwilling Doctor and Jess back in time to save its race from extinction by advancing Cyberman technology in a complicated, ambitious and often genuinely funny story featuring four different kinds of Cybermen, all played by Luke Newman (albeit voiced by Daniel J Patton). Watch for a glimpse of a stop motion/action figure Cybercannon-man a little homage to his prior work with action figures. The Ryan Hennessy Doctor returns at the end.

Into the Mind (April 25, 2015, 29 minutes)- A 'ship in the bottle' episode, literally, set in and taking place almost entirely in *the Tardis control room, with some flashbacks and inserts to liven things up. The trouble is that the inserts are weak and don't do much, and since they're just memories, no real tension. Shortest episode of the second series, and perhaps the weakest. It's purpose is mainly to set up Dark times.*

Dark Times (May 9, 2015, 51 minutes) - *From the first episode on, the series 2 opening theme features the Tardis leaving Earth and spinning through space, passing through a field of Asteroids and a Dalek fleet. This is actually an Easter egg that pays off in the series finale. Davros and the Daleks invade Earth. Wacky hijinks ensue, old faces return, plot threads are resolved and the underlying arc lurches into the next series. Jess disappears early in the episode, and the two Doctors end up in different locations. The episode is relentlessly grim, Earth is literally burning, the air is full of cinders and ash, and a sense of fatalism is everywhere. Extremely well done.*

Along the way there are missing seven minisodes, notably *Tardis in Need,* an eight minute *'Children in Need'* special, with Daniel J. Patton as a future Doctor; *As One Chapter Closes* which covers the departure of the 'Other' McGuinness Doctor, and *Two Great Minds,* re-introducing the Hennessy Doctor, and a lead in for Into the Mind.

I don't know whether we'll ever see the lost episodes of Series 1 and 2 remade, or Newman following through on his threat to remake series 3.

We're promised a revised, re-created Series 2 for 2024. On the one hand, fan history is littered with failed and abandoned projects, and I think Series 2 and 3 are fine the way they are, flawed sure, but charming. On the other hand Luke Newman and company have an impressive track record, and if this is what they want, so be it.

Frankly, I'll agree some bits of Series 2 could stand to be tinkered with, despite their charms. Newman was still learning, there are structural issues in some of the stories, he was beset by various disasters, I can appreciate the urge to go back and do it again.

Dark Night of the Scarecrow and *Into the Mind* are both weak short pieces, they're bridging episodes where nothing really happens, and conceivably they could be rethought and redone better.

Days of Forgotten Past could stand to be restructured to merge the mirror demon story with the 2nd Doctor story, and build drama *Peril of the Unknown* could be improved with a three minute prologue scene to establish the monsters, and the monsters are actually pretty tosh paper mache. But otherwise they need little improvement.– there are also a lot of very nice things in these episodes. Criticisms aside, they're engaging, watchable and successful.

Nightmare Within is an effective piece. *Destiny in Metal* works and the dodgy Cyberman actually contribute the humour. *Dark Times* is a satisfyingly grim closer on its own terms.

The second series, overall, despite a couple of dodgy filler episodes holds up well. By no means is it a loss. The first and second series were overall strong and held together as entirely watchable. As much as a replacement series would be intriguing, it would be a shame to lose the original versions.

2019 again seemed to be a shaky year for DW2012 and Newman, between the transition to a new Doctor and new Doctor's stories and the quest to revisit old series. This was followed immediately by the disruptions of Covid, which shut everything down, and inspired an audio series of vignettes.

Maybe Newman's moved on from trying to Remaster his old stories, because in 2022, Series 5 finally begins after what's effectively a four year hiatus, and the Dominic G. Martin Doctor is taking the stage.

Apart from that, he's also branched out a bit. You can find his writing credits or other credits on other Who fanfilm projects, notably Fractured Timeline. His Tardis set has been used for other fan productions. In the peculiar world of Doctor Who fan films, the Little Red Doctor is a giant.

In the meantime, over the past decade, Luke Newman and DW2012 is really one of the most remarkable bodies of work in fan films today.

&&&

SERIES ONE REVISED (4 episodes)

DAWN OF THE DOCTOR, Series 1, Episode One, Original version September 28, 2013 / remastered version September 28, 2019 (54 minutes)

We open with the Doctor regenerating from an incarnation apparently wearing Capaldi's costume. There's some retcon here – in the original version, the Newman Doctor was wearing Matt Smith's togs, and tells Jess he's 1600 years old. That got adjusted, in *Scarecrow* the Doctor announces he's about 10,000 years old, and the concept is he's on his 39th regeneration.

It's a rough regeneration, as the Tardis messes up, crashes on Earth and the new Doctor staggers out and falls over in front of Jess, played by Chloe Naughton. Cue the eventual 'meet cute' banter and bickering, but it's actually engaging, the script is strongly influenced by Matt Smith's stories, you can almost hear Smith speaking these lines, and while Chloe Naughton is not the best actress, she's got charm, timing and a nice comic sense.

Anyway, Plot: Jess has phone problems, it gave her a painful hypersonic jolt, courtesy of International Electromatics. Her phone even fries the sonic screwdriver. Meanwhile, the Doctor is being watched by an evil CEO, Dickinson, who is actually a pawn of the Cybermen who are holding his daughter hostage. It turns out International Electromatics has been inserting lethal microchips into all sorts of appliances, as part of the usual evil Cyberman scheme. The Doctor figures things out a little too easily and the solution has a little too much technobabble, but otherwise it's well written, well-acted and well shot with a lovely series of twists and some nice CGI. It's an auspicious debut.

The original version was also fairly well done. To my recollection, the big difference was that in the Remastered version they've got an actual Cyberman costume, worn by Dale Smith, who normally plays the Brigadier. In the original version, Luke Newman was rather more short-handed, so he built and wore a Cyberman suit made of corrugated cardboard and duct tape painted silver... and it was the cutest thing ever.

Dickinson in the original version was played by a different actor, and the character wasn't given a daughter – he was just a jerk.

Newman's Doctor in the original version was considerably more bloodthirsty, he shows up on the Cyberman ship with a severed Cyberman head. It actually made him more fun.

&&&

WHISPERS IN THE WOODS, Series 1, Episode 2, Original October 12, 2013, Remastered October 26, 2019 (43 minutes)

On their first jaunt together, they end up back in 1897 (ignore the anachronistic phone booths). Hearing of people going missing in the forest, the Doctor senses an adventure and goes there. It turns out that there's a dimensional portal in the forest to the realm of the Wisps, mostly benign, but a really bad one has crossed over and is eating people.

There's some nice location work here, notably the forest, but also a set of ruins for the meeting with the Great Wisp, and an older street passing for 1897 London. The CGI is sparse but effective.

On the downside, this is one of the few episodes where Newman ventures outside his acting range, hamming it up a bit when he's tempted to sneak off on another tempting adventure, in the midst of his current adventure, and then when he gets caught. He's a bit silly, the script is trying way too hard to do the Matt Smith Doctor and it doesn't come off for Newman, he doesn't have Smith's lightness.

Apart from that, this is a nicely creepy episode, spooky in the right places and the right ways. The relationship between the Doctor and Jess develops nicely. Several plot-arc elements get laid down, first with the first appearance of mysterious portals, then when Jess gets bitten and poisoned by an alien plant, and finally when the Great Wisp gives the Doctor a peculiar fragment of stone with unearthly properties.

The differences between the original and remastered edition are small, generally, it's a matter of polish. One thing that's very apparent is that both Newman and Naughton look very visibly young in this first series. Naughton is still wearing braces. From original first to fourth series – a five year span, you can literally watch them grow up from teens to young adults.

Another interesting difference is that the first series is more prone to greenscreen and CGI landscapes. The original version has the Doctor coming upon an actual temple complex rendered in CGI. In the remastered episode they physically go to a set of actual brick ruin from some long fallen building. In contrast to many of his peers, Newman seems to deliberately move away from green screen, preferring real sets and locations and more careful use of CGI in this and other remastered versions.

&&&

The Last Pirate's History, Page 258

BLOOD HUNTER, Series 1, Episode 3, Original October 26, 2013, Remastered November 16, 2019 (24 minutes)

While the Doctor is trying to figure out the magic rock he got from the Wisps, an evil bounty hunter named Zardox sneaks up on the Tardis with his ship. Zardox manages to dope the Tardis into shutting off its shields, so he can teleport aboard.

After that it's cat and mouse as Zardox chases the Doctor through the Tardis. Until time begins to break down around them, weird things start to happen, and the Doctor persuades Zardox that they need to work together to save themselves.

In the original version, it was Luke Newman in the Zardox costume, chasing himself around through the magic of careful editing. In one memorable close up shot, Zardox and the Doctor are face to face, and you can tell Newman is literally holding up the Zardox mask just out of frame, it's weirdly charming. In the remastered edition, it's James Sutton who gives the role some panache.

The original version also depicts the Tardis interior through greenscreen, whereas the remastered version uses actual locations – a library, and sets – drywall with paper plates to simulate rondels.

But fair is fair, Zardox's original uniform was cardboard. A bit more goes into the costume in the remake. Overall in both versions it's a pretty good alien bounty hunter costume.

Beyond that, there isn't much change. In both versions, this is a smartly written, clever little two-hander, moving along briskly, balancing tension and dialogue and continually throwing out little twists to keep the audience engaged. It's a nice example of doing very good work with limited assets.

&&&

ETERNAL DARKNESS, Series 1, Episode 4, Original November 23, 2013, Remastered, December 7, 2019 (74 minutes)

At home, scary ghosty things are happening to Jess. She calls the Doctor who shows up brings her to Tardis, just in time for the whole Tardis to be zapped away by a beam of blue light.

The Krystal Moore Doctor from *Velocity* appears on the viewscreen to mention that soul snatchers are after Doctors and he needs to run and find more versions of themselves to fight the enemy. The Doctor's Tardis materializes in a vast graveyard copied from Earth (actually a really nice effective location shoot, it's hard to go wrong with a good graveyard), littered with crashed and burning Tardises. The Doctor meets several other incarnations, notably the Gudera (Blonde) Doctor who takes the role previously played by Ryan Hennessy, the Patton Doctor (aka the Irish Doctor from *Tardis in Need* and *Fractured Timeline*) and the Dominic G. Martin Doctor with MeganShirley.

The cemetery is full of graves of Docs companions, and looming over everything is a nicely rendered giant stone Dalek monument, presiding over Dalek catacombs. The Doctors are pursued by Daleks and by black robed corpse figures, falling one by one, all at the machinations of a sort of half skeletal, decomposing villain.

Both versions of this are nicely shot, making very effective use of location. On the downside, they're really talky and they both drag a bit. The original version was an anniversary story so the entire point was to unite a lot of Doctors, the story was secondary. The remastered version is significantly more concise (but still drags).

Overall, it's an effective piece of work. In particular, the villain in the remastered edition is truly terrifying, and his revelations, while not making a lot of sense when you think about it, digs deep into Who lore.

&&&

SERIES THREE, 8 episodes, 3 minisodes

THE ARKHALLON TRANCE, Series 3, Episode 1, October 31, 2015 (39 minutes)

K9 warns the Doctor of an alien ship, the Arkhallons, on the way to Earth. Their shtick is to cause humans to fall asleep. They announce that they're just here for 'minerals' and warn humanity not to resist. If not for the particular 'mineral' this would be most low key alien invasion ever. But there are complications.

Jess is back, the Brigadier (Dale Adams, originally appearing in the lost *Peril of the Unknown*) is back, the cast expands, which builds a sense of a world nicely. The Brigadier for instance meets the Prime Minister to reactivate Torchwood. Jess has a boyfriend. There's a woman called Violet who meets the Doctor, but also talks to her friend Sarah Whitehouse. All these people give a sense of a world beyond the Doctor.

The Arkhallon ship and costumes aren't bad. A lot of the action takes place in and around Paradise Forum plaza in Birmingham, which is a nice mixture of old civic and new public architecture with lots of steps to convey a sense of dimension to the geography.

It's not a bad little episode.

&&&

AGE OF HUMANITY, Series 2, Episode 2, November 7, 2015, (34 minutes)

The Doctor takes Jess on a trip to the Cretaceous to picnic among dinosaurs. That's just the coolest thing ever. And I guess it means that dinosaur CGI must be dirt cheap, accessible and available. They watch Brachiosaurs, encounter a T-Rex and are menaced by a Spinosaurus. Wandering into picturesque woods where the trees are overgrown with vines, they find a primordial 'tree of life' a 'regeneration tree' pollinating the planet. A moment later, they find a portal to another dimension and a Timebot pops through to clean up the timeline. The Timebot gives chase, but they escape. A moment later they're racing back to the Tardis to escape the planet killing asteroid that eventually snuffs the dinosaurs.

Eventually, plot happens when they discover that the Tardis can't leave, it turns out the Timebots here are scrambling the future, preventing the rise of humanity, and the Doctor and Jess need to stop it and close the portal. Before they can, a mysterious robed figure, the Annihilator, played by Jay McGuinness in a silver mask, comes through the portal on a quest to eradicate humanity before it starts.

Overall? I'm a sucker for dinosaurs, even if you've composited them onto what seems to be a golf course green (you can see a hiker in the far background of one shot). The forest location is visually cool, the CGI Timebot is a nice piece of work, and the Annihilator costume isn't bad. The Doctor and Jess bounce off each other nicely. The Doctor debates the Annihilator rather than stopping him. The 'tree of life' idea doesn't make any sense, and that undermines the logic of the plot. The story doesn't amount to much, but I'm fine with that. It's a charming enough piece of work.

&&&

POWER OF THE PUPPETEER, Episode 3, Series 2, November 14, 2015 (44 minutes)

This is kind of a paradox, which is perfect for a show about a time traveller. This is an excellent episode, but in order to fully appreciate it, you kind of needed to have watched the lost episodes.

Let's start with the beginning - we open with shaking camera in the control room (always an easy but effective dramatic start) a portal opens up in the Tardis library, and Violet, who the Doctor met briefly in *Arkhallon* pops out - except that she remembers being a longtime companion of the Doctor, and she says her name is Robyn, not Violet. Before the Doctor can wrap his head around this, he's contacted by a menacing figure calling himself The Hood, who threatens to blow up the Doctor's friends with clever planted bombs. The Doctor must race against time to find and disarm each bomb, going from the Brigadier to Jess, before confronting the Hood in an alley. This part is not bad at all, there's mystery, tension, weird things happening and a sense of danger. It's a little hammy but it's got momentum.

But in the alley, we get the big payoff. The hood throws off his cloak, revealing himself as...some guy we've never seen before, played by Jay McGuinness. Unless, of course, you happened to have watched the second series episodes *Days of Forgotten Past, Perils of the Unknown,* and *Into the Mind,* at which point we're all shocked to discover that the Doctor's enemy is... the Doctor, his prior incarnation! Shock! Except, he reveals, he's not the Doctor, he was the Master all along! Double shock! He's got some scheme involving the Doctor's daughter, a plot thread that was laid down in *The Nightmare Within,* and *Dark Times,* both of which are also lost... But triple shock! The Master is on the trail of those mysterious portals, first seen in *Whispers in the Woods* and *Age of Humanity,* which you can actually watch, so at least that's nice. And those two mysterious other-dimensional stones, both the one we saw in *Whispers in the Woods,* and the one we didn't get to see in *Dark Times,* are involved. This would be spectacular, it's the big revelatory payoff that pulls two and a half seasons of episodes and minisodes together and turns them on their head, except that it's dependent on episodes that aren't available.

As it is, it's....sort of cool and impressive, but probably a bit confusing for those who haven't seen the second series.

Luckily, Luke Newman and Jay McGuinness as the fake Doctor/Master have terrific frenemies chemistry together, and we're hit with enough weirdness so fast it basically works.

Anyway, the T-Rex from *Age of Humanity* makes a welcome surprise entrance and it turns out Robyn is from another universe.

There's a very funny, but too long, conversation with the Doctor and Master whispering to each other while standing in front of the T-Rex debating what to do. It's a great scene, but the problem is that they're doing it standing in front of a crazed, time-shifted T-Rex. Personally, I'd be focused on running, screaming, being bitten in half. Apparently, T-Rex's were a lot more polite and well-mannered than Jurassic Park would have us believe.

With or without the background, it's still a fun episode.

&&&

REFLECTION, Series 3, Episode 4, November 21, 2015, (35 minutes)

We open with the Doctor playing chess with K9, and losing. The Tardis gets sucked into one of those annoying portals and is temporarily disable. Luckily, the Doctor has some emergency gear from Doc Brown and his Delorean, and uses it to jumpstart the Tardis back to Earth, where he encounters a ghost and a mysterious haunted house.

It's the return of the Mirror Demon from *Days of Forgotten Past*, the lost second series lead episode. Aidan Beardsmore, who appeared in Arkhallon as the Prime Minister, plays a different role as Professor Henry Vancouver.

The most notable new face is Megan Shirley, playing Megan Williams, who will become the companion, through the rest of the series, and the single most important person, on screen and back stage after Newman himself.

Overall, it's a haunted house story with the Doctor playing something very much like a chess game with the Mirror Demon, and it's a hard thing to say which one of them is scarier.

The episode starts with a creepy vibe it essayed successfully in *Whispers in the Woods* and not so successfully in the lost *Dark Night of the Scarecrow,* and manages to build into something complex and effective.

It's a bit talky, a chronic thing with fan films. But overall, it works nicely, the house is spooky, the actors know what they're doing and they work well together, Newman is actually chilling and the script both calls back to previous episodes and scenes and advances the accumulating story arcs.

&&&

WAR SALVAGE, Series 3, Episode 5, November 28, 2015 (31 minutes)

Megan's maiden voyage on the Tardis. She opts to visit the past of King Richard III.

Then it gets weird. King Richard knows who the Doctor is, it turns out he's well versed on aliens, and he's hooked up with a Rutan who he thinks will win him the battle of Bosworth. The problem is that this will make Earth a battleground in the Sontaran-Rutan War.

The Doctor opts to sneak the Rutan off planet, wearing Richard as a host, but before they can get away, they're captured by a Sontaran, who teleports them all to their spaceship and to the Rani...

It's a fairly smart, ambitious episode let down by production values. Lauren Garnett turns in a mostly decent performance as the Rani, and manages to be a highlight of the episode.

On the other hand, Jordan Jones struggles with the role of King Richard, but his costume, particularly his wig does him no favours. (Jones returns to play the Master in *Fall of the Doctor*, and does much better with something to work with) Despite being a King, it's hard to overlook the fact that he has a total of one retainer, played by Kai Nelson (last seen as Jess's fiancé) doing thankless journeyman work.

The big handicap are the Rutan and the Sontaran, both papier mache constructs gone horribly wrong. In particular, the Sontaran looks like a giant evil chipmunk. There's an attempt to find locations that might evoke 15th century England, but mostly not enough use is made of it, with the shots being tight and cramped (probably to avoid the nearby 20th century buildings and fences getting in the frame).

That's how it is - sometimes you go hunting and you get the bear, sometimes the bear gets you. It's not a bad story on paper, and there are things to like about some of the execution. But it does demand forgiveness and tolerance from the viewer.

&&&

BIRTH OF AN ANGEL, Series 3, Episode 6, December 5, 2015, (44 minutes)

It turns out that garden gnomes are a larval form of Weeping Angels or something of that sort, a stroke of genius that is both funny, sublime and disturbing.

Jess wakes up to discover the Doctor in her room, watching her sleep. Admittedly it's a creepy start, but the episode segues into lighthearted humour, as the Doctor turns out to be oblivious about the simplest things in domestic life - toasters, shower privacy, details like that. It's enjoyable, Newman and Naughton have always had terrific comic timing together.

On board the Tardis, the Doctor is puzzling over the magical rock from previous episodes when Meg walks in.

Hello paradox! Or pair o' Docs!

The Doctor finds his Tardis being dragged and drained to 2014, where there's a massive build-up of time energy. The Tardis lands, but when the Doctor steps out, the Tardis shuts, locking Meg inside, and takes off on its own. Trapped on earth, the Doctor searches out Jess, it was a flashback all along, not a paradox.

The source of time energy turns out to be Weeping Angels, in their Garden Gnome form. We're all set for an adventure with the Doctor and Jess, and Jess's annoying little sister, Sarah, played by Elizabeth Kirk, who has a secret, and then it just goes off in a totally unexpected direction.

Bottom line, it's a worthwhile episode shifting tone smoothly, moving from humour to drama to revelation to pathos, never quite going where you expect it, but never cheating, always pleasantly surprising, and in the end passionate.

&&&

JOURNEY TO THE MULTIVERSE, Series 3, Episode 7, December 12, 2015 (35 minutes)

The Doctor returns to Gallifrey with his daughter, Scarlet, an event which results in an immediate family blowout and reconciliation. Elizabeth Kirk who plays Scarlet brings a fascinating combination of fierceness, vulnerability and sheer neediness to the roll.

Meanwhile, Romana, President of the Time Lords, played by Hannah Padley, send the Doctor out on the most quixotic mission ever: Rescue the Master who has vanished, but was last seen on Skaro. The Time Lord costumes are achieved with liberal amounts of duct tape, spray paint and corrugated cardboard. It reminds me of my favourite Cyberman.

Meanwhile, Gallifrey is depicted by an Anglican Church interior - the vaulted ceilings, arches and grandeur carry off well. They try to keep the shots tight, so as not to make it too obvious, but it is a trade off.

Off the Doctor and Meg go to Skaro, which turns out to resemble an English meadow, and the inevitable confrontation with Daleks. Luckily, they manage to escape through one of those mysterious inter-dimensional portals that have been popping up since *Whispers in the Woods.*

This takes them to an alternate Earth, where they find the Master, the final magical space rock and a terrifying alternate version of the Doctor.

Seriously, Newman can do scary very well, we saw him do it in *Reflection,* and he does it again here. Maybe he should try doing the Master sometime.

The episode ends on a cliff hanger with the Master lost in another dimension, the evil Doctor loose on our universe and the real Doctor killed by Daleks.

Despite the shifts in pacing, the episode holds together and moves quickly. Plot threads laid out in the first and second series are picking up pace and moving to the fore. There's an accumulating tension picking up speed.

&&&

DARKNESS RISES, Series 3, Episode 8, December 19, 2015 (52 minutes)

The Doctor is dead, but somewhere else the Doctor is alive and facing off against the Valeyard, played brilliantly by Dokka Chapman.

It turns out to be complicated, for reasons that date all the way back to *Eternal Darkness* in the first series. I like the depth this gives the series overall, the way plot threads gest established and weave in and out unexpectedly.

Also, the Valeyard is screwing with the Doctor by stealing Earth and slowly, steadily shrinking it into a paperweight. Stop and think about that one for a second. Okay. So that's a thing. Oh well, the BBC series did goofier things.

Meanwhile, the other characters, the Brigadier, Romana, Meg and even Jess struggle to find their way through the crisis.

Anything more?

Sorry, spoilers.

Overall, it's an effective closing to the third series, and illustrates that the Doctor doesn't just succeed on his own, but succeeds because of his friends. The episode is driven by solid performances, not all of them, but everyone gets moments and opportunities to make whatever they can of those moments.

Luke Newman has his Doctor down of course, but he goes a little overboard.

Megan Shirley excels as the key mover, her character is clever and resolute and very well depicted.

The big surprise is Dale Smith, who was unbearably wooden in his first appearance in DW2012, in *Peril of the Unknown*, but has steadily grown into something of an actor, with real rapport with Newman and other characters. One of the small pleasures of DW2012 is watching Dale Smith's performance develop over the course of the series. It turns out that his character is the son of the original Brigadier and brother of Kate Stewart, a nice bit of retconning.

Dokka Chapman has the standout turn, his Valeyard is a triumph of malevolence, and although he turns out to be the warm up act for the main villain, he's got one of the best performances in the series. He'll be back, and he's always a pleasure to see.

For once, the cast and crew have filled out, and their number opens up both storytelling possibilities, and more production resources.

And we're on to the fourth series.

SERIES 4 (8 episodes, introductory minisode)

ESSENCE OF A LEGACY, Series 4, Episode 1, October 29, 2016 (59 minutes)

This one is 59 minutes of a bad road in a school zone, not much happens, and it happens slowly.

Basically, the Doctor got mopey over the events of the series three closer, and decided to hide out.

Everyone's looking for him, particularly the Time Lords, led by a Castellan with the most ridiculous fake beard on Gallifrey. They decide to set Megan on the trail.

That's a good choice, both for the Time Lords and the story. Megan's an everywoman, we see her at home, we see her working at a coffee shop; she is intrinsically part of the normal world, a recognizable sympathetic character. But she's also part of the Doctor's world, and completely un-phased by it, whether confronting alien kidnappers, bargaining with Time Lords or stealing her own Tardis.

Her hunt for the Doctor is the best part of the episode as she relentlessly tracks down a series of clues, each one leading to the next. It's path that takes her from the Brigadier to Benton, to Gallifrey and the Doctor's daughter and finally to some obscure nowhere world where she confronts a hermit with the second most ridiculous fake beard in the episode. Along the way, we see that not only can she pilot a Tardis, she can steal one from Gallifrey under the noses of the Time Lords. It showcases the character of Megan Shirley wonderfully, her intelligence, strength and resilience, and it gives the actress Megan Williams real room to work.

Things slow down though, when she finally tracks down the Doctor and tries to talk him out of his emotional funk. She does it eventually, but not before Dalek saucers show up, the Time Lords abduct them, the Doctor is sentenced to death. Eventually, he has all his future regenerations stripped from him.

But there's an escape clause, if he can hunt down and kill or contain Omega, they'll consider giving them back. Basically, this is the soul-searching, redemptive, renewed conviction episode.

Ironically, through the rest of the series, the Doctor's not particularly bothered by his loss of regenerations, nor does he actively search for Omega, both are back-burnered. He just goes on regular adventures without a care.

It's a slow episode, heavy on emotion, and it's largely built on the accumulated good will and the story arcs of the three previous series. It's not really a stand-alone, or even a normal season opener, but a continuation, a deep breath, from the baggage that's gone before. It's a 'great big plot arc' story.

Downside? Those ridiculous fake beards. Upsides - they have real Time Lord head-pieces (not cardboard and duct tape), and bonus - K9 has been refurbished into the Australian television series version.

Long on angst, short on action. If that works for you, good.

Otherwise, watch it for Megan Williams.

&&&

PLANET OF THE CYBERMEN, Series 4, Episode 2, November 12, 2016 (49 minutes)

After some rough, but unseen, adventures it's time for Megan and the Doctor to take a break and relax. They accept an invitation to a high class gallery show from the Doctor's friend, Nova, played by Steven Jeffries.

When they arrive, however, they discover that the centerpiece of the show is a recently excavated Cyberman chassis, and what a mess of a Cyberman, motley, jury rigged shambles, with awkwardly joined parts from every version of the Cybermen.

Bad news, turns out it's not dead. Worse news, it's been sending a distress call. Even worse news, armoured Cybermen show up to rescue it because it's the Cyber-God, the incarnation of all phases of the Cyber-race, and its recovery prefigures a whole new Cyberman Jihad to convert whole planets. Worst news of all, the armoured Cybermen don't intend to leave witnesses.

Luckily, the Doctor, Megan and Nova are saved at the last minute by a couple of warriors, 409 and 715, played by Harry Calder and Richard Griffiss, part of a war against the Cybermen. The war hasn't gone well, they find they're all that's left. But the Doctor and Megan are on the job...

Meg and the Doctor's relationship continues to evolve, and unknown to the Doctor, we receive hints that there's more going on with Meg than meets the eye.

It is not any kind of insult to call this an extremely conventional episode. There's no angst, no drama, no person development or evolution. This is a straight up adventure, as the Doctor, Megan and their new friends head to Telos to infiltrate the Cyberman base, overcome a series of obstacles and complications, discover and foil the their evil plans. It would be perfectly at home in both the classic and new BBC series.

For once, we have a large cast. Often Newman's struggled to get people to help out, and then struggled to find something for them to do. But here we've got three full supporting roles in Nova and the two rebels, topped off with a whole mess of Cybermen.

The nice thing about Cybermen is that they all look alike, so one Cyberman costume used carefully can seem like an army. Indeed, there's not just one Cyberman costume, there's at least two of Armoured Cyberman costumes (clearly handmade but serviceable), and at least one of the *Earthshock* Cyberman suits, plus whatever unholy mess the Cyber-God is. This, together with some judicious set construction, allows for a real feeling of presence, the sense that the place is just teeming with them. In turn, it allows the episode to really carry some weight.

The episode is well placed with appropriate twists and turns, but still taking time to develop its characters. Genuine tension and action is balanced with moments of lightness, particularly in scenes where Meg, having donned a captured Cyberman suit to infiltrate, completely fails to act like a Cyberman, exhibiting completely human body language.

Oh, and there's a little arc-plot point going, there's a moment where Megan apparently has glowing eyes. I'm sure that little incident will soon be forgotten and never be referred to again.

&&&

BLOOD TIES, Series 4, Episode 3, November 19, 2016 (37 minutes)

A mysterious entity, calling itself the Consequence, pursues a fleeing Megan, casting her back to 1996, where she meets another woman with a baby daughter, who she feels strangely connected to. But it's not just any date in 1996, it's the date of her mother's mysterious death, and it's her mother that she's encountered.

It seems that there was something paranormal involved in her mother's death, and reports of a mysterious woman spotted at the scene. Megan's grandparents ended up raising her and her grandfather was always obsessed with the unanswered questions around his daughter's death, particularly the paranormal aspects. In turn, he passed that obsession with the paranormal on to Megan. That's how she ended up assisting Professor Vancouver, and why she followed the Doctor the minute she met him. But now it's all come full circle.

Given the nature of this story, comparisons to *Curse of Fenric* are inevitable. That's the McCoy serial where Ace, played by Sophie Aldred, travels back to WWII and meets her own mother. Indeed, Ace is actually referenced in a line of dialogue.

Uniquely in the DW2012 canon, this is the only episode not written by Luke Newman. Instead, it's written and co-directed by Megan Shirley. Susan Shirley, Megan's mother plays Grandmother Williams, all of which suggests it's a very personal story. It's definitely her character's story and heavily freighted with emotional weight. The Doctor is very much a supporting and supportive character.

It's not a perfect episode, there are some problems with the dialogue between Megan and her mother Nessa, played by Sarah Poyser, but given the emotional freight, that's understandable.

More problematic, the character of the Consequence is mostly acted by a mannequin in a mask, draped with a gauzy black road and draped with CGI smoke - in most scenes, its visibly immobile, and simply voice-overed by Dave Nyra. There are only a few scenes where an actor, probably Newman himself, wears the costume.

But the mysterious Consequence is ultimately just a McGuffin to drive the story forward. We don't care about him. We care about Megan's story.

This is simply an excellent episode, small, human and deeply heartfelt. It's hard not to get at least a little choked up.

&&&

GLITCH, Series 4, Episode 4, December 3, 2016 (37 minutes)

The Doctor and Megan receive a distress call from a 22nd Research station orbiting Jupiter, a mysterious creature has gotten on board the station and is killing the crew. The Doctor and Meg show up to the rescue, but it's too late, the crew is dead, and only the station's artificial intelligence, Cavi, is left to talk to them.

The monster is still on the prowl though, and is invisible to the station's sensors. Indeed, entire sections of the station are inaccessible to Cavi's sensors. Things go from bad to worse, when they learn the station will fall into Jupiter's atmosphere in an hour.

The clock is ticking down for the Doctor and Meg to solve the mystery of what killed the crew and escape. However, their efforts only lead to them getting split up with only Cavi to talk to. But as the scenes shift back and forth between the two, the audience starts to realize that Cavi isn't telling the entire truth, and Megan starts to ask some pointed questions...

The script is literally perfect, there's not a wasted line of dialogue. It marshals information carefully, with each character slowly peeling back layer after layer, revealing Cavi's plans and malevolence. There's no real action, it's entirely set in hallways, but the tension ratchets up continually through the interplay of the three characters.

Physically its low fi, it's mainly shot on location in the access hallways of what appears to be a shopping mall parkade. If you watch the dark windows carefully, you can see the parkade, the pillars, the floor lines, at one point you can even see a car coming in to park. But that's fine - the space consists of a series of stark white halls and corridors, there's a rigorous antiseptic quality reminiscent of 2001: A Space Odyssey that works very well. It's an inspired shooting location, and one that supports without distracting.

Good performances all around, particularly from Lucy Klam as the malevolent AI, who manages to slowly infuse the pleasant monotone with evil glee.

Megan has evolved far beyond a companion, no longer a sidekick but a full partner to the Doctor, and watching their interactions is a treat. Oh, and she's still manifesting superpowers, but this time, the Doctor has noticed, even if he's not mentioning it.

This is my favourite DW2012 story, a virtuoso example of building drama with almost nothing to work with but three characters and some hallways.

&&&

THE NIGHT BEFORE CHRISTMAS, Christmas Special, December 25, 2022 (25 minutes)

Check the date, four years after release of The Fall of the Doctor. Luke Newman returns to the Little Red Doctor to do a special story of how the Autons almost stole Christmas. According to the notes, this is intended to be set between *Glitch* and *War of the Daleks*, so I've inserved.

Christmas stories can be hard to do, the subject matter is really narrow, the vibe is focused, and it is so easy to tip over from sacharine to shmaltz. Having said that, this is just wonderful.

A few random thoughts. Has someone got themselves a drone to play with? I'm seeing some really interesting altitude and tracking shots, that really add production value. It's amazing how this technology is really opening up genuine cinematic possibilities.

Absolutely loved that DW2012 opening, the music, the christmas lights log. Perfectly captures and sets the mood. Really liked that tracking shot from the top of the Christmas tree all the way around to Megan at home. That's some fluid camerawork. Beautiful and assured. That's better than professional. Professional simply implies technical competence. This, this is a film maker's eye, it's an artist at work.

It looks like Luke and Megan managed to talk their way into a department store after closing time to do some shooting. I wonder how they managed that. Did one of them work there. Or did they find a sympathetic Manager / Clerk / Janitor? In any case, to steal a Smith "Brilliant!" The inherent production value is amazing. It's a complicated, textured three-dimensional space which allows for endless visually interesting shots, a unique depth and background in every frame, the opportunity to do all kinds of things.

The scenes of the Auton coming alive, or the Doctor stalking or being stalked, the cat and mouse, this is great. It's a wonderful example of low budget or no budget film making managing to be visually big in scope.

There are some great shots. The black hand coming alive, the black auton smashing through a window, the window store dummies turning their blank heads. All of the auton shots manage to be creepy in unique ways. The Auton in the department store slowly coming alive and struggling to walk is the best, there's a sense of something being born in uncanny valley.

There is so much story going on, that really, all there is room for is to tease us with the various short Auton awakening shots. The story has to move - to the Doctor's counter-move, the confrontation with the Auton, the Christmas resolution. As always, the by-play between Megan and the Doctor is a pleasure, whether it's the Doctor spinning yarns about knowing Kris Kringle, or the scenes at the gift exchange, there's a chemistry there and a genuineness to the banter.

The Doctor effectively becoming Santa Claus one night, visiting every home, is cleverly done. It's a bit techno-babble, but it makes sense within the context of the story, and there's nothing there that hasn't been established in previous episodes.

The Nestene Consciousness scheme makes sense, what better time for a plastic monster to insinuate a trojan horse? It's also very 70s, it's such a nostalgic callback to the old Holmes stories, particularly *Terror of the Autons*. The department store Auton freezing back into immobility had just a touch of pathos.

The emotional core, of course, are the final Christmas exchanges, with an effective call back to an earlier conversation. The sentiment feels genuine. I could imagine children watching this over and over and over, or families making it an annual part of their Christmas. It can readily take its place shoulder to shoulder with the professional Doctor Who Christmas episodes.

As always, not quite perfect, the economy of the production does show through here and there, the realities of not having (functionally) unlimited budgets or resources or crews, and the need to tell stories within limitations show through. But despite that, what we have here is something amazingly polished. There are commercial and professional productions which simply don't reach this level. Once again, we see what two people with genuine skill and talent (and modern technology) can achieve.

&&&

WAR OF THE DALEKS, Series 4, Episode 5, June 3, 2017 (41 minutes)

The Doctor and Megan are taking some time apart, nothing negative, just doing stuff. Megan's doing fine, the Doctor's not, he's got it bad. It's a throwaway opening, but it's a fun picture of their evolving relationship, and just how strong Megan is. She's living life exploring New York, but the Doctor is bored and pining for her. When he talks her back aboard the Tardis, she's almost annoyed, and when he takes them on a trip she complains she's just gone from one room in a spaceship to another room in a spaceship *"I gave up New York for this?"*

In a nicely unremarked bit, as the Doctor starts piloting the Tardis, she starts helping with the controls and settings. She's already been established as being able to pilot a Tardis, but here they operate it as a couple, so familiar with the controls and each other, that they don't have to talk.

Anyway, once again, Megan and the Doctor go back to Skaro, this time on a mission to stop the Daleks latest doomsday weapon. They don't go directly or intentionally, the ship they're on is a warship on a mission and it crashes with them on it.

Skaro was last glimpsed in *Journey to the Multiverse*, the penultimate episode of series 3, But this episode is really a sequel to *Dark Times*, the lost closing episode of series 2, when the Daleks invaded Earth, with direct call-backs and some recycling of footage. As per usual, it didn't go well, the invasion failed, the Daleks blew up, and Davros got away.

One of the plot threads that got lost back then was the Supreme Dalek organizing a conspiracy to overthrow Davros.

Well, it turned out that the coup worked - sort of. Dalek Supreme made its move, created an Emperor and engineered a revolt. Davros survived with the aid of loyalists, but wasn't able to put it down. Instead, Skaro was divided between two cities of warring Daleks, Davros and the Supremes, each bent on universal genocide, each claiming to be the true Dalek race.

Anyway, the Doctor and Megan get separated early on. Megan is captured and is taken to the Dalek Emperor. Meanwhile, the Doctor and K9, searching for Megan, infiltrate the wrong city. K9 throws down against Daleks while the Doctor kidnaps Davros. The Dalek civil war heats up. In the Imperial city, Megan escapes provides mercy to a Dalek victim, and then gets satisfyingly grim. While the story feels a lot like Classic Who, a lot of the story is a character showcase/development arc for Megan which is very evocative of New Who.

For once, the Daleks are pretty good, both CGI and real work. DW2012 has found some very good locations that they've dressed well, or they've actually built sets or pieces of sets. The Emperor Dalek is based on Troughton's Evil of the Daleks version, and might be a tabletop model. The production values are pretty good, doubly impressive, considering Newman's penchant for doing questionable things with corrugated cardboard and papier mache.

Again, like *Planet of the Cybermen*, this is a very good conventional episode, modelled on the classic series. It moves briskly, looks good, with plenty of twists and some very good character moments.

&&&

THE MYSTERIOUS CALLING, Series 4, Episode 6, June 17, 2017 (52 minutes)

If *Planet of the Cybermen* and *War of the Daleks* feel like call backs to the classic series, *The Mysterious Calling* is very much at one with the flavour and sensibility of the new series. It's up there with *Glitch* as one of the best offerings.

It starts with a cold open, a woman named Annabelle is walking when she notices that the phone booth on the corner is ringing... The next thing she knows is 35 minutes is missing, and she's been probed.

Meanwhile, back in Potters Lane, a postman delivers a 450 year old letter to the Doctor, an ancient letter written by a woman named Annabelle. Well, a mystery like that is catnip to the Doctor and Meg, so they track her down. Of course, Annabelle leads them to the mystery of the phone booth on the corner which, in the course of her entire life, she can't remember anyone using it. Turns out on examination that it's deactivated. On further examination, it's never been activated.

Because it's not a phone booth at all.

It's an elevator.

See what I mean? It feels like Newman is channelling Moffatt or Davies here, where with the Cyberman and Dalek episodes, he was channelling Holmes and Dicks.

Oddly, there are some genuinely funny bits here, including literal slapstick. Early on Annabelle whacks the Doctor in the face with a frying pan, and it and his reaction is hilarious. At another point the Doctor sticks his head out of the Tardis' phone drawer and has a surreal conversation with the postman. The characters and situations are such that the actors are able to play for laughs, and it feels natural and unforced.

Despite this, the episode is able to shift tones smoothly, transitioning to serious and even dramatic. When it gets serious, it gets serious. It's not jarring, but an acceptance that the stakes are real and dangerous, that lives are at stake. Strangeness gives way to tension, and while the Doctor is confident, there's a real sense that the outcome is very much an open question.

Beyond that, the production values are good. The alien costume is convincing, the only problem being that sometimes it's hard to make out the whispering. The underground base is shadowy and indistinctive, but that adds to the mystique.

What really makes the episode is the wonderful performance by Melissa Collier as Annabelle, with only one episode to work with; she hits it out of the park. Her delivery is accomplished and fluid, it doesn't feel like acting. Kai Nelson, who's shown up through the series as Jess's fiancé, Time Lord General Maxill, King Richard's bondsman, etc. delivers a wonderfully comic turn as a Post-man. Luke Newman and Megan Shirley as the Doctor and Megan work together like a Swiss watch.

Well written, well directed, well-acted despite a 52 minute running time, it never really lags. Once again, this is simply a pleasure.

&&&

THE FATALITY TRAP, Series 4, Episode 7, July 8, 2017 (38 minutes)

This one's a bit of a three card monte. Okay, here's the deal: You're coming up to the end of the series, you have a penultimate episode, you need to lay out some plot points, set up for the big finale, but at the same time, you can't give too much away. It's a filler episode, how do you make it interesting?

Well, if you can't work with content, then work with structure.

It's interesting that in a show about time travel, all the episodes are pretty straight narratives - they start at the beginning and then proceed to the end. Except for *Fatality Trap*, the closest DW2012 has come to a genuinely experimental episode.

The story opens with the Doctor and Megan trapped under a pile of rubble, badly injured, perhaps dying. Flashback two hour...

The Doctor and Megan are about to head off on a trip when they get a call from the Brigadier. The Tardis has been found at the bottom of a lake. Creepy! The Doctor takes it in stride, he's a time traveller, and this is just the Tardis from his future. But when they open it, they find the skeletal corpses of the Doctor and Megan.

Flash forward, the Brigadier is down there in the rubble with them, also badly injured.

Flashback half an hour. The Doctor is desperately trying to figure out what happened in the future, and as if he doesn't have enough problems, a series of cloaked spaceships are descending on Earth. Daleks, Sontarans, Cybermen, all preparing to throw down. As they do, Unit Headquarters collapses, and the Doctor, Megan and Brigadier are all caught in it...

Spoiler - we don't solve the riddle of the corpses in the future Tardis, they're saving that one. We learn more about Meg's powers, the Doctor's Daughter comes back, a mysterious figure from *Essence of a Legacy* reappears. There are some nice character bits. But not a lot happens, not a lot gets resolved.

The whole thing turns out to be a shell game, designed to lead into the next episode. But it's well done and it keeps your attention.

&&&

THE FINAL ENIGMA, Series 4, Episode 8, July 22, 2017 (65 minutes)

Series finales are not normal episodes. Typically, they should be the showstoppers, bigger and more epic than a regular episode. You need to really pull out the stops, and preferably, you should lay some ground in previous episodes, maybe pull the whole previous series together, and set up the next big story, which in this case wraps up the entire project.

That's a bit of a challenge, particularly in a series that's already had strong outings with Silence, Cybermen and Daleks, typically, each of them are capable of being big closers. But here they're the warm up acts?

In *Essence of a Legacy*, first episode of the fourth series, Megan is briefly kidnapped into another dimension by a mysterious deformed figure who commands her to find the Doctor, and then returns her back to reality.

Then he sort of disappears until the penultimate episode, the *Fatality Trap* where he shows up and kidnaps Megan from the hospital.

The finale starts with a time jump, its two months later; the Doctor is travelling with his daughter and searching desperately for Megan, beating up Arkhallons and generally being unbalanced. He's contacted by Olivia from Torchwood, who reveals that they've detected time and void energy, suggesting that Megan's been abducted to another dimension. Finally, with a solid lead, the Doctor sets out like the wrath of god, he's going to find Megan, and someone's going to pay!

Meanwhile, in another dimension, Megan is captive of the deformed stranger, who turns out to be something of a dick, and she's giving him the gears at every opportunity. She even attempts to pick her manacles with a piece of chicken bone. But he's almost gleeful, because his endless plotting is finally coming to fruition. It seems that since the beginning, he's been manipulating Megan with post-hypnotic commands, and now he's got what he's wanted all along. The DNA of the Doctor!

The stage is set for shocks, thrills and epic confrontations as the hidden enemy is exposed, Megan is killed, the secret of her superpowers is revealed, a steampunk version of the Doctor appears, Omega makes his move and summons his armies. Good and evil face off in preparation for the final battle.

The series finale manages to pull everything together and set us up for the big conclusion. Quick note – watch for the 'blink and you'll miss it cameo' from Jessica Prestage, who plays the 2nd series companion, Lily.

&&&

FALL OF THE DOCTOR, Special - Sep 29, 2018 (140 minutes)

According to video diaries, Luke Newman had the *Fall of the Doctor* planned out before he even started shooting Dawn of the Doctor. All these plot threads across four seasons, the multiple Doctors, the death of Jess, the Master, the Doctor's daughter, even the Mirror Demon and Blood Hunter have all been laid out deliberately, all leading up to this epic finale.

Not everything was according to plan, the falling out with Jay McGuinness forced a huge swerve in second and third series, and the arrival of Megan Shirley turned out to be a major addition to third and fourth series. Some stories like *Curse of the Mummy* got abandoned, even with the stories that got made, often they were just stories told along the way, inspired by circumstance or opportunity. That always happens, but there actually was a plan, and if it wasn't always followed, Newman kept sticking to it..

What we've been doing is watching a 28 chapter, 15 mini-chapter, 23 hour long television novel, created over a period of four years, all leading up to this final story. Literally, a singlehanded achievement by one driven individual supported by a close circle of friends and supporters. That is a hell of an achievement. If you're not impressed, you should be.

And what we've been watching is five years of Luke Newman painstakingly learning the art of writing, the art of film making, the intricacies and challenges of telling a story, composing narrative over 21 stories, until finally, he's tackling the project that was in his mind from the start, building up skills, and building a network of friends and associates and supporters to help see it to completion.

And trust me, given that fall of the Doctor is almost two and a half hours, that's a good thing, it means that he's been developing the skill to match the ambition.

Fall of the Doctor is the final epic of the Little Red Doctor. It starts off almost quietly.

The stage has already been set, the mad god, Omega is loose, the Daleks, Cybermen, Sontarans and Silence are his armies, he's passed a death sentence on the universe, intending to unravel history all the way back to the Big Bang and rewrite existence from the beginning. Even the Time Lords are running scared. Against him is the Doctor, stripped of regenerations and condemned to death, and a handful of friends and associates, Megan, his daughter, the Master, an other-dimensional counterpart, other versions, and anyone he can enlist to his cause - not nearly enough.

The opening is almost a dirge as the outmatched Doctor contemplates mortality and morality and looks for help anywhere he can, approaching the Ice Warriors, trying to enlist Davros and even the Valeyard. Off camera, Omega has already devastated Gallifrey, killing half the council and forcing Romana into a new regeneration. There are comic moments, as they defenders debate increasingly ridiculous plans to defeat Omega. And there are poignant moments as the Doctor moves through a series of goodbye scenes with each of the people in his life, Megan, the Master, Scarlet, an avatar of Jess, the Valeyard.

The monster costumes, Sontarans, Daleks, original Cybermen, Sontarans, Ice Warriors, Silence and Arkhallons are reasonably effective, probably the best versions DW2012 has produced, and are replicated through CGI into a decent sized crowd for some scenes.

There are some complaints; chiefly being that Omega with his giant oversized bucket head is kind of ridiculous. It's a thing, you either go with it, or you don't, that's all.

The rest is mainly the product of the limitations, no real budget, no resources, even with all the cast and crew it's tiny and unskilled for the scope of the project. There's a lot of talking, a lot of melodrama, the choreography is a bit wonky, the location, some sandy beach region, isn't all that epic.

But the reality is that so many, many others have done so, so much less with so, so incredibly much more, I'm all right with the shortcomings. Newman has earned forgiveness.

The battle, missteps aside, carries off well, with a nice mixture of group scenes and individual moments. There's a lot of action and events, the balance shifts back and forth. There are last minute saves.

Is it worth watching? Well, two hours and twenty minutes are a big ask, but yes. Still, no need to take the leap, there are a lot of episodes along the way to this point, try some of them out, and if those work for you, commit to the whole novel.

In fact, thinking it over, I'd recommend not taking the leap into *Fall of the Doctor* straight away. The trouble is that if you go into it blind, without the backstory, you're going to get lost. Why is Megan throwing force blasts from her hands?

Who is Scarlet? The long haired guy is the Valeyard, why is he here? You'd have no idea who Crowvax unless you watch *Blood Hunter*. There's so much backstory, that really, to watch *Fall of the Doctor* and not get lost, you really should make it the end of the journey, not the beginning.

But I'll give away the ending, the good guys, the ones that survive, win. Omega is defeated. The old Doctor dies, a new Doctor rises. We all knew that. It's getting there that's worthwhile.

CAST: *Luke Newman - The Doctor, 'Doctor Who;' Megan Shirley - Megan Williams; Elizabeth Kirk - Scarlet, Sontaran, Dalek Operator; James Sutton - Omega, Arkhallon, Voice of Alpha Centauri; Jordan Jones - The Master, Elder Silence; Jack Batron-Highfield - Timelord General Maxill; Dokka Chapman - Valeyard; Sophie Flanagan - Romana; Dale Smith - Brigadier; Harry Calder - Crowvax; Chloe Naughton - Jessica Whitehouse; Daniel Patton - Irish Doctor, Voice of K9; Aine Coyle - Maggie May, Akhallon; Claire Andrews - Eliza; Melissa Collier - Annabelle McKenzie; Sian Kumar - Robyn; Mickey Wildman - Future Doctor; Ben Walden - Cyberman; Dominic G/ Martin - Next Doctor, Ice Warrior; Craig McDowall - Silence; Geoffry Allen - Davros; Sara Poyser - Nessa;*

CREW: *Luke Newman - Producer, Director, Writer, Editor, DOP, Visual Effects, Set Builder, Prop Maker, Music, Costumes, Marketing and Publicity; Daniel J. Patton - Director, Editor, DOP, Visual Effects, Graphic Designer; Megan Shirley - DOP, Set Builder, Costumes, Make Up, Marketing and Publicity; Dokka Chapman - DOP, Photographer; Dominic G. Martin - DOP, Marketing and Publicity; Ben Walden, Visual Effects; Kireon Holmes - Stunt Double; Ned Warren - Music; James Sutton - Prop Maker; Harry Calder, Elizabeth Kirk, Dale Smith - Runners.*

Reviews: The Purple Doctor (2022-Onwards)

Dynamic Works 2012
Series 5 and Onwards

Dominic G. Martin, whose Doctor Who career also includes being a freelance Producer for Big Finish productions, is officially the DW2012 Doctor as of September 29, 2018 and the conclusion of the *Fall of the Doctor*.

But actually, his first appearance is in the *Arkhallon Trance*, released on October 31, 2015, in a blink and you'll miss it moment. There's a shot of the Brigadier unconscious on his desk, and fallen from his hand is his smartphone. On that smartphone is an image captioned 'The Doctor' featuring Luke Newman, Ryan Hennessy and Dominic G. Martin. Another bit of evidence as to how far ahead Newman planned out.

Following that, Dominic G. Martin appeared in his first solo outing in *How Time Flies*, on June 29, 2019. Which was remastered and re-released on April 30, 2022.

He then reappeared as one of the Doctors in the remastered version of *Eternal Darkness*, technically Series 1, Episode 4 of the DW2012 series, December 7, 2019, remastered from an original from November 23, 2013.

Meanwhile, from 2020 to 2022, the Purple Doctor appeared in a series of short audio plays, several written and narrated by Dominic Martin himself, among others. Covid turned out to be a big pain in the ass, for DW2012 and everyone else.

What this all means is that the Purple Doctor is living his career out of order in his own past and future, which is oddly appropriate for a time traveller.

Currently, the Purple Doctor stars in two full length stories, *How Time Flies*, April 30, 2022, *Vengeance of the Bloodline*, July 16, 2022, and a six minute minisode on June 11, 2022, called *Mad Man With a Broken Box*.

Anyway, this basically means that Dominic Martin have been a Doctor for four to seven years by the time the first official lead Black Doctor, Ncuti Gatwa comes along. And he even beats Jo Clayton's January 26, 2020, appearance as a Doctor in Fugitive of the Judoon by years. That's pretty cool.

Although he won't have been the first Black Doctor, he will have been preceded by Jevocas Green, the '*Forgotten Doctor*'' who appeared in a series of episodes starting May 28, 2013. And by Spencer Kennedy who first appeared August 16, 2012, in the *Mystery of Rorrim* and then in *Untimely Death*. And of course, the original Black Doctor Who was Sir Lenny Henry Himself, who played the Doctor in a sketch on his variety show, all the way back to 1984.

As the future of DW2012, Dominic G. Martin's Doctor, has a hard act to follow. The four series and 28 stories of Luke Newman's Doctor amount to a television novel, it's a huge body of work, and a coherent body, the whole greater than the sum of parts. It can even be considered epic.

How do you follow up on something like that? How do you establish yourself? How do you get out from under that shadow? Will the Martin Doctor have his own arc? His own epic? We're literally at the beginning, so it's hard to say.

With only two full adventures, there are signs of a larger arc, and clearly a lot more technical ambition.

At this point, the Dominic G. Martin Doctor seems trapped on Earth, the Tardis disabled, a situation that has persisted through two episodes and a minisode and is likely to evolve as a storyline.

Megan Williams, the character, is struggling with a changed relationship with a changed Doctor, and with feelings of betrayal. A well-established character with a strong identity and a strong actress, Megan is likely to be even more prominent in the series going ahead.

Supporting characters are coming forward. At this point, it looks like this new Doctor and new series will establish a distinct identity and style separate from what has come before.

Behind the scenes, the hand of Luke Newman remains. His name is everywhere in the production credits. But there are signs of letting go, or at least loosening. Green's name shows up in writing credits, Megan Shirley shows up in editing.

One key distinction is that there are a lot more people involved, in front of and behind the camera. Gone are the days when Luke Newman was playing both the Doctor and the Monster, and doing everything else single-handed. More actors means that they need more lines, they need things to do, that affects storytelling. More people behind the scenes means more opportunities and options. Martin's stories seem to be moving towards a cinematic feel.

The question is what kind of Martin will be. It's hard to say. He's off to a good start. His character is more expressive than the Newman Doctor, more fluid and emotional, but also more overtly analytical. I think that as an actor, Martin may have more range than Newman, which offers opportunities, but more risks of going off a cliff. In terms of comparisons, I find myself reaching for everything from Richard Ayode's Moss to Benedict Cumberbatch's Sherlock. It'll be interesting to see what he does with the role.

Martin, co-writing Time Flies, as well as his minisode and audio shorts also seems to have established some chops as a writer. Add production experience through his work with DW2012 and Big Finish, and he seems to have the makings of a formidable and worthy successor to Luke Newman and his Doctor. Certainly, his two stories have been among the most ambitious of DW2012's impressive history.

If the tangled past is a predictor, Ncuti Gatwa may have some real competition. It's something to look forward to.

&&&

ETERNAL DARKNESS, Series 1, Episode 4, Original November 23, 2013, Remastered, December 7, 2019 (74 minutes)

We've already covered this one, but we're circling back to touch on it again. Dominic G. Martin doesn't appear in the original version of Eternal Darkness; he wasn't even a glimmer of a Doctor then. But when the episode was reshot, it opened up an opportunity to include him and Megan Shirley into the narrative. This is one of those great multi-Doctor epics, so basically it's putting in an appearance on a crowded landscape with a lot of things going on. This appearance is set much later in Series 5, or perhaps even Series 6, so this is later in the Purple Doctor's timeline than we've actually seen. The big takeaway is that the relationship with Megan is or has been awkward and careful.

&&&

HOW TIME FLIES, Series 5, Episode 1, (67 minutes)

The story opens with a framing device, Megan Williams is meeting with a therapist to work out some issues, which shows us that this story is as much Megan's as the Doctors.

And yes, that's how it turns out, as Megan literally falls out of the sky without a parachute in a truly terrifying sequence, deals with that trauma, wrestles with the respective challenges of getting to know a resurrected mother and a new Doctor, makes new friends and gets possessed by the latest alien menace.

First appearing in *Reflection* in the DW2012 third series, Megan Williams established herself as fearless, confident and quick witted; a character as strong as the Doctor, more partner and colleague than sidekick or companion. All that, and her formidable history with the series, makes her a dominant presence, and her actress, Megan Shirley delivers a forceful performance.

In contrast, Dominic G. Martin, playing the Doctor in his regeneration story, has to establish himself and his character. So we get what have become the usual post-regeneration jitters and trauma, and then the central mystery and confrontation as the Doctor settles into his new identity, discovers skullduggery afoot and proceeds to solve the riddle, confront the monster - in this case Time Flies - and fix things, which he does, of course. A co-writer for the episode and actually playing the Doctor as far back as 2019, Martin-Green has a grip on a Doctor that is looser than Newman's, more naive in some ways, more emotionally open, but also more intellectual. It's an engaging, watchable performance.

Beyond that this episode feels cinematic. In the early scenes, the Tardis explodes, and there are scenes of Meg falling through the sky, screaming in terror, while all around her fragments of Tardis interior the size of buildings fall all around her. It's a spectacular scene. There are multiple characters, complex shots, some visually effective locations, and very good effects all giving the story pace and weight. Sure, there's the usual fan film/no budget issues, notably a spot of wonky acting or two, some dodgy casting. But it's astonishing how much these issues don't even amount to a speed bump in a production which is very well put together and a story that manages to keep a number of balls in the air, both developing characters and telling a good story.

It's what we'd call an auspicious debut.

CAST: Dominic G. martin – The Doctor; Megan Shirley - Megan Williams, Voice of the Time Flies; Ben Walden - Tommy Benton; Dale Smith - Brigadier; Molly Reed - PC Lauren Miller; Jack Reeves - Ashley Jones; Michael Seagar - Ned; Sarah Poyser - Nessa Williams; Steph Barker - Therapist

&&&

MAD MAN IN A BROKEN BOX, Series 5, Minisode 1, June 6, 2022 (Six minutes)

&&&

VENGEANCE OF THE BLOODLINE, Series 5, Episode 2, (67 minutes)

What strikes me most strongly about this episode is how cinematic it is. From the shots of an asteroid scorching its way across the night sky over a city, to a series of careful shots showing the Brigadier at his hobby and looking up to notice, this often feels more like a theatrical movie rather than television.

There are differences; television is shot to a rigorous schedule and a small screen, so that biases a lot of decisions as to how shots are set up, how many shots you do in a scene, and what kind of choices you make. A cinematic approach with more time and money offers more freedom for complexity. Apparently, the DW2012 gang was using downtime during the Coved pandemic to up their game.

This is also a little reminiscent of the Pertwee era, not just in that both Doctors are trapped on Earth for the time being, but that they both head up an ensemble of continuing characters, all of whom, more or less, have lives of their own. The Dominic G. Martin Doctor is less of a star or dominating presence, than he is the head of the ensemble. But oddly, this works, with more characters to have relationships with them, and allows Martin-Green opportunities for a more nuanced palette. Thinking out loud, this is probably the backstage reason why the Tardis is stuck on Earth – it's hard to have an ensemble cast if you are gallivanting around the Universe. It's much more viable to build a diverse ensemble around the Doctor and Meg if they're stuck on Earth for a while.

This time the monster is another Slitheen, familiar from appearances in the Ecclestone era and the Sarah Jane Chronicles. The Slitheen are an interesting monster, a mix of baby features, unsightly fat and scary claws, and they consistently manage to be almost sympathetic but blow it by being predatory jerks, and as Sarah Jane demonstrated, they're easily dispatched.

The Slitheen monster here is really well done, terrifyingly so. It's kind of like this, you've been watching a bunch of kids building go-carts, at first crude, but gradually getting better, and you turn your back for a second, and when you look back, they've built an F-16 fighter jet. Apparently, the head was sourced from Ebay, the right arm and hand was by Philip Robinson and Luke Newman built the body.

The bare bones of the story are typical, disguising as an obnoxious human, the Slitheen try and take over, are eventually exposed and exploded. This time, the Slitheen gets a lot further, and is only halted by group effort. The execution balances tension with humour and even sadness. It's not a brilliant plot, but what the episode is really about is the emerging chemistry and genuine emotions of the characters, Doctor included.

We'll see what comes next.

CAST *Dominic G. Martin – The Doctor; Megan Shirley - Megan Williams; Ben Walden - Tommy Benton; Dale Smith - Brigadier; Sarah Cooper - Angela Fletcher; Sarah Poyser - Nessa Williams; James Sutton - Captain Fraser Ward; Molly Reed - PC Lauren Miller; Steph Barker - Therapist; Sophie Bridgewater - News Reporter Luke Lane - Unit Trooper, Radio News reporter;*

&&&

HAPPY BIRTHDAY MEGAN WILLIAMS, Series 5, Minisode 2 (6 minutes) 2022

&&&

INTO THE TIME LOOP, Series 5, Episode 3 (62 minutes) 2023

The Clockwork Androids from Girl in the Fireplace and Deep Breath are back in an episode which amounts to another version of Groundhog Day.

This may be the highlight of the season with not a foot put wrong. The Androids are brilliantly realized, applied sparingly and effectively, the performances are rock solid, the story develops perfectly with an accumulating sense of dread and emerging body horror that draws you in. The episode belongs to Megan Shirlley, giving a standout performance. If you want to introduce someone to the Purple Doctor, start here.

CAST *Dominic G. Martin – The Doctor; Megan Shirley - Megan Williams; Ben Walden - Tommy Benton; Sarah Poyser - Nessa Williams;*

&&&

BODY SWAP, Series 5, Minisode 3 (7.5 minutes) 2023

&&&

The Last Pirate's History, Page 296

THE MOST HATED MAN ON EARTH, Series 5, Episode 4 (58 minutes) 2023

Made a full year in advance, this episode feels and works a lot like The Giggle.

Essentially, the Doctor wakes up one morning to find that he is literally hated and despised by literally everyone on Earth. A godlike nemesis has taken control of reality, and pointed it at the Doctor like a gun.

A nice slow start, establishing a slice of life normality, and then with the twist this slowly escalating sense of dread as events build up. It reminds me of an old Harlan Ellison story.

The cat and mouse through the house is extremely well conceived, not quite as well executed, but I award the points anyway. The Doctor and Meg hiding in a hole is actually gripping, because there's no way out. It's a situation which leads to a series of disorienting surreal twists that build tension nicely.

Call outs to Dale Smith's performance as the Brigadier, he radiates seething malice locked under professionalism, complete control. Smith's evolution as an actor of genuine subtlety is one of the reasons to watch DW2012. He balances Martin perfectly in their scenes together. Megan Shirley turns in a great, natural performance - she's in my top tier of companions - BBC or fan, and she's got some great lines. Shirley's also the writer, and it's a solid ambitious script. James Sutton as the villain turns in a solid performance.

Something to call out are appearances by real life Youtube stars, who blur the lines between reality and fiction, appropriate for this episode.

Overall, I'm consistently impressed with the professional quality of the Purple Doctor's stories - writing, cinematography especially, composition, etc. It's a far cry from some of the dodgier episodes of the Little Red Doctor (although I love those episodes dearly).

CAST *Dominic G. Martin – The Doctor; Megan Shirley - Megan Williams; Ben Walden - Tommy Benton; Dale Smith - Brigadier; Jacob Kay – The Magician; James Sutton-The Trickster; Sarah Poyser - Nessa Williams; Michael Seager- Ned; James Sutton - Captain Fraser Ward; Molly Reed - PC Lauren Miller; Sophie Bridgewater – News Reporter; Martin Theobald – Viewer; Rachel Ward – Radio Presenter; Allen Raferty – Studio Extra; Benji Clifford – Studio Directorl*

&&&

A RADICAL BOND, Series 5, Minisode 4 (12 minutes) 2023

&&&

THE SUMMER OF '82, Series 5, Episode 5 (53 minutes) 2023

The Tardis is finally fixed and the Doctor takes it out for a spin. Of course, things go wrong and the Doctor, Megan and the Brigadier are accidentally dragged back to 1982.

But this isn't quite the 1982 that we remember, it's a sort of hyper-realized 1982 where pop culture is wildly smashed together. The problem turns out to be a wannabe screenwriter trying to complete an action adventure move – 'Ghost Terminator From the Future.' Somehow, time begins to disintegrate. The Trickster is behind it all, and the Doctor is in over his head.

It's a fun journey into genuine nostalgia, as our characters wander through an era which is simultaneously familiar and gorgeously extravagant and alien. The re-creation of the 80s is vivid and authentically haunting. The actual plot, on the other hand is a bit wobbly, and perhaps doesn't quite hold.

The episode ends with moments of genuine shock, and the haunting realization that the Doctor doesn't always win..

&&&

VENUSIAN AIKIDO, Series 5, Minisode 5 (9 minutes) 2023

&&&

FLATMATES, Series 5, Episode 6 (71 minutes) 2023

This is the Nightmare Fair, the moody, surreal, jaunty excursion to the Blackpool holiday fair, and the encounter with the Celestial Toymaker in the midst of an existential crisis, that Colin Baker deserved – instead of what got written for him, and fortunately abandoned back in 1985.

There is so much in this story that is so reminiscent of that abandoned serial – the setting, the villain, the loose structure where the companion and her friend are separated from the Doctor for much of the episode. It's hard to imagine that Newman and company weren't aware of that lost story. Regardless, they've transcended it in every possible way.

Blackpool and its locations and imagery are clearly established, and sensibilities of the theme park carry into other visual elements of the episode. There are a number of shots and locations, and there's a huge diversity, including the black abyss of the Toymaker's lair, but it actually fits nicely. Overall, the visuals and character bits are excellent. I loved the opening scene with Meg in medieval times, that's a perfectly done throwaway bit. The scenes of banter inside the Tardis are lovely. The scenes inside the Toymaker's realm are also well done. It's black and vast and gloomy, reflecting the

Toymaker's existential ennui, but with traces - toys and robots and clowns that hint at a more expressive past. Particular favourites are the Robot - a human sized version of a child's toy, but somehow imbued with personality; and the creepy doll, who manages to go from terrifying to sympathetic.

One particular scene stands out. When Meg goes up to the Doctor standing at the window. That's just an amazingly creepy and well done scene, filled with mounting dread and menace, and when the 'Doctor' turns around, I actually jumped. The 'fake Doctor' was a terrifying creation, reminiscent of the clockwork androids we saw a few episodes back, both visually and in terms of movement, but with an exaggerated creepiness of its own.

Along the way, the evolving relationship between Megan Williams and the character of Tommy Benton continues to mature and deepen, while Dominic Martin's Doctor, beneath his glibness and theatricality grows ever more haunted.

I'm regularly impressed by genuine cinematography in the Purple Doctor era. A lot of fan films just hold the camera. The DW2012 crew have, time and again, proven increasingly adept at framing cinematic images, and building on that to create professional scene compositions.

The return of Johnathan from the previous episode, in the form of the Toymaker, was an interesting choice. The character didn't survive, one of the Doctor's notable failures, and there's a bit of guilt there. Oddly, the Toymaker didn't seem to pick up on it, so it really does seem to be the Doctor's guilt and reservations expressing themselves.

A reflective almost pensive episode, perhaps a calm before the storm.

CAST *Dominic G. Martin – The Doctor; Megan Shirley - Megan Williams; Ben Walden-Tommy Benton; Allen Ravferty – John*

Clark/Toymaker/BoBo; James Sutton – VOC Robot; Davin O'Keeffe – Knight; Hannah Shirley – Dolly; Harry Namwen - Robot.

&&&

TIME CRISIS – PART 1, Series 5, Episode 7 (74 minutes) 2023

Reviewing only the first part of a two or three part story is hell. The first episode only deals the cards, sets up the situations, but it's hard to assess the story.

But here goes – through the actions of an enemy the past is constantly being rewritten, changing the present moment by moment, as seen with people continually having different clothes and hairstyles, and time and space are on the verge of collapse. The Weeping Angels get involved, sending Tommy Benton back to WWII where he encounters a Silurian uprising, and Megan Williams to 1973, where she encounters the Cybermen of the Invasion and the Troughton Doctor. Meanwhile the Tardis is out of power and down to its final trips, the enemy is closing in, and the Universe is ending.

As always, the production values re remarkable. Downside, the cast is sparse, and the story feels like it's moving slowly. I guess we'll have to wait and see how it all turns out.

CAST Dominic G. Martin – The Doctor; Megan Shirley - Megan Williams; Ben Walden-Tommy Benton; Chris Walker-Thomsson – 2nd (Troughton) Doctor; Joe Street- Harry/UNIT Trooper; Brian Cooper – Peter Holmes;. Stephen Higginss-Field Marshal Pearce; Jack Debbage – Captain Evans; Molly Reed – Lauren Miller; Sarah Poyser – Nessa Williams; Elizabeth Kirk – Scarlet; Dale Smith – The Brigadier; James Sutton – Fraser Ward; Lisa Twigger – Olive Benton; Sophie Bridgewater – Lucy Grace; James Sutton – The Trickster; Matthew Whitehouse – 70s Shop Keeper/The Movement; Kevin Twigger – Soldier.

Reviews: The Velocity Doctor (2017-2024)

Breaking the Barriers in Boise, Idaho

It seems fitting that having begun this series by exploring the ground breaking impact of the first Woman Doctor, that we should close out with another woman Doctor doing brilliant work.

I bring you, Doctor Who: Velocity, featuring Krystal Moore, which premiered just before Jody Whitaker, and whose stories will hopefully continue after the Whitaker era. Velocity is one of the most interesting Doctor Who fan film productions of the modern era.

According to a Wiki article, *"Doctor Who Velocity started when Krystal Moore, a comedienne and performer resident in Boise, Idaho, had an idea for a comedy sketch after Matt Smith departed from Doctor Who, believing it would be funny if the Doctor was female. The thought returned when Peter Capaldi was leaving Doctor Who, so she mentioned the idea to her partner Chris Phillips, who loved it."*

I'm not sure if I believe that. It smells a lot like *"Wow, I'd really love to play the Doctor, but I might get laughed at if I say it out loud, so I'll present it as a joke thing, and that way if people laugh it'll be okay, ha ha."* A defense mechanism.

I'm not sure I fully believe it, because Krystal Moore is really really good at playing the Doctor. It's possible the story is dutch because she is a comedian and performer. But she's a really good Doctor. Now, to be completely fair, she's not the actress that Jody Whitaker is, you can spot that as you go through, lines that aren't delivered convincingly, bits of woodenness, timing issues. But it seems to me that you can't be as good as Moore is about playing the Doctor, if deep down, she wasn't passionate about the idea.

The thing with Moore's performance, and Moore's version of the Doctor, is that she's absolutely confident. Whitaker's Doctor sucks her cheeks and frowns and often comes across tentative and uncertain and covers that with being frantic. Not so with Moore's Doctor, she's absolutely confident, even when she's completely wrong. In her first episode, Moore's Doctor screws up completely, and you know what, it doesn't even dent her confidence, she just fixes things and keeps on going. It's a completely different take on the Doctor from Whitaker, and it works as well or better.

Moore's Doctor is also absolutely competent and deeply compassionate. She wanders through a dangerous universe with a kind of joyful, wide-eyed knowingness, that can seem naive, but really is just a product of her confidence and ability. She's not blind to evil, but she's not bothered by it, and particularly, she's enthralled by the beauty and possibility of the Universe. This is a Doctor that can rescue a 16th century witch and save the Earth, but can also go to a rave and dance her ass off, or enjoy visiting lonely friends on Christmas.

Personally though, through the process of doing these reviews, I've had the chance to see several women, Barbara Benedetti, Sharon Horton, Lily Daniels and Krystal Moore take on the role, each amassing a body of work of at least an hour and a few stories each, and I've found a lot to like and admire in each. So even if you're a big Whitaker fan, that's cool, but I'd say give the Moore Doctor a chance and I think you'll find something enjoyable in her approach to the character.

Not everything about Velocity works. I'll admit, the American accents, particularly Moore's, threw me. I'm just used to the Doctor sounding British, but I can get past that. Moore, Phillips and her friends come across as young, though not the youngest. Basically, it's an ongoing production by a group of friends, with no money to speak of, in the middle of Boise, Idaho. It's Boise Idaho, there's no 900 year old churches, antique sailing ships, submarine museums, Roman amphitheatres, Mayan (or any other ruins) to shoot around. There are all kinds of limitations and shortcomings, in locations and resources which are inevitable.

There are occasional strange choices. In the middle of a smashing title sequence, there's a flaming skull. Why is there a flaming skull, and how exactly does it fit? It doesn't really, but I think it's there because a) they had a flaming skull CGI graphic, and b) they thought flaming skulls were cool.

Although incredibly heavily dependent upon CGI, they're also working with low end, consumer accessible CGI software packages, and perhaps figuring things out as they go. So if you watch it a second or third time, or have a very critical eye, you can see the seams and limitations, the flatness of some effects, the telltale composition. Some of the effects don't necessarily work well at all, particularly skeleton robots.

The episodes are short, averaging fifteen minutes. And perhaps that's not enough time. Generally, there's a lack of narrative tension or dramatic pacing. Maybe that's a factor of how short the episodes are; it can take time to build up momentum. The episodes play like BBC minisodes. There's seldom a sense of tension or danger, a sense of threat, that builds up to a payoff. The Doctor is generally solving her problems at arm's length which undercuts the dramatic impact, she seldom feels like she's at personal risk.

Ultimately though, Velocity has three things going for it. The first of course is Krystal Moore's understated but endlessly charming and excessively confident performance as the Doctor, she sells the character, and she solidly anchors every episode.

The second is an amazing visual sense, often rendered through CGI, which is imaginative, innovative and unafraid to take chances. Whether it's cavernous Tardis interiors, Dalek complex, a Tron-cyberspace, an 80s rave at Stonehenge, or the dream dimension of a 15th century poet, the series consistently gives us visuals which are striking and at times feel almost cinematic, which feel huge and colourful and unconventional. There's a level of sheer imagination and creativity, a willingness to let loose here that compares very well to the BBC's own productions. As CGI software becomes more widely available, more and more amateurs are working with it, but it's rare to see it used so creatively. I'm sure that a lot of people, including Krystal Moore, have a hand in the editing and the visual effects in some way, but I'll put a lot this down to Chris Phillips as an artist.

Finally, Velocity tells interesting stories, both in terms of its subject matter, and how it frames things. Its stories are often quirky and fun, and quite often, there's a heart to it. Going back to the early fan Doctors, what I liked about Barbara Benedetti or Rupert Booth's work, was that every adventure they had, every story they told, was wildly different. Velocity has that - whether it's Davros latest scheme, a Christmas episode with surprising depth, or a rendition of Tron, it's all interesting stories, and often told in interesting ways - an episode about a 15th century poet is livened up with a dream dimension, a story about a rave at Stonehenge employs a shotgun narrative technique. There is at times, real research in the writing, quite often some sly and subtle humour and social commentary, and at times some genuine emotion to tug at your heartstrings.

THE WITCHFINDER GENERAL - Episode 1, October 31, 2017 (13 minutes), Written by Krystal Moore, Directed and Edited by Chris Phillips

The Moor Doctor regenerates from the Capaldi Doctor and ends up with a whiny companion, Carl, who has important news about the Master and Gallifrey. An attempt to reach Gallifrey ends up in 16th century England, where the Doctor is taken for a witch and put on trial. There she meets and rescues Agnes Waterhouse, played here by Jen Potcher, also charged with witchcraft. Unfortunately, the miraculous magical rescue and escape changes history, and they end up in a future Earth ruled by a high-tech, extremely misogynous, witch-fearing future... And that's all I'll tell you, except that we end on a cliff hanger.

Agnes Waterhouse (1503-1566) was a real person, the first woman to be hanged (not burned) for witchcraft in England. She actually owned a white spotted cat that she named Satan, which was kind of asking for trouble. The lurid details of her trial, her confession and the evidence against her, as reported and circulated in the pamphlets of the day became the source of much of the English lore about witches.

Was she really a witch, or did she really believe she was? Well she confessed in detail, though a lot of the confession seems fanciful, and I suspect a certain amount of torture. Or perhaps a lot of literary license by the pamphleteer who is the source of the information, it wouldn't be the first time that the media of the day inflated a story.

Still, there were elements, abortion herbs, unwanted pregnancies, stealing sheep, thieving for food, praying in Latin, chronic injuries which may imply a hardscrabble life of folk remedies and opportunism and family traditions, which might be the basis for the lurid stories.

The Velocity folk did their homework, and they go with the theory that Agnes believes herself to be (and that might well have been the case, though it's pretty iffy), an actual witch. But in the story, written, overt supernatural elements are eschewed in favour of portraying Agnes' witchcraft and Satanism as a sort of proto-feminism. Despite being pretty upfront about the whole witchcraft/Satan thing, Agnes is never portrayed as mean or less than kind and open minded (if slightly deluded), and she embraces the idea of a positive future for women with genuine hope, even if she has to go back to die for it.

In contrast, the Witch-hunters of both Agnes time and the dystopian future come across as narrow minded, harsh and gratuitously cruel. There's no question as to where the episodes sympathies lie, and this coming out of Boise, Idaho, not what you'd think of as a pro-witch, or even pro-feminism country.

Relatively unusual for Velocity, this episode uses a fair number of location shots. Notably, there are some very nice scenes of the Doctor and Tardis out in the forest, and some very carefully selected, minimally altered locations standing in for a 16th century court building and chamber, and even a dystopia future.

One of the big visual highlights of the episode is the Tardis interior, which amounts to a relatively small console in an absolutely cavernous space. Literally, the Tardis control room is the size of an aircraft hangar, it's immense, white and striking, and the Doctor and Carl are shown as tiny figures in that vastness. It's gorgeous.

&&&

DAVROS AND THE DALEKS & THE MASTER TAKES REVENGE! - Episode 2, July 15, 2018 (14 minutes); Episode 3, October 31, 2018 (15 minutes) Written by Krystal Moore, Directed and Edited by Chris Phillips

These are episodes two and three, and while they're distinct episodes, they function well as a two-part serial. I kind of have the feeling that this was the original Doctor Who story they wanted to tell all along. Witchfinder General was sort of 'proof of concept' testing out whether they could do it at all. But this was the big story they wanted to do, and after that it was, 'hey we can handle this; you know what else would be fun?'

This is also the most conventional of the Velocity stories, and when I say 'most conventional' that's not disparaging. What I mean is that this feels like the most mainstream or typical of the BBC's styles of Doctor Who stories, it's got the Master, Davros, Daleks, a fiendish plot threatening Earth, and the Doctor being the Doctor, saving the day. After this, they'll drift towards more experimental or unconventional work.

Chance Fuerstinger plays the Master, lacking the dignity or malevolence of a Delgado or Ainsley, but with an unmatched fussiness. This version of the Master isn't so much evil, as just very frustrated, annoyed and full of himself, his main weapon as a blunt sarcasm. Interestingly, Fuerstinger's Master seems to have a genuine love/hate thing with the Doctor, not just hate. When he loses his memory, they're actually good friends.

One of the standouts of these episodes is Davros. Traditionally, Davros is a withered husk, trapped in his chair, near blind, almost unable to move, a tremulous shrieking figure with a malevolent mind. Yeah, that's out the window.

This version of Davros, played by Scott Grady, comes across as a decomposing surfer dude, gray skinned, trapped in his chair, visibly rotting, but the eyes flash, the voice is strong and commanding, and there's a malevolent confidence to the character. This Davros, for all that the appearance is different, is as ruthless and brilliant as the one we know, absolutely capable of weaponizing the Doctor's morality back at her, and as relentless as they come. It's a pleasure to watch him.

I think it was a brave decision to just throw out the classic image of Davros, and I love the boldness of both this new concept and the execution.

And for once, Davros has got a good idea. Instead of forcibly converting Earth's population, why not just offer it to them? Who would want a personal tank/battle shell, protecting them from all harm, and capable of dealing out destruction? Well, it turns out, just about everyone. It's the ultimate in safety and 'self defense.' Davros argues that he's not being evil at all, it's a good thing, he's saving humanity, and he does it with conviction. Classic Davros, you'd never believe, but this version is very close to convincing.

This is a satirical riff on America's gun culture sly and subtle that I have no idea whether it was deliberate or not. But it's there. Everyone that gets their Dalek shell raves about safety, about protection from a dangerous world, and almost immediately you've got a guy, invulnerable in a Dalek shell, shooting a parking offender for a trivial trespass.

Of course, it's Davros and the Daleks, so of course there's an evil scheme that goes without saying, but it's engaged effectively and resolved in a satisfying way.

Assisting Davros on Earth is tech billionaire Kevin Apiary, played by Paycen McGahey, a man deeply in over his head, but who only comes to realize it when Kevin's slightly smothering mother, Gloria, played by Jen Potcher, tries out her own Dalek shell, courtesy of Davros, and is slowly taken over.

Because this is a two part episode, the story has time to breathe, taking twists and turns, with the Doctor's capture, the Master's amnesia, Davros plan, and so forth. Move and countermove happen logically, with events growing organically from preceding events. This allows the episodes to build and several plot threads to evolve. There's twists, turns, ups and downs. It's a fun story.

Visually, there's a lot of very cool stuff - from utterly vast Tardis interiors, the control room and the library, the immensity of Davros base, the ships, and all kinds of CGI Daleks, and cool shots. It's a visually rich episode. Admittedly, some of the new Dalek designs look a bit goofy, and they don't actually look like a person would fit inside them as a protective shell. But that's a small quibble. On the other hand, the special Battle Daleks are nicely scary.

Overall, it's a delightful riff on the BBC series, a good story, well told.

&&&

THE ACE CAMEO - SOPHIE ALDRED IN VELOCITY - Episode 4, August 1, 2019 (17 minutes), Written Directed and Edited by Chris Phillips.

Yeah, sort of. It's actually an audio participation, with a couple of stills and photo-manipulations from the 80s Sophie thrown in and slightly animated. On the other hand, they've got a major companion from the classic series volunteering to participate in their fan film? That's a hell of a thing, and they have every reason to be chuffed.

Honestly though, that's just the tip of the iceberg of crunchy goodness. We have Stonehenge, dance parties, sly humour and funky visuals, and weeping angels. This episode is set in 1989, and is built around the "*Summer of Rave.*" That was a real historical thing, a culture and a wave of illegal (occasionally drug fuelled) dance parties, which were to culminate with a rave at Stonehenge. Unfortunately, the resulting moral panic brought about a police crackdown across the country, so no wild orgiastic dance party at Stonehenge.

Except that in Velocity, with the help of Jeremy, a slightly sleazy, somewhat mercenary promoter, played by Dylan Wood, his assistant and the creative side of the business, Ashley played by Denae Gardner, and the early early internet, the Rave comes together. The Doctor, up for a good dance party joins in, and we discover the rave at Stonehenge is taking place in a dimensional pocket, it turns out that the weeping angels are up a nefarious scheme.

It's a retro period piece with a strong sense of 80s fashion and aesthetics, supplemented by a lot of stock period footage. There are some nice touches, if you watch for it; you'll notice the scruff of VHS tracking. There's a gag about dirty photos sent through the internet. Stonehenge is an inspired setting, both conceptually and visually, rendered through compositing of real photos, a cardboard monolith, what looks to me like a tabletop model and some effective CGI modelling. There's also a very gritty take on a Weeping Angel, built around actress Miranda Palacio, which you'd hate to meet in a dark alley.

Not everything works. This is an incredibly intensive use of CGI for a no budget production, and some of it, particularly the shot of Weeping Angels flying off comes off as flat. The episode moves through easily through a series of tonal shifts, from documentary realism, to the lighthearted banter of Jeremy and Ashley, to the psychedelia of Stonehenge, the doctor's growing disquiet, to genuinely tense scenes pursued by an angel. I think though, that the shifts in tone undermine the overall dramatic pace. In the end, the Doctor sorts it out, without any sense of danger - there's a problem, she figures it out, and she solves it, it's not a nail biter by any means. But then, there's only seventeen minutes to work with and no budget, so you can't do everything. In a perfect world, this would be three or four times longer, and they'd have real money to work with. What they've actually achieved is amazing.

And to be completely fair, without revealing too much, they've managed to write a bit of a heart wrenching ending, which actually casts a shadow back over the rest of the episode, and leaves you re-evaluating events.

&&&

ETERNAL DARKNESS, Remastered DW2012 - December 7, 2019 (74 minutes), Written and Directed by Luke Newman

This one is actually the product of the Birmingham UK fan film group Dynamic Works 2012. A mysterious force which turns out to be the Valeyard sends a legion of Soul Stealers out to attack all the incarnations of the Doctors. Krystal Moore's Doctor sends out the alarm, warning all the incarnations of the Doctors, many of whom end up in a picturesque cemetery and then helps to coordinate the response, advising and telepathically linking. Starring Luke Newman, the story is actually an excuse for many of the major current fan Doctors to get together in a story. Krystal Moore's Doctor is in a supporting role, but it's a critical and prominent supporting role. Obviously, a troupe centered in Boise, Idaho, weren't making the trip to Birmingham, UK, but participated just the same through the magic of the internet.

&&&

THE VASHTA NERADA RETURN -Episode 5, December 30, 2019 (14 minutes), Written by Krystal Moore and Chris Phillips, Directed and Edited by Chris Phillips

The Vashta Nerada were the rather vaguely defined monster of the Tenant episodes, Silence in the Library and Forest of the Dead. They're kind of particles of darkness that are everywhere and normally don't amount to much, but which occasionally eat people. In the Tennant episodes, as people's bodies get eaten, their souls or something are dumped into a library's computer system.

That's sort of the basic premise here. The episode is a sequel or sidequel to the Dalek two-parter. Kevin Apiary, former tech billionaire, is now a bit of a fugitive, hiding out in the tropics. This leaves his mother, former Dalek and current empty-nester, Gloria Apiary, played Jen Potcher, facing Christmas all alone.

And wouldn't you know it, the Vashta Nerada eat her and her consciousness ends up getting dumped into an unbearably saccharine Hallmark Christmas Movie, where she has a romance with a Christmas Prince named Noel Sleight Kringle, played by Brett Dayne. Luckily, the Doctor likes to look in on her friends, particularly the lonely ones, and she's soon along to sort things out...

In some ways, this is the weakest episode of the velocity series. Clocking in at just under 14 minutes, the story is threadbare, the CGI robot just looks wrong, the visuals are weapon and not much goes on. Compared to what's gone before and what comes after this feels like a filler. Of course, any fan film is so much hard work that nothing is really a filler, but this has that feeling.

If the story feels weak, the subject matter is thematically interesting. This is an episode about a middle aged woman being left behind by the world. Gloria is a person, but she's not special, she's not remarkable, she raised up Kevin Apiary, who almost conquered the world for Davros, but he's out and moved on, and their relationship is 'Hi Mom, Merry Christmas, see ya later.' She's kind of left behind, with nothing and no one in her life. In literature, characters like that have literally served their purpose, so they just go offstage and die quietly. But she's a person, and she has a life, empty as it is. I suppose the emptiness of her life is why the Vashta Nerada get her; she's not supposed to be missed. And I suppose she ends up in a hallmark movie because she's already been spending time a lot of time there already, devouring treacly Hallmark fantasy as a substitute for the emptiness in her life.

So this is really a story about a person that stories aren't supposed to be about, about the people, the women, we're all supposed to forget about and leave behind. I rather like that, actually. It's Gloria's story. The Doctor is there, of course, visiting and trying to visit with Gloria, not out of pity, but out of a belief in Gloria's worth and genuine friendship and she sorts things out. But it's really Gloria's story as I've said, and the focus is on her overcoming the diabetic fantasy she's been abandoned in, and with the help of her friend, getting her life and a future of her own back. Which, when you think about it, is a heartwarming Christmas story.

&&&

TRON - Episode 6, September 11, 2020 (17 minutes), Written Directed and Edited by Chris Phillips

Our old pal Jeremy is back, having bought a defunct video game company, and once again out to make a fast buck. Unfortunately, the game company he bought was the maker of Tron, and before you know it, he's digitized and catapulted into the Day-Glo, wire frame reality of Tron's version of cyberspace. Luckily, the Doctor comes to the rescue, but only gets digitized herself and sucked into the game. Can the Doctor, trapped on the inside, manage to win the games with the help of her allies on the outside? For a sixteen minute episode, there's a surprising amount of plot going on.

To be honest, I never particularly liked the original Tron movie from 1982, for all its neon brilliance, the story seemed wafer thin and mainly an excuse to launch an arcade game. It felt like Disney trying to jump on an idea, without actually understanding it. I think a lot of people felt like I did since it took 28 years to spawn a sequel, Tron Legacy, in 2010, and thirty years to spin off a cartoon series in 2012, set between the two movies (as is this episode). So I was kind of dubious about it.

Oddly, I ended up liking this episode a lot more. The Doctor and Jeremy in Tron-space genuinely feel like the movies, and it ends up being a lot of fun. Maybe it's the shorter running time, or the fact that I'm watching it on a smaller screen so it manages to feel visually big but not overpowering, or maybe it's Crystal Moore's endless charm as the Doctor. But whatever reason, it works quite well, all the familiar elements are there, the neon-highlights to everything, the wire frame world, the 'video-game' shtick, but it feels fresh.

The entire episode, even the 'real world' stuff, is entirely CGI. It was the Covid Pandemic; no one could actually work in the same room, so literally everything has been composited together. That's an insane amount of work, and they carry it off more often than not. There's some lovely attention to detail - in one scene, the Doctor is confronted by coloured wire frame versions of Weeping Angels, Sontarans, Cybermen and Daleks, each with their own colour and movement, and you can actually see their blurry reflections in the floor of Tron-space. As episodes go, this is pretty much eye candy, its light and superficial, despite the stakes and the relative story complexity; you never have any sense of the characters being in danger. It's just a fun romp, but that's cool, I'm okay with that.

Apart from that, this is a reunion episode. Jen Potcher is back as Gloria Apiary, last seen in the Christmas episode, now wearing a robot body; Paycen McGahey has a cameo as former mogul, Kevin Apiary. Dylan Wood and Denae Gardner are back from the Weeping Angels episode as Jeremy and Ashley respectively. Even Chance Fuerstinger is back as the Master. Rounding out the cast is Nick Gill as the programmer, Corey, Tom Sanford as Flynn (also credited with Production), Chris Phillips as the voice of the Master Control Program, Erick Gutierrez appears as a game opponent and there's even a cameo from Megan Shirley from DoctorWho2012.

Throw in Matt Gillikin as the prop maker, and this is a relatively huge cast and crew, particularly for a film made during the Covid Pandemic lockdown. They've got an interesting making of feature, which explores not just Day-Glo world of Tron, but the difficulties and measures for working in the pandemic.

&&&

THE SILENCE - Episode 7, January 30, 2022 (16 minutes), Written by Gavin Cummings, Directed Edited by Chris Phillips

This is an interesting, poignant meditative little piece built around a 15th century Mexican/Spanish poet, played here by Monica Aguilar, was a real person, and one of the key figures in Spain's literary golden age. Juana Ines was one of those gifted polymaths, reading at age three, and growing up to be a major figure in the literary world of the day. Unfortunately, her brilliance brought her up against the regressive male dominated society and Catholic religious conservatism of that age, she was forced to abandon literature and music and become a nun and many of her works were tragically destroyed. What survived assured her legacy.

In a sense, this is Velocity's 'Historical' episode, not unlike the Hartnell historicals; or Whitaker's Rosa or Demons of the Punjab. But this gives us a much more intimate and personal story, one woman's aspirations and oppression (as engineered by the Silence for their own mysterious purposes). It's actually refreshing for exploring a topic or character that's not widely known, but which is also poignantly universal.

Of course, building an entire episode in 15th century Mexico might be a challenge. I suspect that there's a shortage of appropriate locations for that kind of thing in Boise, Idaho. Instead the they just go all greenscreen and CGI, crafting a visually glorious and evocative dream dimension, full of luminosity and floating crystals, which is where Juana Ines poetry takes her when she sleeps, . The dream dimension is wonderful to look at and almost overpowers the story. It's remarkable what you can do with sheer creativity.

The dream dimension is also where she meets a more benign and obviously gay version of Father Nunez, played by Enzo Benzo here once again is a sly acknowledgment of the cost of sexual repression, this time around sexual orientation. In both worlds, Nunez is gay, but in the real world, he's repressed and constrained; both a victim and instrument of repression. In the dream dimension, he's free to be his own self and he's a genuinely happier and holier man. It's a nice little throwaway bit that's not given any emphasis at all, but is allowed to breath, and it works perfectly for that.

The Silence, played by Magdalene Schernthanner and Chris Phillips, appearing in both the real world and dream dimension is well realized. The button down black suit and gray alien face, with a bit of Edvard Munch's The Scream, thrown in make it very effective as agents of the Patriarchy. They're not so much alien as ultimate expressions of an establishment so remote, arbitrary and inflexible, it seems alien. The Doctor confronts them, but doesn't so much overcome as evades them. Not dramatic, but it works for a meditative episode.

In the end, The Silence is hampered by a too many roving floating camera angles, too little time to develop the story fully and the limitations of amateur actors in a no-budget production. But all of that is forgiven. It's an episode with glorious visuals, an interesting idea and subject, and a story with a certain poignancy that, if I had any human feelings at all, would have left a lump in my throat at the end.

&&&

THE BOGLINS, Episode 8, September 1, 2022 (17 minutes). Written, Directed and Edited by Chris Phillips.

The latest episode of Velocity has the Doctor facing off small troll-monsters called Boglins, 80s era rubber monster puppets.

Boglins are actually real, not made up for the episode. They date to 1986, and were created by a trio of Jim Henson (The *Muppet Show, Fraggle Rock, Dark Crystal, Labyrinth*) puppeteers, Tim Clark, Maureen Trotto and Larry Mass, although these days, it seems to be mainly Tim Clark pushing They're hideously ugly and ungainly looking in the sort of way that twelve year old boys love, with grotesquely distorted facial features colourful lumpy warty skin. I'm told that they were somewhat inspired by Olmec heads. Behind the head are two frail arms, a short body and a sort of fishlike tail, to me they vaguely resemble a fish called a mudskipper.

The Boglins were an attempt to cash in on the 'little monster' wave that was going on back then, which included *Gremlins, Critters, Ghoulies, Charles Band's 'Puppet Master'* and so on. They were distinctly second tier creatures in never getting a B-movie franchise or a Saturday morning cartoon series, or even a comic book so they never really had much of a backstory beyond some superficial box copy.

What made the Boglins distinctive was that they were actually rather cleverly designed for hand puppets. Sure, you stuck your hand in the bottom to make the mouth move. But there was plastic armature to make the eyes move back and forth, and a pair of plastic levers to move each eyebrow. The original design even had a lever hidden in the tail to make the arms move. So with a bit of practice, you could actually make it pretty lifelike. This cleverness extended to the packaging, the Boglins were sold in a square cardboard box made up to look like a wooden shipping crate. The box had a perforated circle in the bottom to cut a hole with you could puppeteer the Boglin in its crate. The front of the crate was twisted metal cage bars that you could lift straight up. Inside the box was a sign saying 'gone for lunch' visible when the Boglin was removed.

Anyway, the Boglins were initially picked up by Coleco unsuccessfully, then marketed by Mattel in 1987. There were three initial Boglins figures, but they diversified rapidly into different variations, including ones with hair, ones that spat. There was a line of mini-Boglins with eyes that weren't moveable, and a line of mini-mini versions. I'd never heard of them, but they'd apparently been popular in Europe, and they had a decent run through the 80's and 90's. There was apparently a re-release in 2010. Robot Chicken did a sketch on them. These days, Tim Clarke seems to be pushing a revival with Chris Cofoni and Tri-Action Toys.

I assume that Doctor Who Velocity managed to get permission, or even enthusiastic cooperation as some sort of meeting of minds. Indeed, the opening monologue is straight out of the Boglins advertising copy. I don't know though, I can see how the idea might have been fun, but still, even with their relatively sophisticated internals, they're still rubbery hand puppets. Still, this fits in with Velocity's penchant for retro 80s and 90s nostalgia.

So what's the story? There's a very nice opening, stormy night in some primordial tabletop jungle, a researcher, played by Tom Sandford, narrates his discovery, and things end very badly for him. From there, the story segues into a young man, Ethan, played by Darwin Roy, visiting his school counsellor's office, who just happens to be the Doctor. He complains of hallucinations, she suggests they might be real. There's a clever little riff on an infamous Jody Whittaker scene there.

Ethan goes to a skateboard park (there's a very impressive drone shot descending on the park, watch for it), where he meets Zara, played by Magdalene Schernthanner, and tells her that his father (the dead guy from the opening scene) was studying them. This provokes the watching Boglins to attack, first flying through the air, and then pursuing on skateboards. Zara gets bitten, the wound is multi-coloured and glowing, which doesn't seem good at all. Well, the next thing you know, it's the end of the world. And to make things even worse, the Boglins call in reinforcements – space goblins, riding little combat platforms. Oh no!

The Doctor ends up being a supporting character, a lot of the focus is on Ethan and Zara. But that's kind of the way these mini-monster movies like Gremlins played out in the day, young adults or teens, trying to live their lives and getting embroiled.

There are some very nice shots and scenes here, notably a set of scenes where the Doctor and her knew friends are swarmed by flying Boglins, or a direct steal from a commercial where a child reaches under a bed, a newscaster's broadcast, and an oddly surreal Boglin's rendition of 'When the Saints Go Marching In,' performed by North Gill, while the world burns.

There's a lot here that is simply ambitious. Even things that don't quite come off speak to a level of ambition and daring, of genuinely trying to press the envelope and try something new and different from what they've done before.

But there's some very odd editing choices, and some shots and effects which, while clever, don't quite come off – that, or they're genuinely going for an 80s/90s feel to some of the effects. The puppetry is sometimes more enthusiastic than polished. Roy and Schernthanner aren't really up to the demands of the story, and the script feels unfocussed. The story is truncated, which is a consistent thing with Velocity – averaging about fifteen minutes, stories often don't get the time to fully breathe. You feel like there are missed opportunities. I could have stood to have learned more of the Boglins' backstory and mythology, for instance.

Still, you have to admire the sheer chutzpah of even attempting something like this, the confluence of nostalgia, mixture of puppetry and computer effects, and the sheer campy joy of it all. I'm sure that their 'making of' featurette is going to be absolutely riveting. It's not the best episode that Velocity has produced. But it is fun. So Kudos to Velocity, and Kudos to Tim Clark and Tri-Action toys for making it happen. Maybe we'll see the Boglins return.

&&&

MORE VELOCITY

In addition to the formal episodes, Moore and Phillips have done a short series of audio adventures of varying lengths - A Dalek For Christmas, Club Quatermass and The Bitter End, all featuring the Doctor and DJ Lloyd.

DJ Lloyd is an amiable lunk, he's an antiques dealer slash Deejay, friendly, easygoing, likable and not too bright. Let's just say his sandwich is missing a slice or two, but also his sandwich has a few nonstandard mushrooms in it, if you know what I mean, and I think you do.

DJ Lloyd is also, what we in the business like to call a "weirdness magnet." Through no fault of his own, wacky occurrences tend to occur around him, like a customer accidentally mistaking a snoozing Dalek as a nouveau art piece and buying it as an anniversary gift for her husband, or his pal running a nightclub haunted by an extradimensional creature that eats opening acts, or just happening to give a ride to a time displaced Chaucer and accidentally rewriting history. Through it all, DJ Lloyd is pleasant, meaning no harm and taking no offence. Luckily, he's got the Doctor coming by occasionally to sort thing out and set things right.

They're billed as Velocity's comedy pieces, which is kind of a "yes and no" proposition. Mostly, they're not laugh out loud funny, except for the part where the Doctor is on stage being introduced as an exotic dancer. There's no jokes, no punchlines, no 'drumroll beats.' There's humour, but it's dry and understated rather than broad and over top. Moore plays her Doctor straight on, without any mugging or wisecracks. She's exactly the same as her performances in the episodes, almost a straight man with DJ Lloyd playing the foil.

What this really is, is not so much comedy as 'wacky absurdity.' This is more akin to Grant Morrison's Doom Patrol, or a Far Side cartoon, if that reference makes any sense to you (and I suspect it might not). It starts with absurd premises or ideas, like a Dalek unknowingly brought into a household as an anniversary gift, and just develops it in a completely poker faced way, with an occasional sly wink. The comic aspect is kind of sublime. You get the feeling that the crew has a hoot coming up with the ideas and executing them.

Anyway, it's a thoroughly pleasant addition to Velocity's canon, and I'll happily recommend them.

Finally, like DoctorWho2012, and a number of other modern fan series, Velocity is heavily curated. They have video trailers for upcoming episodes, notifications, and mini-documentaries exploring the making of different episodes and the various challenges, with 'behind the scenes' footage of greenscreens, models, etc.

Chris Phillips talks about searching and struggling with various software packages, Krystal Moore wears glasses, we get to see the development of a Silence or Weeping Angel, the challenges of Tron, a tutorial on how to make a 3D CGI

Dalek with open source software or the writing process for different episodes.

They're typically short, around ten minutes, and they're genuinely interesting, giving us a window into how difficult, and how much sheer hard work and dedication goes into these things. I recommend them.

Overall, Velocity manages to comprise an always interesting, always engaging body of work, that stands as an impressive tribute to the original series, while crafting and exerting its own identity, offering interesting stories and really engaging visuals. It's a brilliant example of the creativity, talent and dedication of fans, and of the potential of Fan Films.

As Joe Bob Briggs would say, check it out.

AFTERWORDS

I have to say, it's been a wonderful time, researching and writing this book. Just between you and me though, I'm glad to be finished.

My first version of this was *'The Greatest Unauthorized Doctor Stories'* Volumes One and Two, in 2017. It was my first attempt at self-publishing. Well, between then and now, there has been a lot of research, a lot of new work reviewed, and a lot of experience, which makes for three volumes, and hopefully a sharper, clearer, cleaner set of books.

Let me take a moment and assure you, by the way, that if you're a Doctor Who fan film maker, and I haven't reviewed or even mentioned your book, it's not necessarily because it was terrible.

It could well have been terrible, that's a very good possibility. But if you loved it, and loved making it, if you and your friends had a great time doing it, if you learned a lot while doing it, and if it's fine for you and your friends.. isn't all that worthwhile in itself? You don't have to be Spielberg or Davies, you just have to enjoy yourself.

Or it might have been really good, and I just missed it. Or watched it and didn't properly understand appreciate it. Or I understood it, but may just not have been to my taste. Or possibly I'm just a jerk.

Who knows?

In the meantime, if you're a fan, if you like the BBC show, if you've read this book, search out some of these films and audios. Go ahead. I didn't write this to hear myself talk. I wanted to make your world bigger. I found these things, and I wanted to share them with you.

They're out there, they can all be found, some of them may be tougher than others, but they're out there.

And hey, just maybe, if you're a fan, and inspired… give it a try.

Build your own Police box. Build yourself a Tardis console and make it any way you want, there's actual plans and software, and people have made amazing works of art.

Be creative. Build Cybermen or Daleks. Put together a costume. Write fanfiction. Find some friends and do an audio. Or create a fanfilm. Don't just watch licensed television. Discover the joy of being creative with something you love.

It doesn't have to be great. You just have to have fun.

All these films and videos, these audios and animations and stage plays, the builds, the costumes, the props and scripts, all of that, that I've canvassed and shown you; every single bit of it, every film maker, every actor, every writer, they all had one thing in common.

There was no money in it, no prospects for the future, no advantages to secure.

They did it for love. That's all, just love and enthusiasm.

And God help me, I can't think of anything more wonderful.

The Doctor would approve.

MORE BOOKS FROM THE AUTHOR

Have you made it all the way here? Have you actually read all this way

Wow. That's amazing. I'm very flattered. I want to give you a hug or something.

Seriously. Thank you! Thank you so much!

I'm going to assume that if you've made it all this way, you've enjoyed yourself. You've learned some juicy new gossip about old Doctor Who, you've found some insights into technology and how it affects what we do, and maybe you found some of the reviews really entertaining.

I will repeat, almost everything I've written about you can find out there, if you look around hard enough. I strongly recommend you do so. I genuinely believe that these films and these Doctors deserve to be remembered.

And I hope you liked my writing and writing style. Because if you did, then I have some non-Doctor Who books, both fiction and nonfiction, that I think you'd love.

They're available on multiple platforms as eBooks, and in some places as print books or audiobooks. Lots of choices.

Please feel free to visit my website: denvaldron.com.

Or just let me tell you about them right now…

THE OTHER
PIRATE'S HISTORIES
OF DOCTOR WHO

You know, when I first started this project, I thought these films were simply cool and wanted to share them. I didn't think there was any deep significance, except that they were worth watching.

But as I dug deeper, I came to realize that the official picture of a wise BBC churning out Doctor Who for a silent audience was wrong, that fans have had a significant influence on the history of Doctor Who, preserving the show when the BBC was throwing episodes away, recovering what was lost, re-creating, saving the show from cancellation, bringing it to stage, to animation, to audio. There's a wonderful history and interesting stories here that gets overlooked or dismissed, a whole set of hidden corners to the Doctor Who universe, and I'm glad to bring it to you.

If you've actually bought the previous Pirate Histories, just skip over this part. Although… if you bought an ebook, I just wanted to mention that I do have print versions. And if you don't like to read, I have audiobook versions. Or if you don't want to spend too much money… ebooks?

If you haven't bought the previous ebooks, hopefully, this will help you make up your mind, one way or the other, because I'll tell you what's in them. That way, you can make an informed decision to say no. Or become wildly enthusiastic for the whole set!

In the first volume, I explain what a Pirates History is. I talk about the general history of fan films or unauthorized pirate films.

We start with the first woman to play the Doctor, Barbara Benedetti, who did a series of films from 1984 to 1988.

I explore the earliest fan films from the Super 8 days of the 70s – films like Son of Doctor Who, Ocean in the Sky, the Image Makers and Doctor Hoo that have been almost completely lost.

In terms of Doctor Who history, there's the cancellation crisis of 1984, the fan rebellion that 'uncancelled' the show, the slow war of the BBC to destroy the show between 1984 and 1989, and the failed revival of 1993.

Then we look at the evolution of a fan culture in the 1980s, the impact of technology, particularly videocassette recorders and camcorders on shaping that culture, and the emerging fan film tradition, along with the best fan films of that time.

Finally, we go into the wilderness years, the 1990s – when Doctor Who was gone and off the air, and when fans started making serious and high quality films.

A PIRATE'S HISTORY OF DOCTOR WHO

REVISED AND EXPANDED

BY
D.G. VALDRON

The Last Pirate's History, Page 329

Before television, there was theatre, so it's not surprising that Doctor Who would appear on stage. The first Doctor Who play didn't actually have the Doctor, just his enemies – Curse of the Daleks. Jon Pertwee was originally going to star in the next Doctor Who play, Seven Keys to Doomsday, but he backed out, and Trevor Martin would become the fourth Doctor, weeks before Tom Baker. In 1989, both Jon Pertwee and Colin Baker returned to their role in Doctor Who, the Ultimate Adventures… and were recorded by fans.

Elsewhere, fans produced their own stage versions of the Doctor, with and without the BBC's permission. Nick Scovell played the Doctor through BBC approved stage plays, and through several classic fan films.

It was the Wilderness years, sixteen years from 1989 to 2005, when the show was off the air, with only occasional flickers of revival.

During this time, due to peculiarities in copyright, fans found a way to make Doctor Who without the Doctor. Sometimes, as with the Stranger series, a Doctor Who actor like Colin Baker or Sylvester McCoy would play a character identical to the Doctor, having Doctor-ish adventures… just under a different name.

Other times, it turned out that you could license characters like Sarah Jane Smith, or monsters like Sontarans and Autons, directly from the creators, and bypass the BBC, for more Doctor Who adventures, featuring companions and monsters.

We'll explore the productions of the BBV, Reeltime Pictures and Dreamwatch, and their skirting of BBC copyrights in Downtime, Shakedown, the Stranger, Daemons Rising and Do You Have License to Save this Planet?

But the BBC's rules on Copyright had a down side. Over two hundred episodes were destroyed. We'll look at how and why this happened.

And we'll explore how, through the efforts of fans, everything that was lost was either recovered or preserved in some form, and how fans worked to re-create lost and abandoned serials through reconstructions and remakes.

We'll revisit the past with *Marco Polo and the Loose Cannons, Masters of Luxor and the Road Not Taken, Yellow Fever and Lost Season, Devious and the Secret of 6B,* and the rise and fall of *Yellow Fever.*

Anyway, if you haven't read them already, I hope you're intrigued enough to take the chance. If not, that's cool. I have plenty of other books that might interest you.

ANOTHER PIRATE'S HISTORY OF DOCTOR WHO

REVISED AND UPDATED

BY D.G. VALDRON

Volume II – Another Pirates History

Introduction - Why Fan Films?
Chapter 9 – Doctor Who on Stage, Treading the Boards
Review – Curse of the Daleks, Remade (1965)
Review – Remembering Seven Keys to Doomsday (1974)

The Last Pirate's History, Page 333

ALTERNATE REALITIES
A Trilogy or Strange New Worlds
The Other books

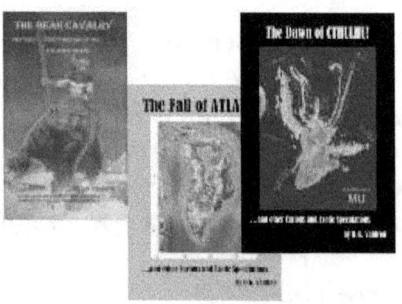

Dawn of Cthulu features explorations of lost continents, both real and legendary; a realistic biology and evolution of muppets and their friends; and the history of the Cthulhu Cult as a real religion.

The Fall of Atlantis includes a geo-historical exploration of a real Atlantis ending in a different kind of tragedy; the Retroverse, a fun the accidental cinematic universe of 50s sci fi films, Ancient Rome plausibly crossing the Atlantic, because of coffee(!!!), and the saga of an Alternate Greenland that was never covered by ice.

The Bear Cavalry, the True (Not!) History of the Icelandic Bears, chronicles a history where travelling Vikings domesticated North American Bears and eventually learn to forge them into the most terrifying medieval fight force ever – with excursions into history, biology and art along the way. Bonus story – the Sharebear Apocalypse, is it really just a hug that feels so good.

AXIS OF ANDES
NEW WORLD WAR
A History of WWII in South America

Berlin, 1937, Adolph Hitler and his cabinet meet with a strange delegation from Ecuador. The delegates from the small South American nation beg for help, fearing an impending invasion from their rival, Peru. What happens at that meeting sets in motion a chain of events that sets the entire continent on fire. By the time it's done, millions are dead, nations are in ruins, and the map of Latin America will be changed beyond recognition.

HEARTS IN DARKNESS

Three Collections of Horror Stories

Featuring riveting stories about a man's cancer learning to talk to him, the ultimate serial killer; Allison, a paralyzed pregnant woman feeling her fetus taking control of her body, a desperate single mother lured down a dark path; the army enlisting the unkillable men in the masks; Silence about a thief hiding in the home of a killer; a ghost that haunts the people around its victim, and many, many more. Melancholy darkness, chilling horror, dark visions.

LEXX UNAUTHORIZED

LEXX a show about a giant space bug that blows up planets, the cowardly security guard who is its captain, and the undead assassin, runaway love slave, and robot head who form its crew.

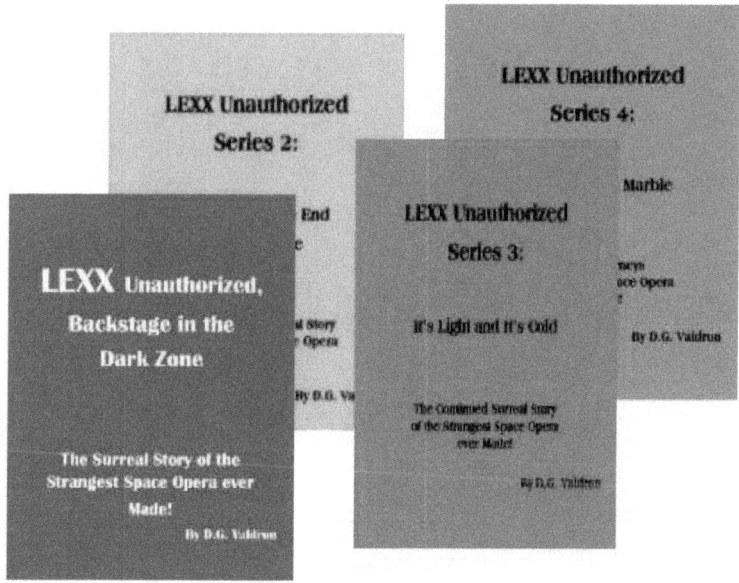

Originally billed as 'Star Trek's Evil Twin,' the cultiest of cult sci fi, LEXX's forte was black humor, startling visuals, big ideas, and a sensibility that had more to do with surrealists like Jodorowsky or Bunuel than mainstream science fiction. And, as unconventional as it was onscreen, the story of how it came to be is even more bizarre.

A Dark Fantasy
of Murder and Redemption

There's a City where all the races come together uneasily.

There's a Civil War gathering, and dark powers assembling.

There's a Mermaid, murdered cruelly, her people distraught.

There's an Orc, lowest and the worst, assigned to solve the murder, before it all comes crashing down.

And there's something else: this world's first serial killer.

The Last Pirate's History, Page 339